GREEN LANTERN
THE MOVIE PREQUELS

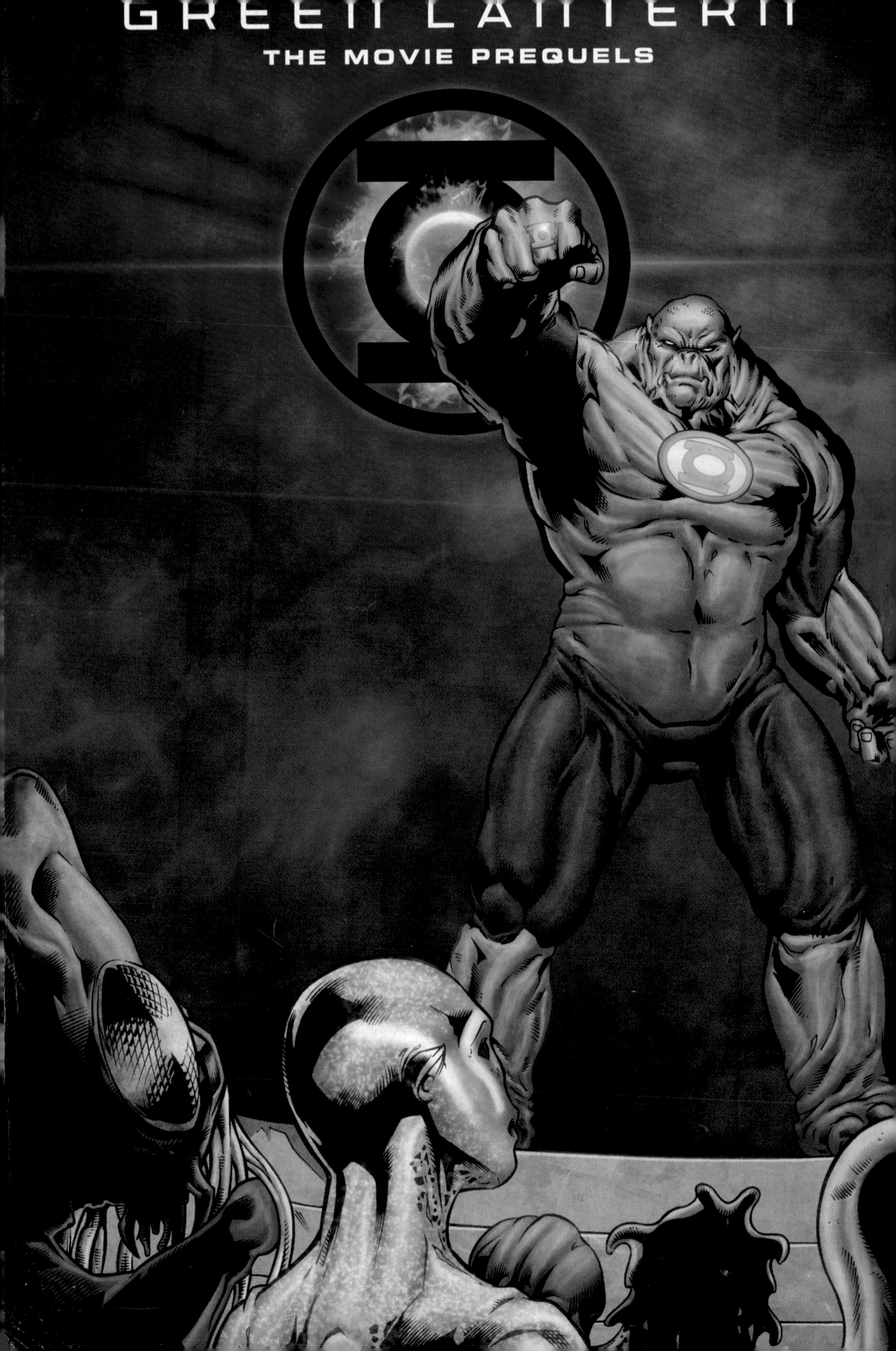
GREEN LANTERN
THE MOVIE PREQUELS

GEOFF **JOHNS**   MICHAEL **GREEN**   MARC **GUGGENHEIM**

PETER J. **TOMASI**   GREG **BERLANTI**   DONALD **DE LINE**

MICHAEL **GOLDENBERG**   ADAM **SCHLAGMAN**

writers

PATRICK **GLEASON**   TONY **SHASTEEN**   CLIFF **RICHARDS**

CARLOS **FERREIRA**   JERRY **ORDWAY**   TYLER **KIRKHAM**

HARVEY **TOLIBAO**   FERNANDO **DAGNINO**   MICK **GRAY**

SILVIO **SPOTTI**   **BATT**   RAUL **FERNANDEZ**

artists

NATHAN **EYRING**   GABE **ELTAEB**

ANDREW **DALHOUSE**   RANDY **MAYOR**

ROMULO **FAJARDO**   PETER **PANTAZIS**

colorists

DAVE **SHARPE**   ROB **LEIGH**

CARLOS M. **MANGUAL**

WES **ABBOTT**   SAL **CIPRIANO**

letterers

EDDIE BERGANZA EDITOR – ORIGINAL SERIES
SEAN MACKIEWICZ ASSISTANT EDITOR – ORIGINAL SERIES
IAN SATTLER DIRECTOR EDITORIAL, SPECIAL PROJECTS AND ARCHIVAL EDITIONS
ROBBIN BROSTERMAN DESIGN DIRECTOR – BOOKS
ROBBIE BIEDERMAN PUBLICATION DESIGN

EDDIE BERGANZA EXECUTIVE EDITOR
BOB HARRAS VP – EDITOR IN CHIEF

DIANE NELSON PRESIDENT
DAN DIDIO AND **JIM LEE** CO-PUBLISHERS
GEOFF JOHNS CHIEF CREATIVE OFFICER
JOHN ROOD EXECUTIVE VP – SALES, MARKETING AND BUSINESS DEVELOPMENT
AMY GENKINS SENIOR VP – BUSINESS AND LEGAL AFFAIRS
NAIRI GARDINER SENIOR VP – FINANCE
JEFF BOISON VP – PUBLISHING OPERATIONS
MARK CHIARELLO VP – ART DIRECTION AND DESIGN
JOHN CUNNINGHAM VP – MARKETING
TERRI CUNNINGHAM VP – TALENT RELATIONS AND SERVICES
ALISON GILL SENIOR VP – MANUFACTURING AND OPERATIONS
DAVID HYDE VP – PUBLICITY
HANK KANALZ SENIOR VP – DIGITAL
JAY KOGAN VP – BUSINESS AND LEGAL AFFAIRS, PUBLISHING
JACK MAHAN VP – BUSINESS AFFAIRS, TALENT
NICK NAPOLITANO VP – MANUFACTURING ADMINISTRATION
SUE POHJA VP – BOOK SALES
COURTNEY SIMMONS SENIOR VP – PUBLICITY
BOB WAYNE SENIOR VP – SALES

GREEN LANTERN – THE MOVIE PREQUELS

DC COMICS, 1700 BROADWAY, NEW YORK, NY 10019. A WARNER BROS. ENTERTAINMENT COMPANY
PRINTED BY RR DONNELLEY, SALEM, VA, USA. 9/9/11. FIRST PRINTING.
ISBN: 978-1-4012-3313-6

SUSTAINABLE
FORESTRY
INITIATIVE
Certified Chain of Custody
Promoting Sustainable
Forest Management
www.sfiprogram.org

Fiber used in this product line meets the
sourcing requirements of the SFI program.
www.sfiprogram.org SGS-SFI/COC-US10/81072

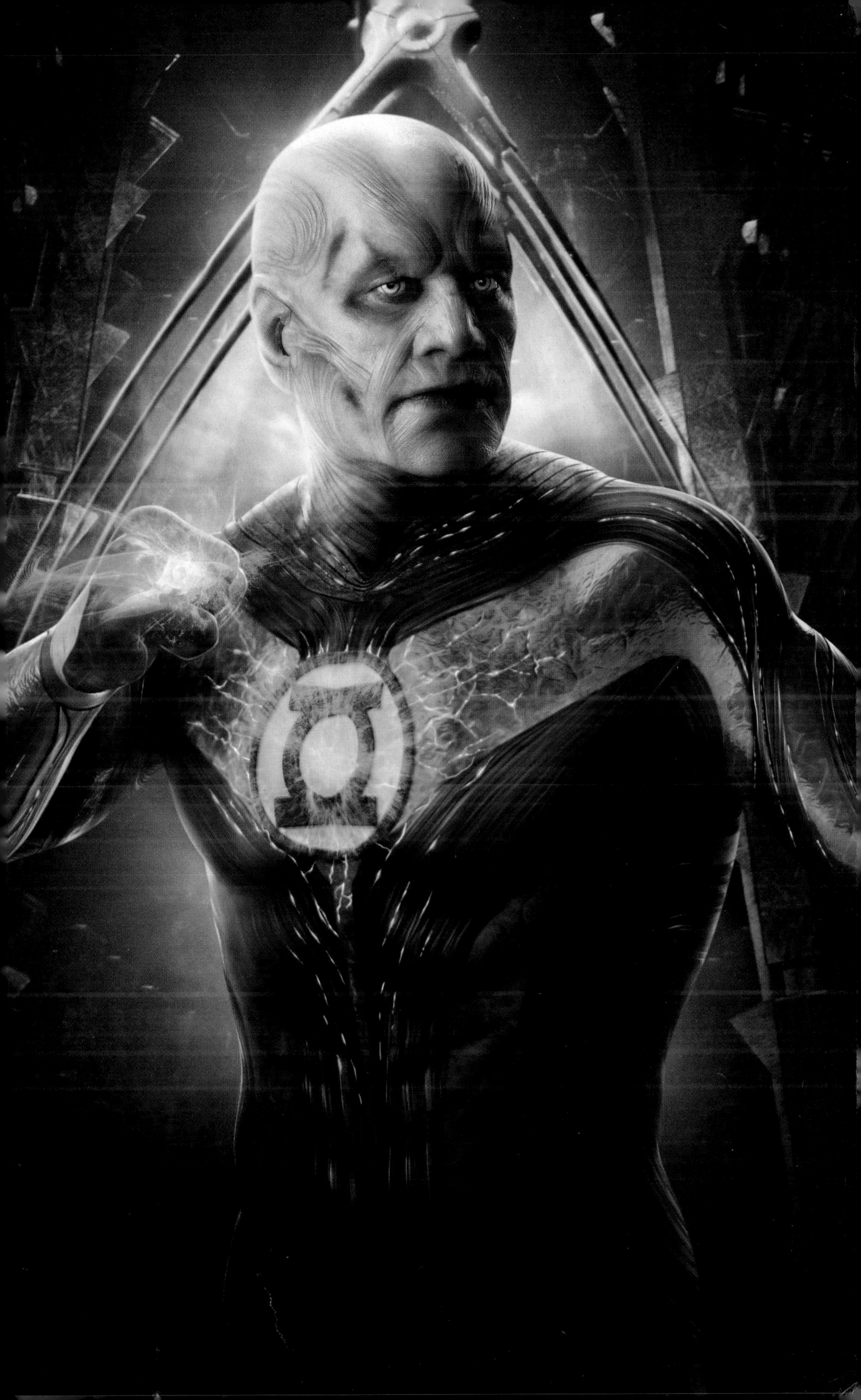

A SMALL, UNREMARKABLE PLANET

MICHAEL **GREEN** writer

PATRICK **GLEASON** & TONY **SHASTEEN** pencillers

MICK **GRAY** & TONY **SHASTEEN** inkers

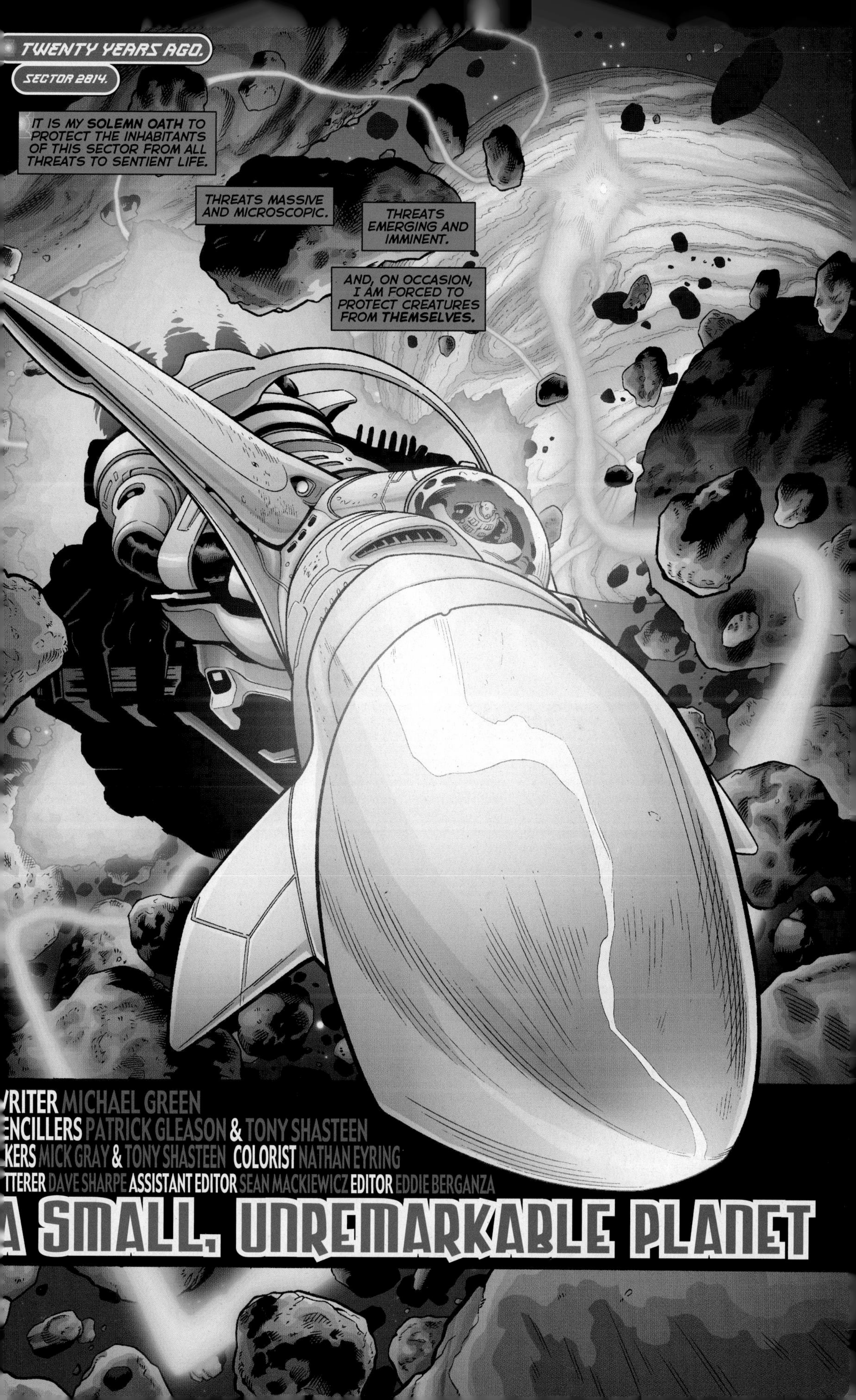
TWENTY YEARS AGO.
SECTOR 2814.
IT IS MY SOLEMN OATH TO PROTECT THE INHABITANTS OF THIS SECTOR FROM ALL THREATS TO SENTIENT LIFE.
THREATS MASSIVE AND MICROSCOPIC.
THREATS EMERGING AND IMMINENT.
AND, ON OCCASION, I AM FORCED TO PROTECT CREATURES FROM THEMSELVES.
VRITER MICHAEL GREEN
ENCILLERS PATRICK GLEASON & TONY SHASTEEN
KERS MICK GRAY & TONY SHASTEEN COLORIST NATHAN EYRING
TTERER DAVE SHARPE ASSISTANT EDITOR SEAN MACKIEWICZ EDITOR EDDIE BERGANZA
A SMALL, UNREMARKABLE PLANET

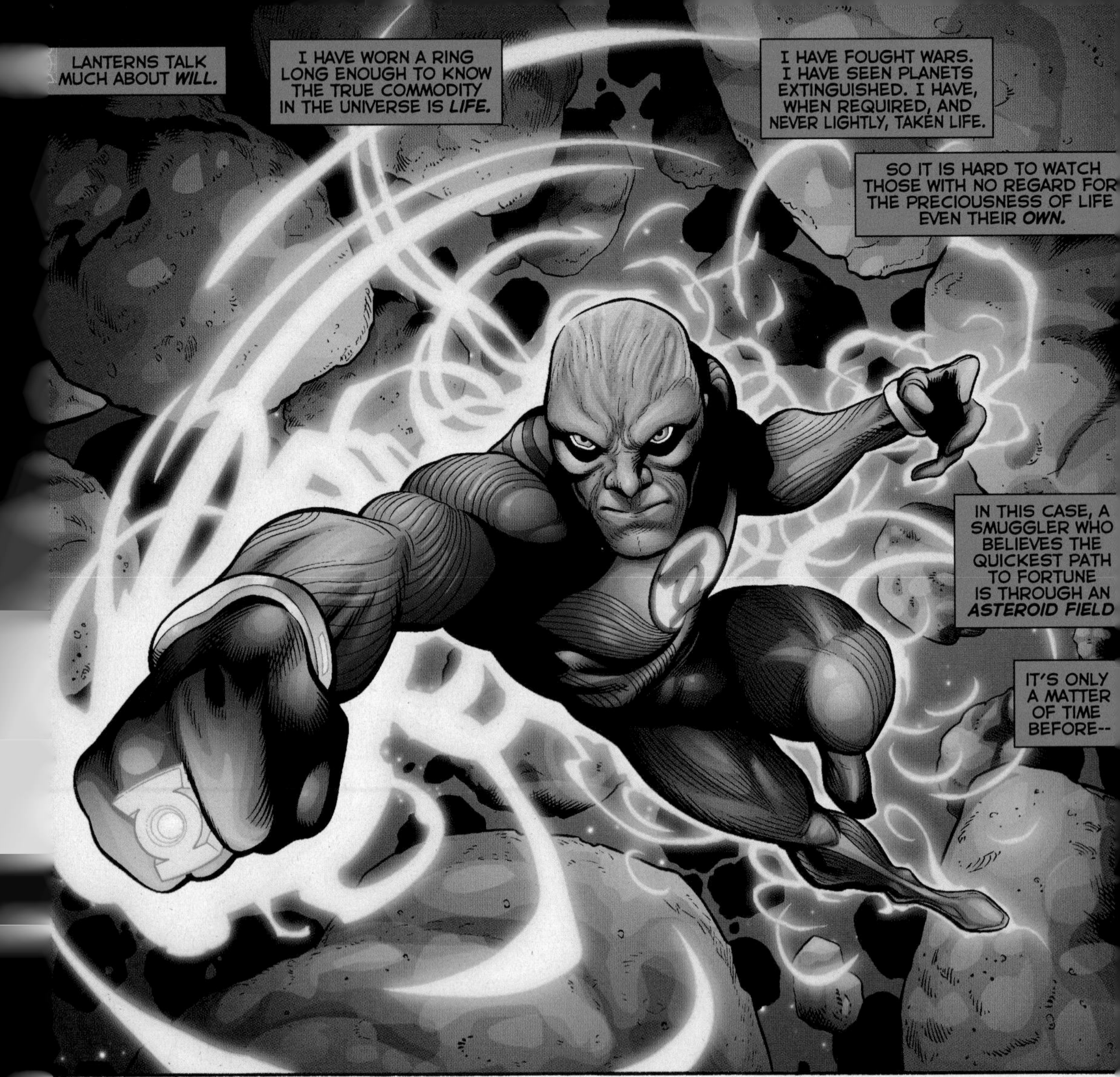
LANTERNS TALK MUCH ABOUT WILL.
I HAVE WORN A RING LONG ENOUGH TO KNOW THE TRUE COMMODITY IN THE UNIVERSE IS LIFE.
I HAVE FOUGHT WARS. I HAVE SEEN PLANETS EXTINGUISHED. I HAVE, WHEN REQUIRED, AND NEVER LIGHTLY, TAKEN LIFE.
SO IT IS HARD TO WATCH THOSE WITH NO REGARD FOR THE PRECIOUSNESS OF LIFE EVEN THEIR OWN.
IN THIS CASE, A SMUGGLER WHO BELIEVES THE QUICKEST PATH TO FORTUNE IS THROUGH AN ASTEROID FIELD
IT'S ONLY A MATTER OF TIME BEFORE--

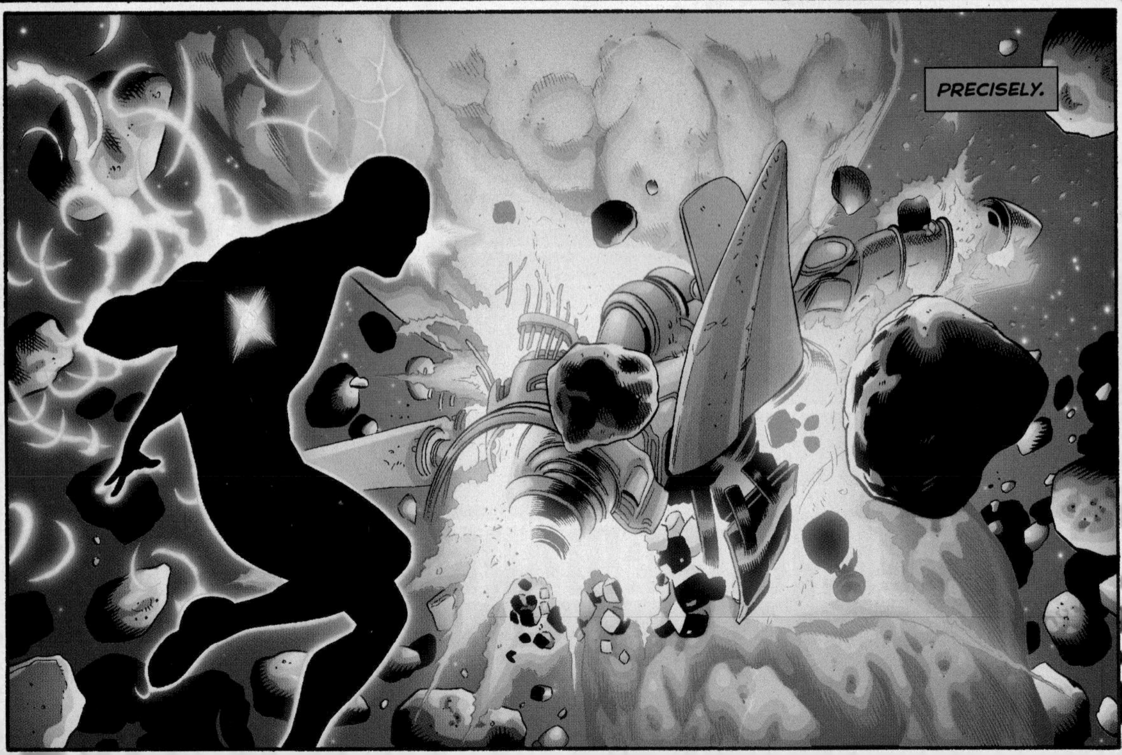
PRECISELY.

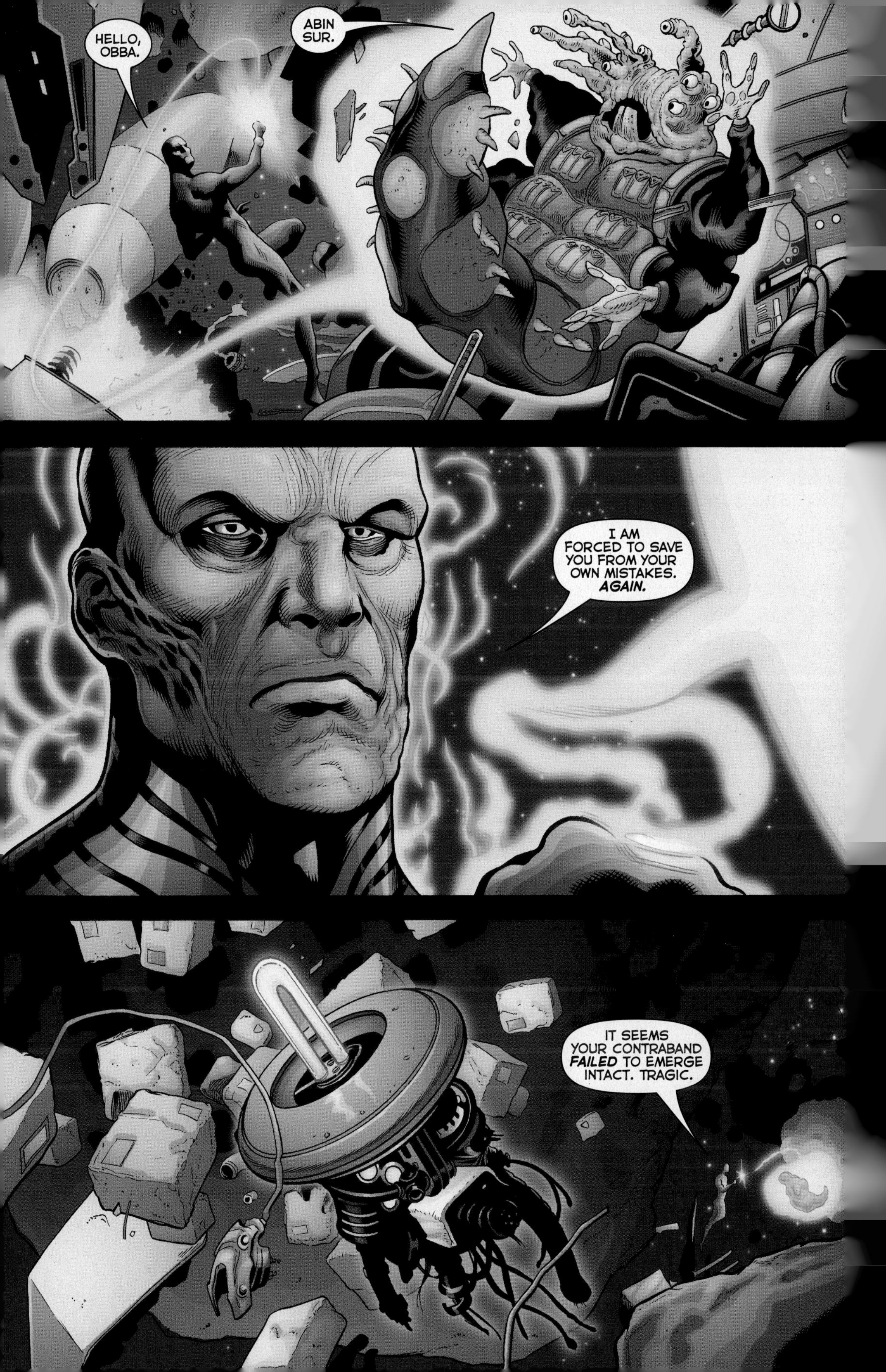
HELLO, OBBA.
ABIN SUR.
I AM FORCED TO SAVE YOU FROM YOUR OWN MISTAKES. *AGAIN.*
IT SEEMS YOUR CONTRABAND *FAILED* TO EMERGE INTACT. TRAGIC.

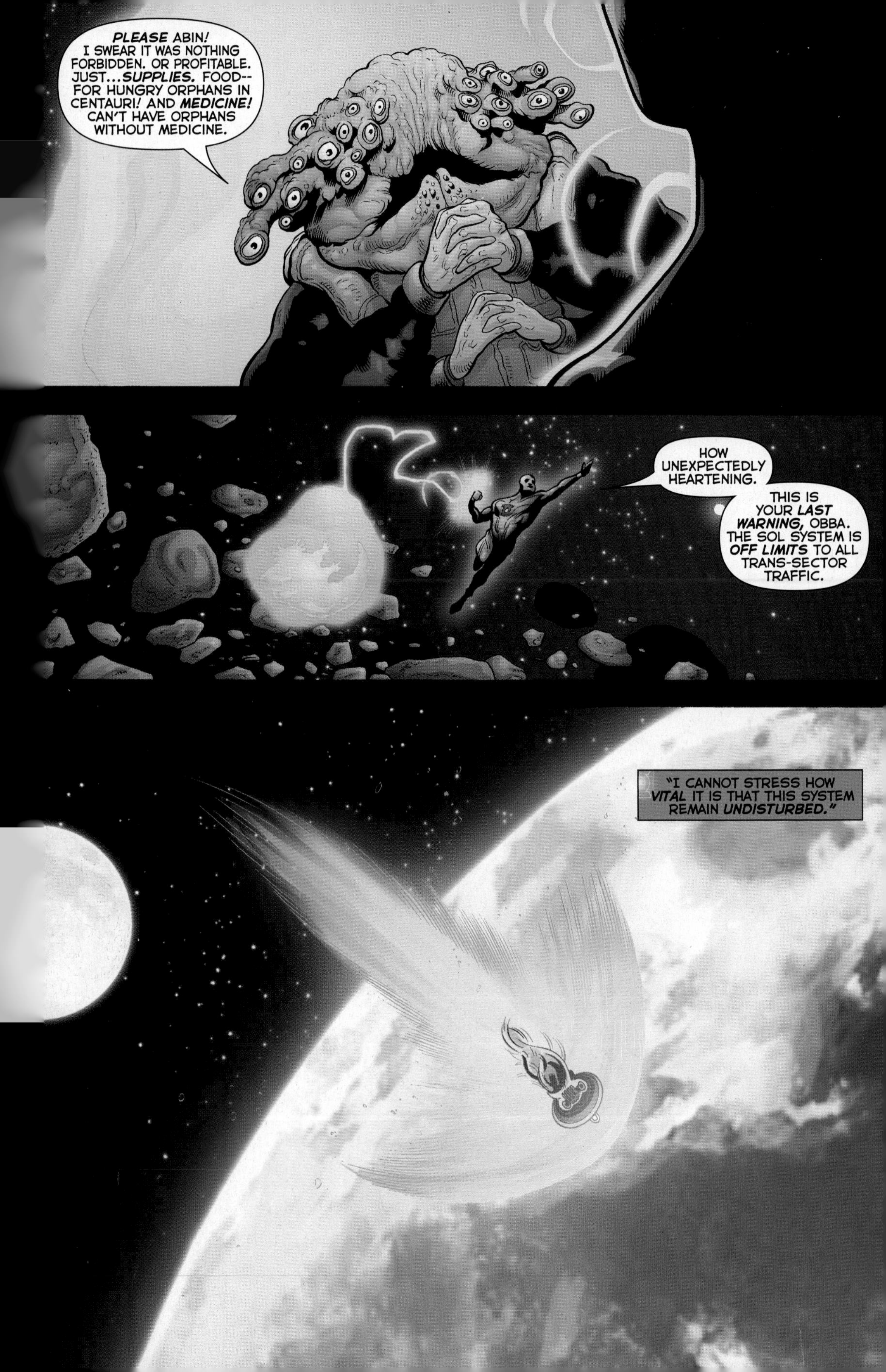
PLEASE ABIN! I SWEAR IT WAS NOTHING FORBIDDEN. OR PROFITABLE. JUST...SUPPLIES. FOOD--FOR HUNGRY ORPHANS IN CENTAURI! AND MEDICINE! CAN'T HAVE ORPHANS WITHOUT MEDICINE.
HOW UNEXPECTEDLY HEARTENING.
THIS IS YOUR LAST WARNING, OBBA. THE SOL SYSTEM IS OFF LIMITS TO ALL TRANS-SECTOR TRAFFIC.
"I CANNOT STRESS HOW VITAL IT IS THAT THIS SYSTEM REMAIN UNDISTURBED."

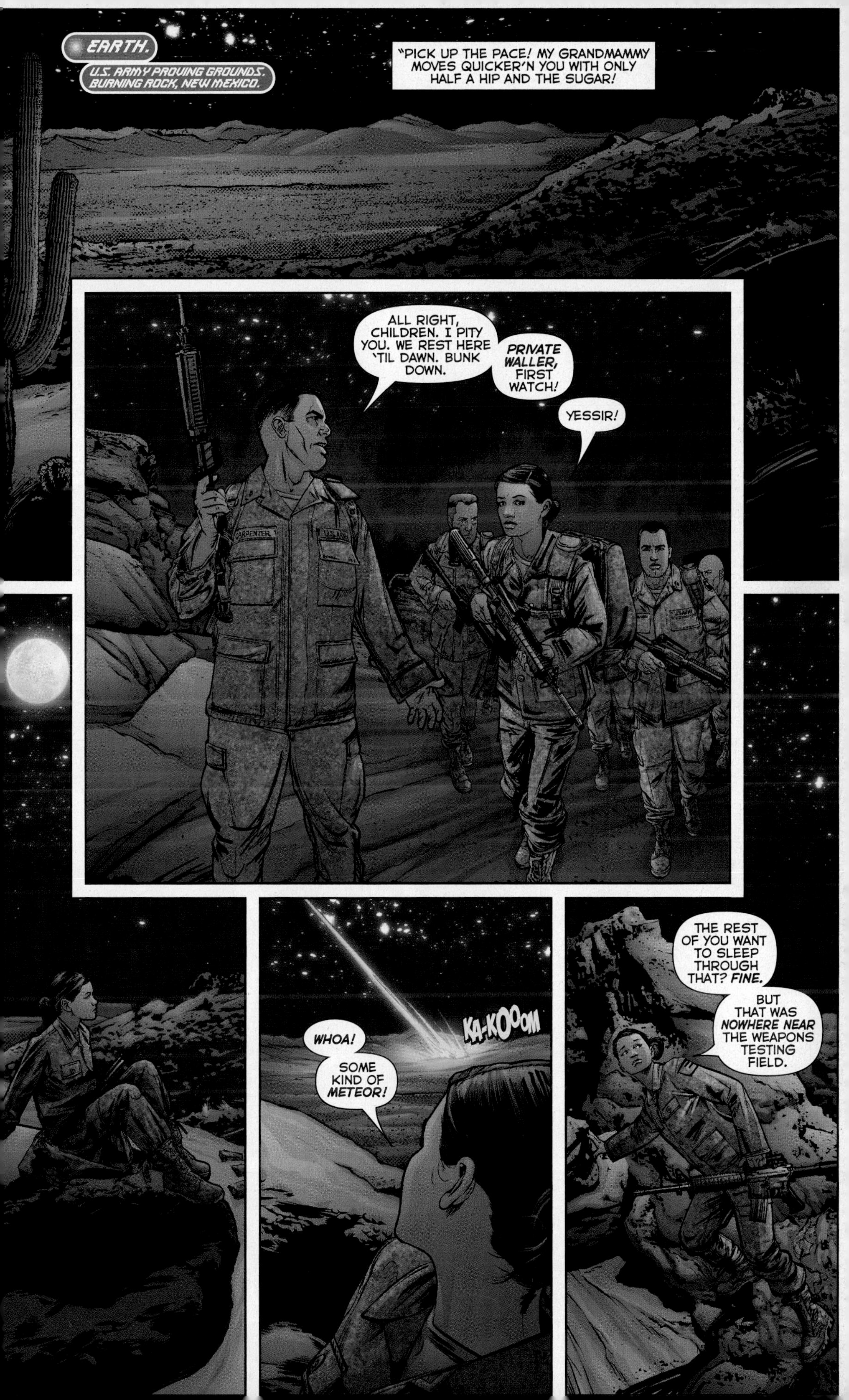
EARTH.
U.S. ARMY PROVING GROUNDS. BURNING ROCK, NEW MEXICO.
"PICK UP THE PACE! MY GRANDMAMMY MOVES QUICKER'N YOU WITH ONLY HALF A HIP AND THE SUGAR!
ALL RIGHT, CHILDREN. I PITY YOU. WE REST HERE 'TIL DAWN. BUNK DOWN.
PRIVATE WALLER, FIRST WATCH!
YESSIR!
CARPENTER
U.S. ARMY
WHOA!
SOME KIND OF METEOR!
KA-KOOOM
THE REST OF YOU WANT TO SLEEP THROUGH THAT? FINE.
BUT THAT WAS NOWHERE NEAR THE WEAPONS TESTING FIELD.

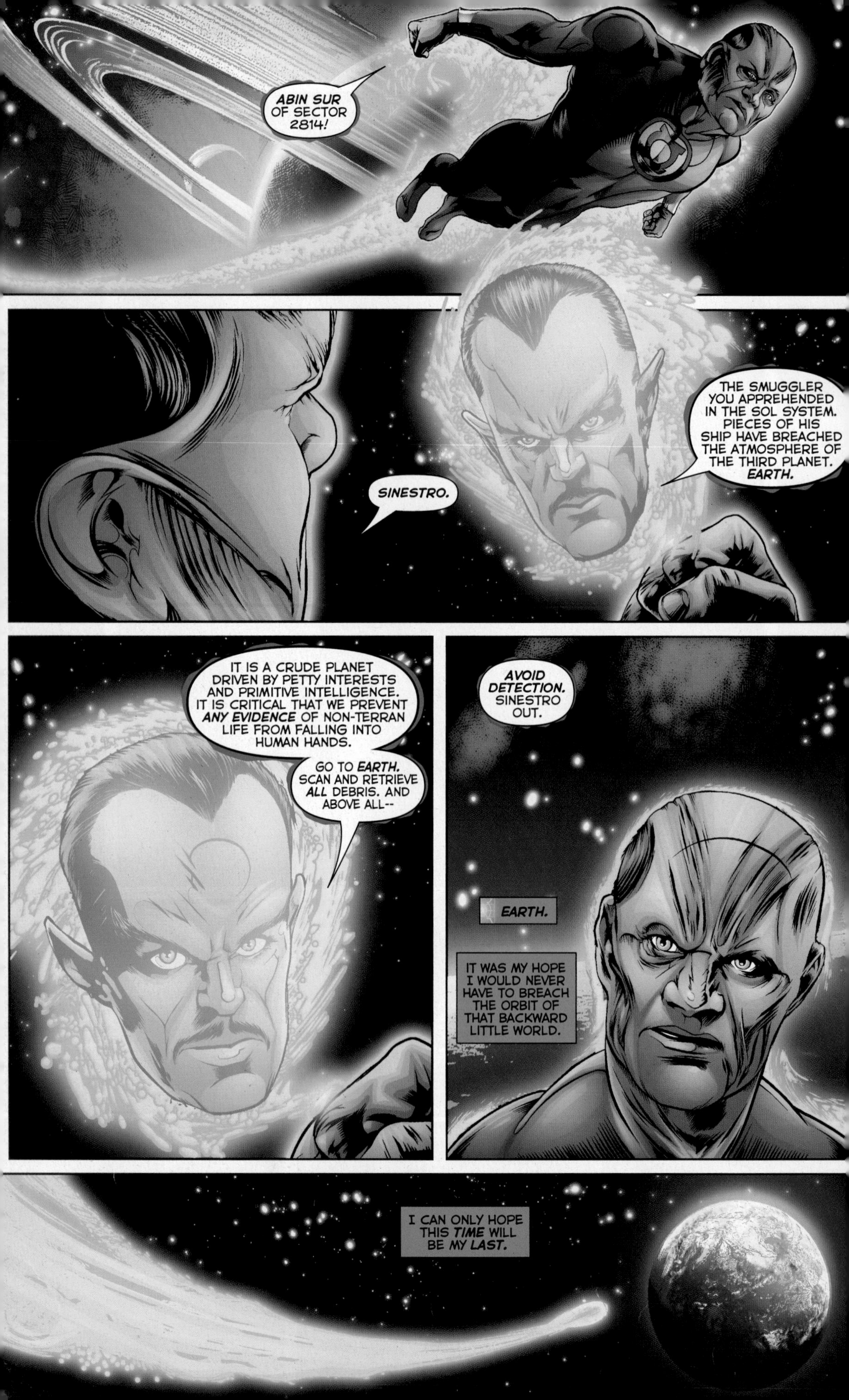
ABIN SUR OF SECTOR 2814!
SINESTRO.
THE SMUGGLER YOU APPREHENDED IN THE SOL SYSTEM. PIECES OF HIS SHIP HAVE BREACHED THE ATMOSPHERE OF THE THIRD PLANET. EARTH.
IT IS A CRUDE PLANET DRIVEN BY PETTY INTERESTS AND PRIMITIVE INTELLIGENCE. IT IS CRITICAL THAT WE PREVENT ANY EVIDENCE OF NON-TERRAN LIFE FROM FALLING INTO HUMAN HANDS.
GO TO EARTH. SCAN AND RETRIEVE ALL DEBRIS. AND ABOVE ALL--
AVOID DETECTION. SINESTRO OUT.
EARTH.
IT WAS MY HOPE I WOULD NEVER HAVE TO BREACH THE ORBIT OF THAT BACKWARD LITTLE WORLD.
I CAN ONLY HOPE THIS TIME WILL BE MY LAST.

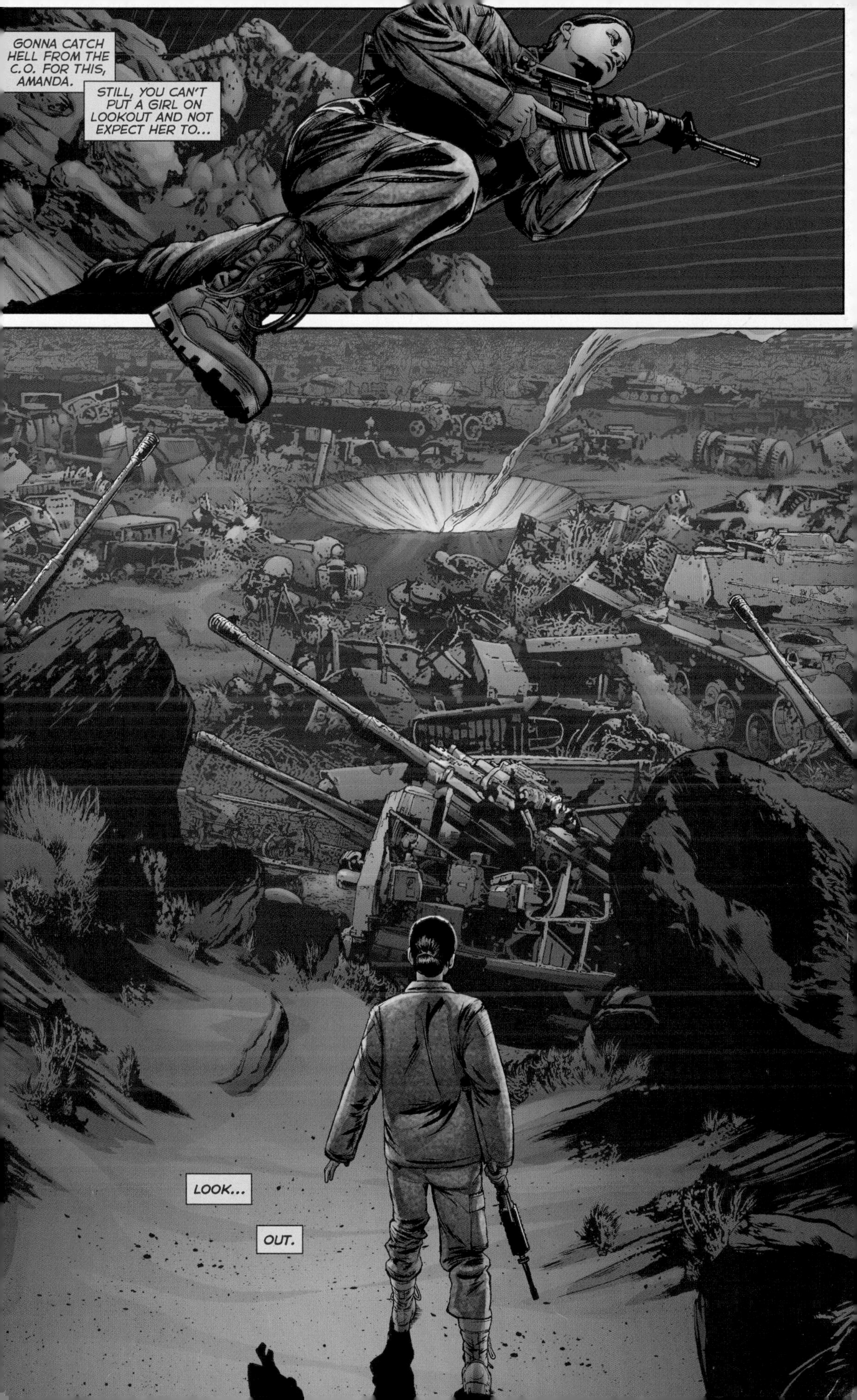
GONNA CATCH HELL FROM THE C.O. FOR THIS, AMANDA.
STILL, YOU CAN'T PUT A GIRL ON LOOKOUT AND NOT EXPECT HER TO...
LOOK...
OUT.

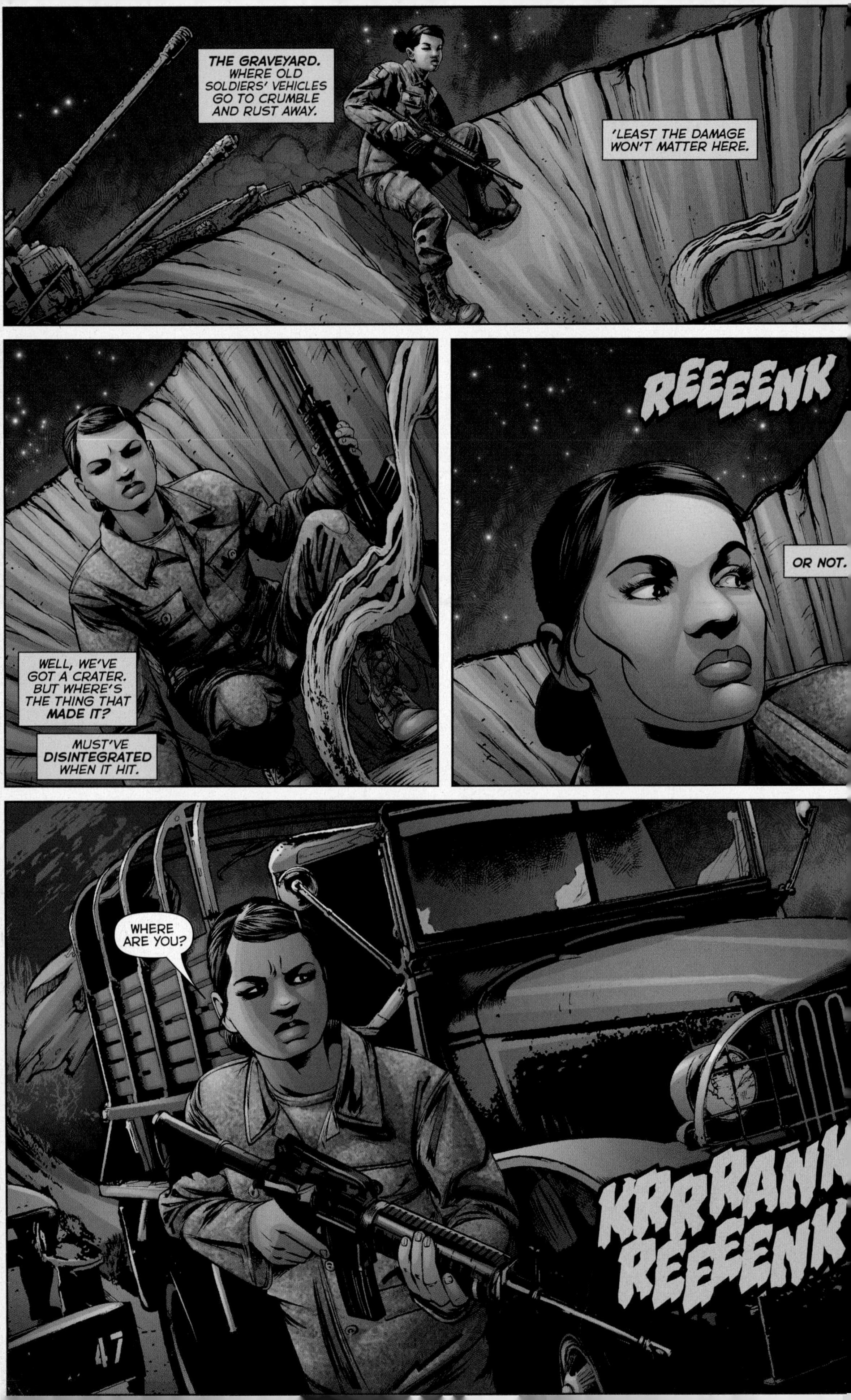
THE GRAVEYARD. WHERE OLD SOLDIERS' VEHICLES GO TO CRUMBLE AND RUST AWAY.
'LEAST THE DAMAGE WON'T MATTER HERE.
WELL, WE'VE GOT A CRATER. BUT WHERE'S THE THING THAT MADE IT?
MUST'VE DISINTEGRATED WHEN IT HIT.
REEEEENK
OR NOT.
WHERE ARE YOU?
KRRRANK
REEEEENK
47

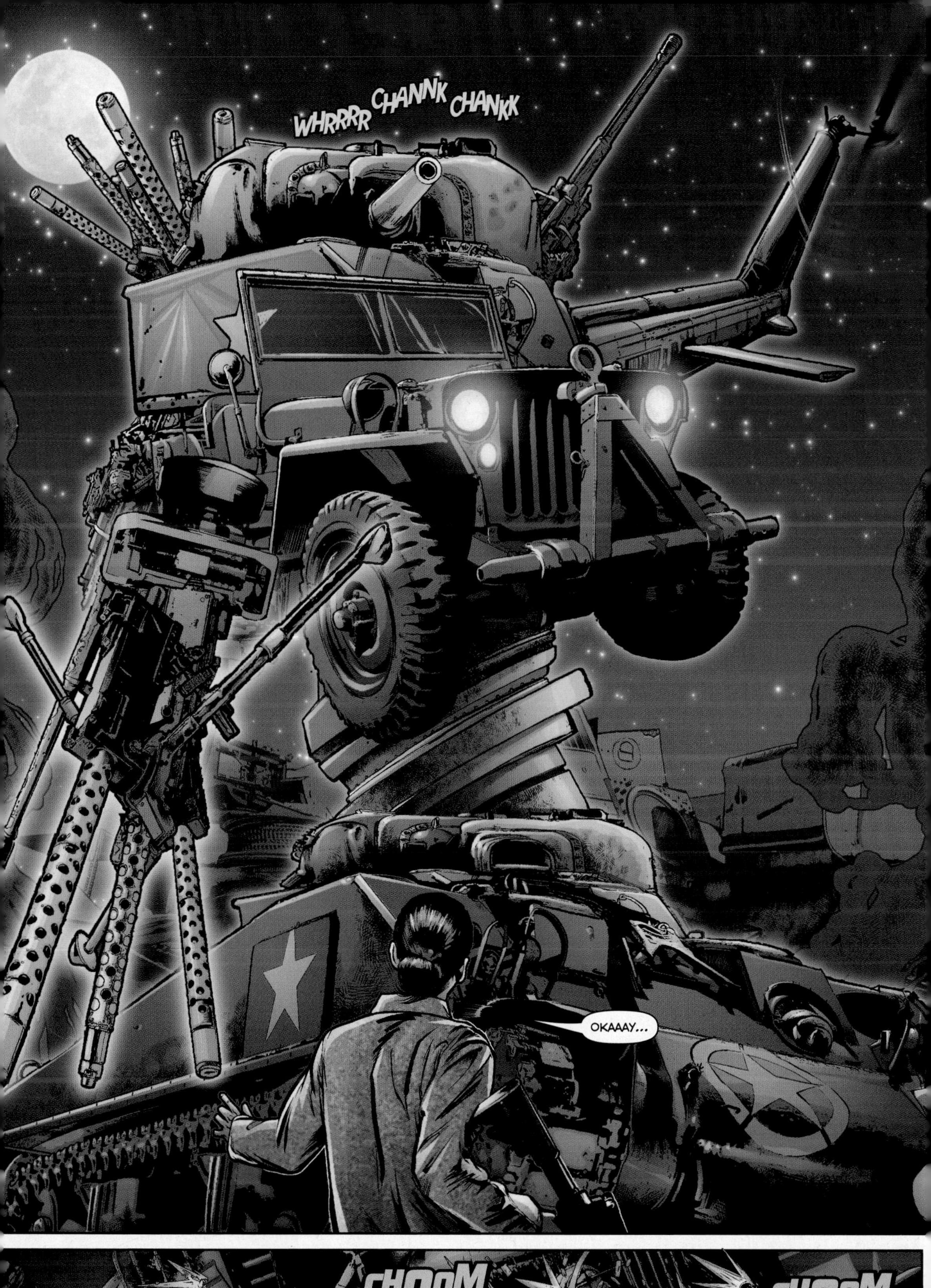
WHRRRR CHANNK CHANKK
OKAAAY...

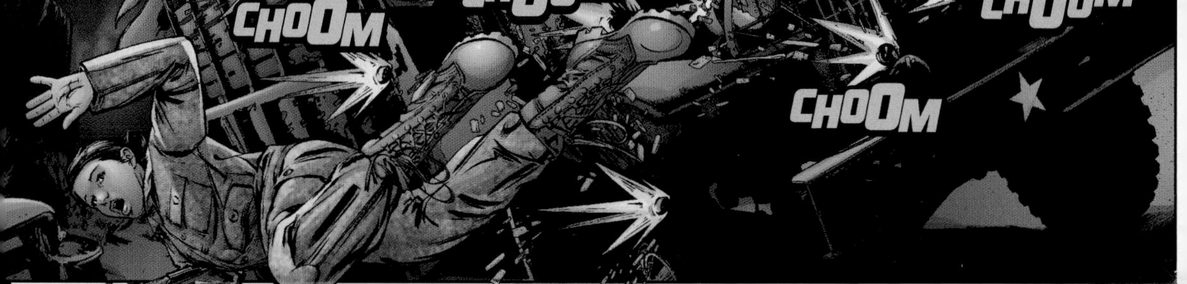
CHOOM
CHOOM
CHOOM
CHOOM

EARTH'S PLANETARY DETECTION SYSTEMS ARE GRATIFYINGLY EASY TO AVOID.

HUMANS FUMBLE WITH THE ELECTROMAGNETIC SPECTRUM LIKE INFANTS.

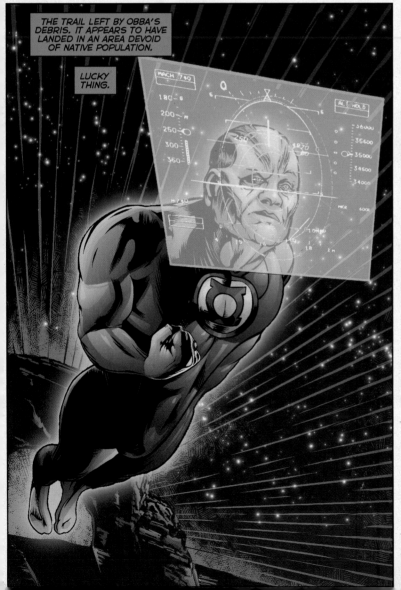

THE TRAIL LEFT BY OBBA'S DEBRIS. IT APPEARS TO HAVE LANDED IN AN AREA DEVOID OF NATIVE POPULATION.

LUCKY THING.

I SHOULD BE ON MY WAY BACK TO OA BY--

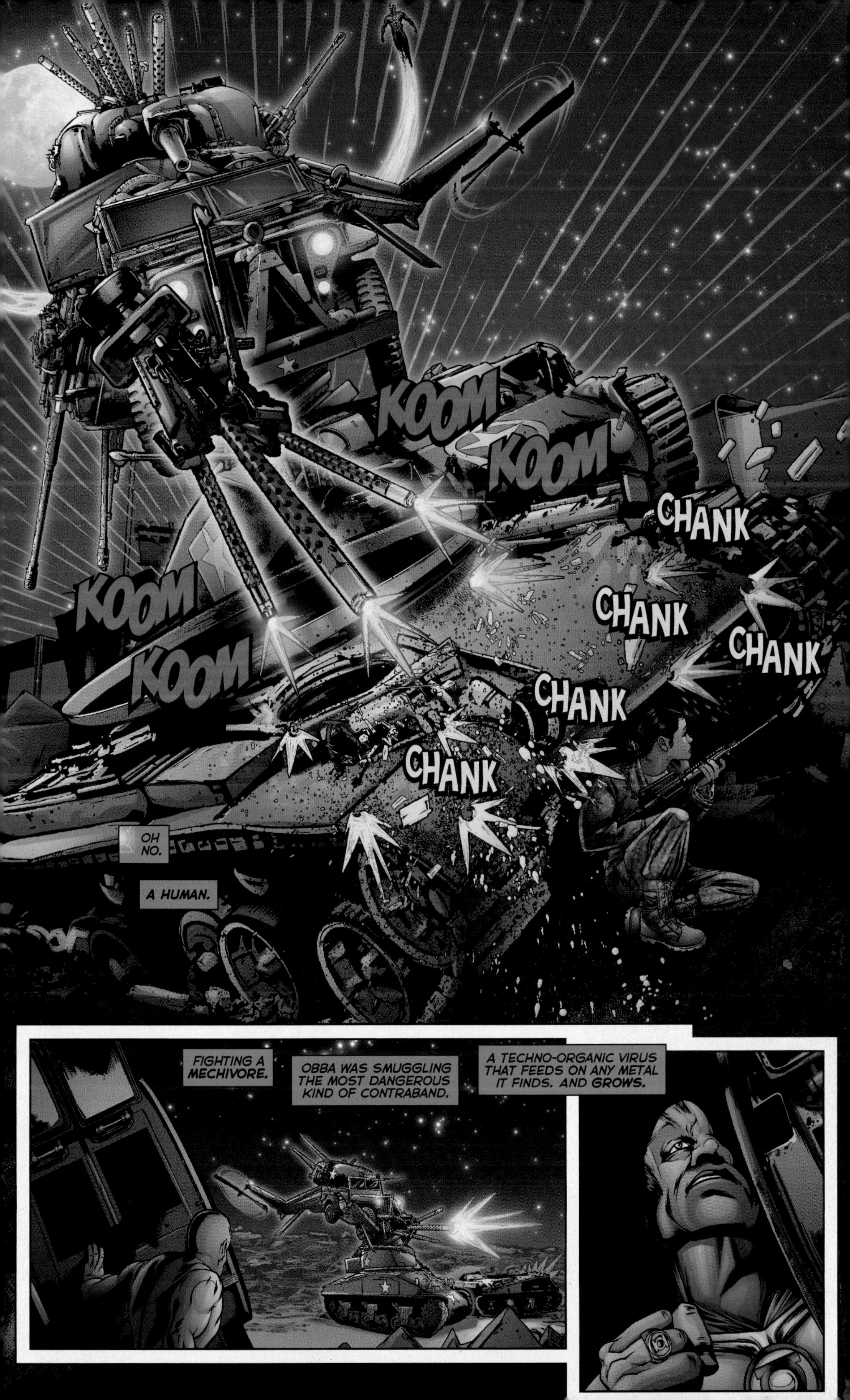
KOOM
KOOM
CHANK
KOOM
KOOM
CHANK
CHANK
CHANK
CHANK
OH NO.
A HUMAN.
FIGHTING A MECHIVORE.
OBBA WAS SMUGGLING THE MOST DANGEROUS KIND OF CONTRABAND.
A TECHNO-ORGANIC VIRUS THAT FEEDS ON ANY METAL IT FINDS. AND GROWS.

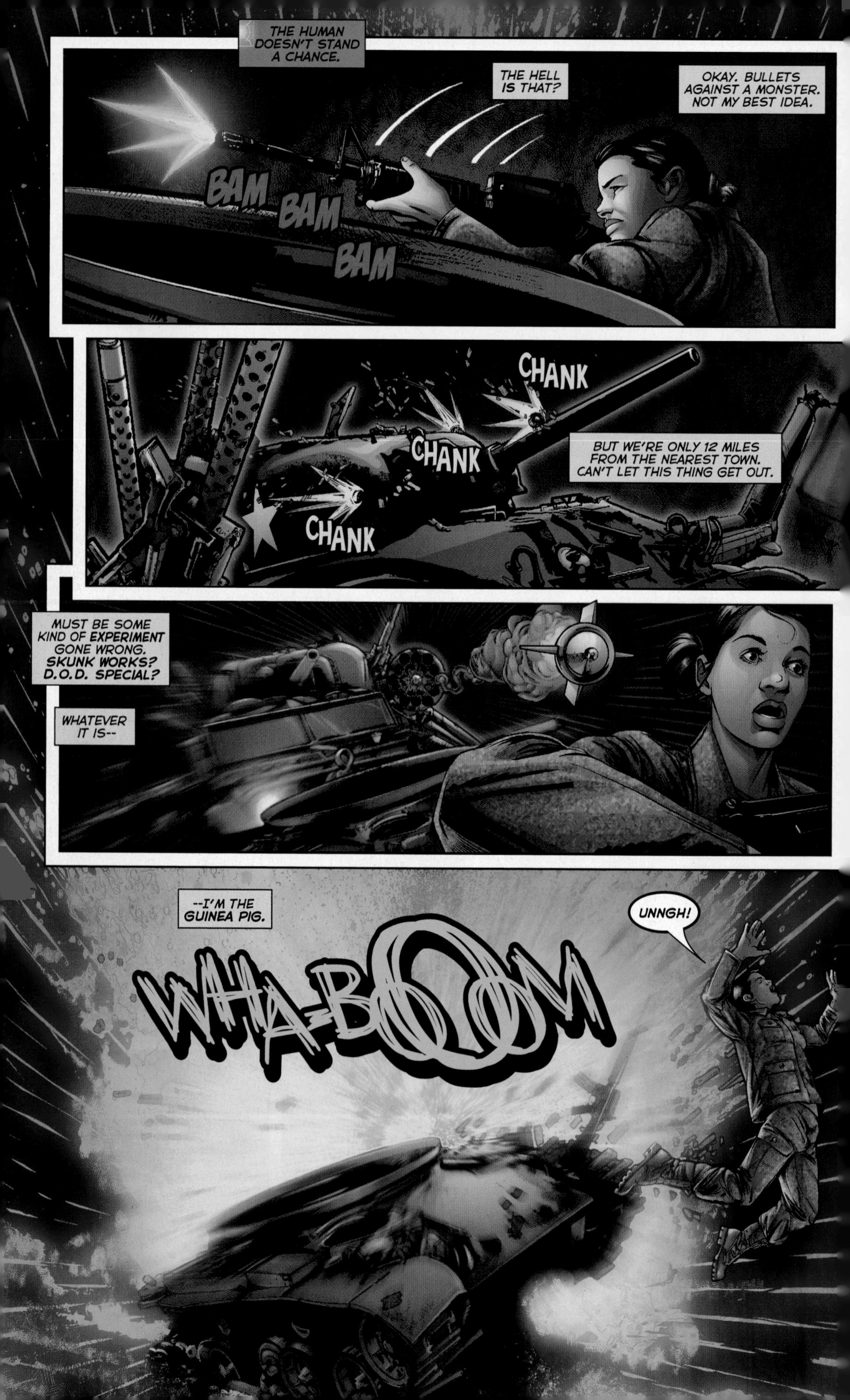
THE HUMAN DOESN'T STAND A CHANCE.
THE HELL IS THAT?
OKAY. BULLETS AGAINST A MONSTER. NOT MY BEST IDEA.
BAM
BAM
BAM
CHANK
CHANK
CHANK
BUT WE'RE ONLY 12 MILES FROM THE NEAREST TOWN. CAN'T LET THIS THING GET OUT.
MUST BE SOME KIND OF EXPERIMENT GONE WRONG. SKUNK WORKS? D.O.D. SPECIAL?
WHATEVER IT IS--
--I'M THE GUINEA PIG.
UNNGH!
WHA-BOOOM

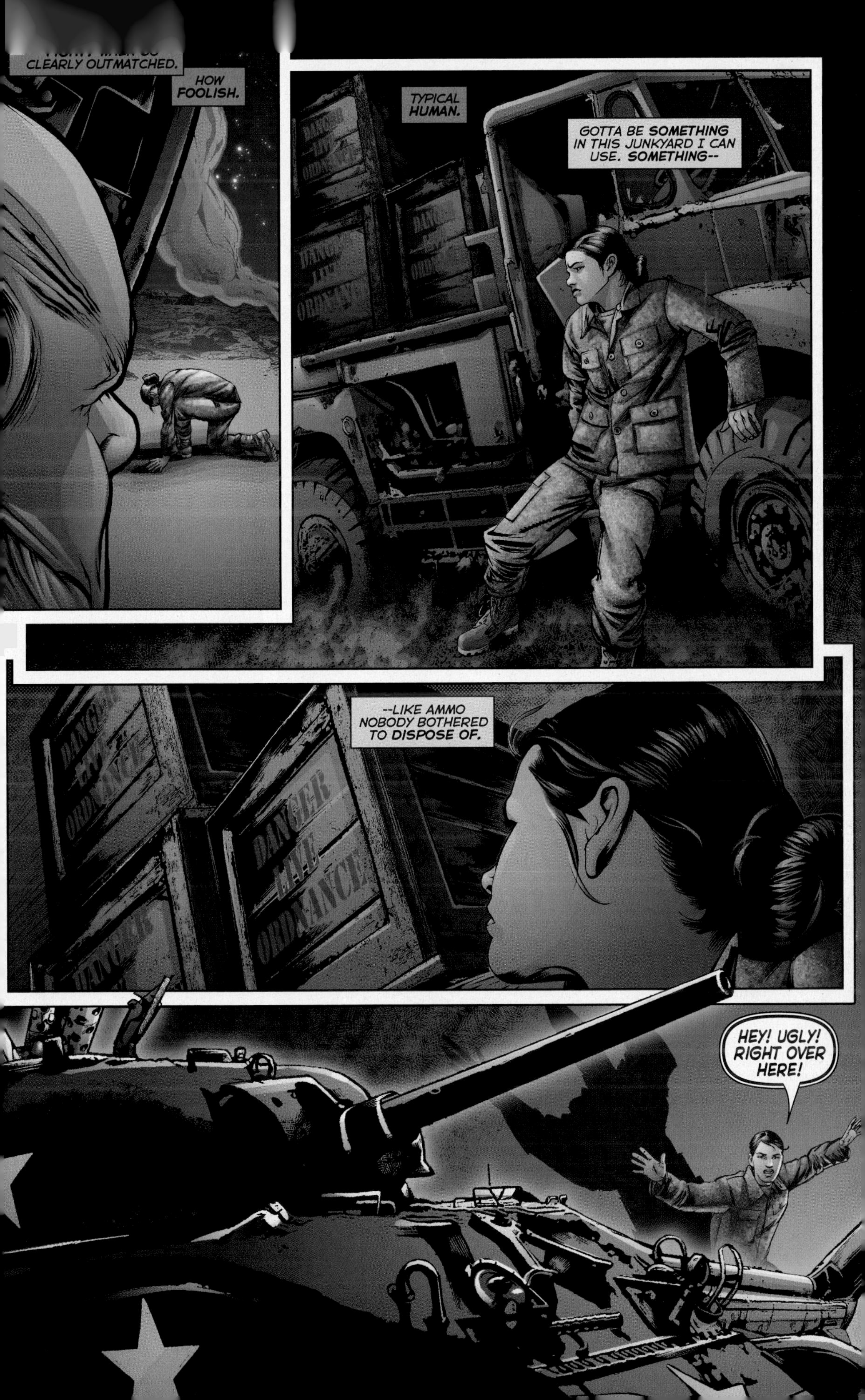

CLEARLY OUTMATCHED.
HOW FOOLISH.
TYPICAL HUMAN.
GOTTA BE SOMETHING IN THIS JUNKYARD I CAN USE. SOMETHING--
--LIKE AMMO NOBODY BOTHERED TO DISPOSE OF.
DANGER LIVE ORDNANCE
HEY! UGLY! RIGHT OVER HERE!

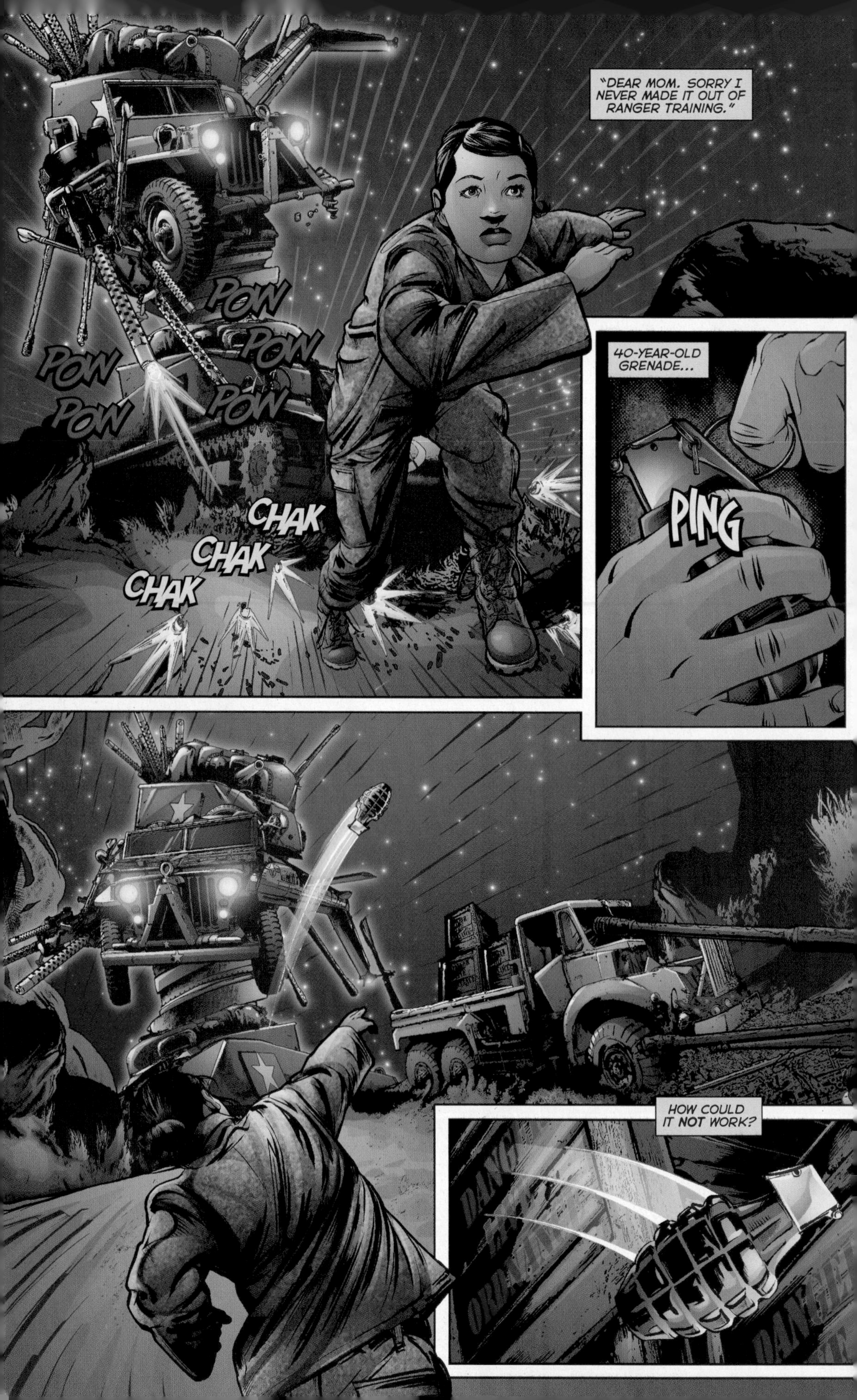
"DEAR MOM. SORRY I NEVER MADE IT OUT OF RANGER TRAINING."
POW
POW
POW
POW
POW
CHAK
CHAK
CHAK
40-YEAR-OLD GRENADE...
PING
HOW COULD IT NOT WORK?

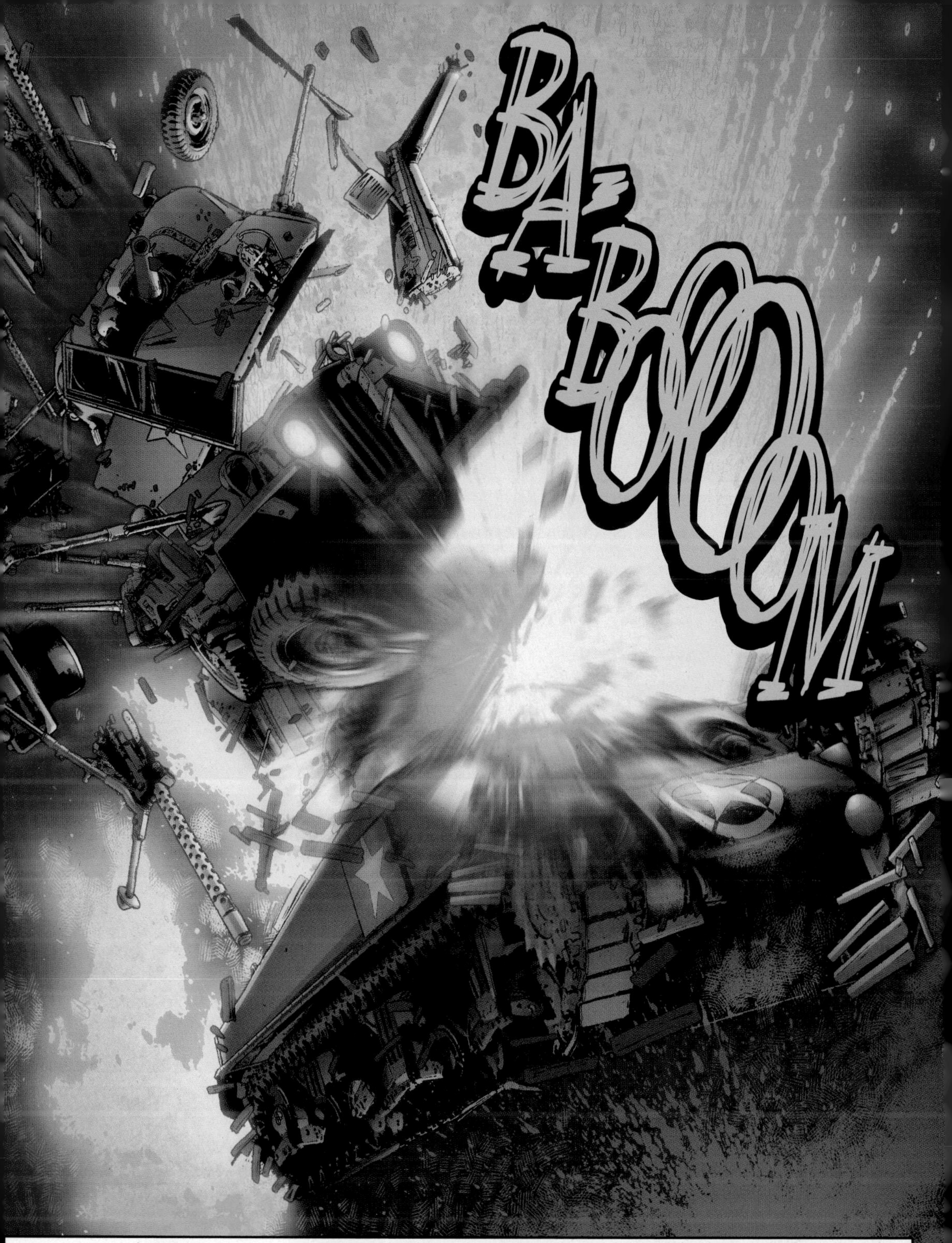
BA-BOOOM

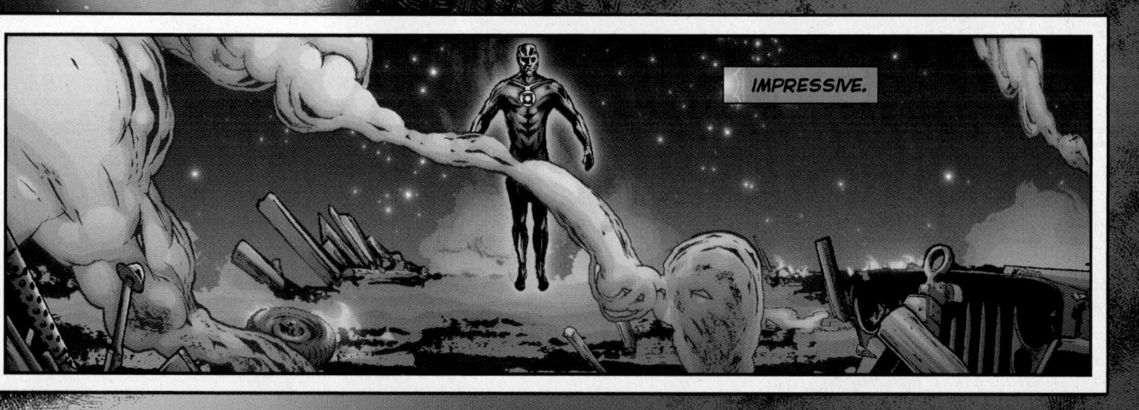
IMPRESSIVE.

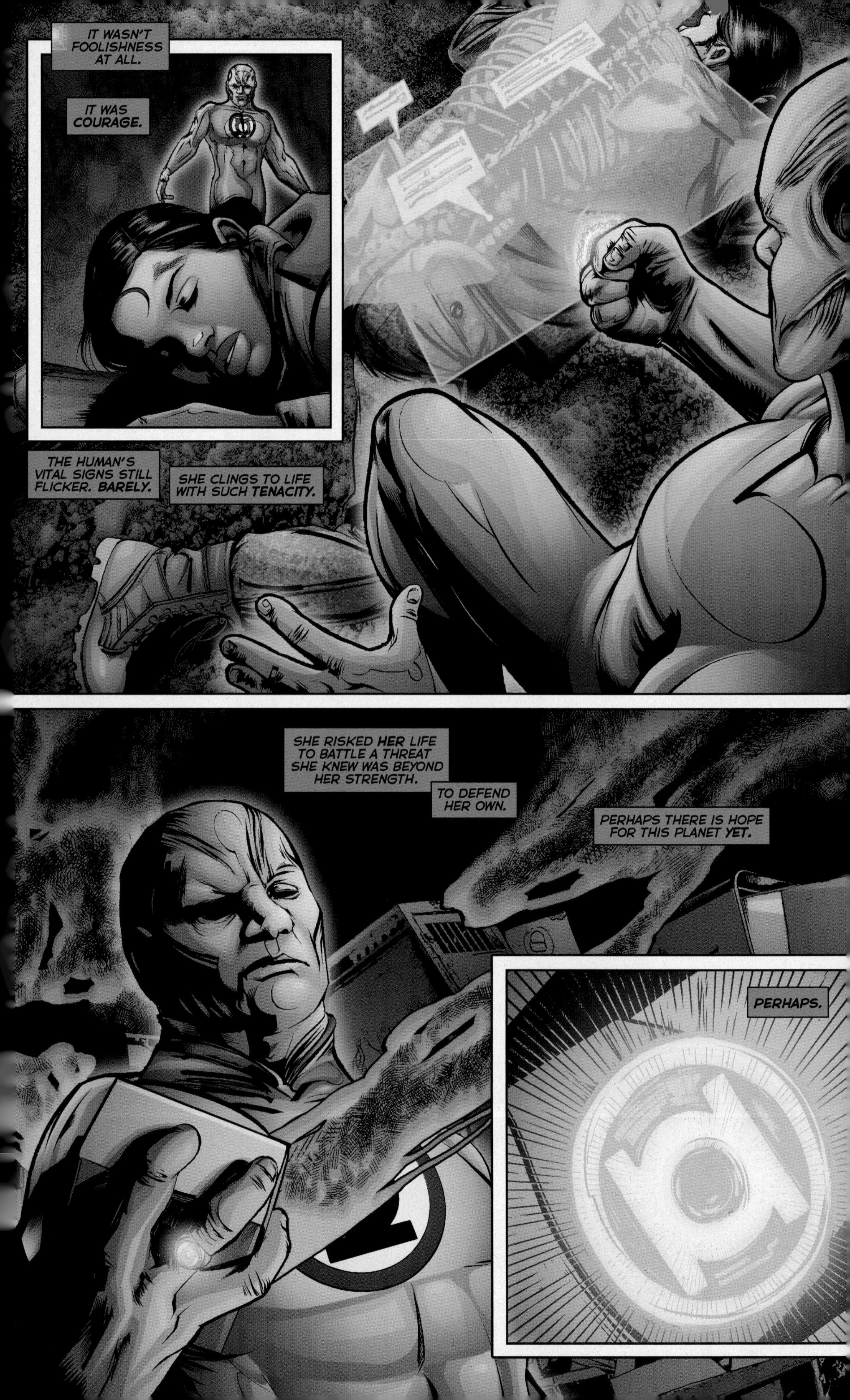
IT WASN'T FOOLISHNESS AT ALL.
IT WAS COURAGE.
THE HUMAN'S VITAL SIGNS STILL FLICKER. BARELY.
SHE CLINGS TO LIFE WITH SUCH TENACITY.
SHE RISKED HER LIFE TO BATTLE A THREAT SHE KNEW WAS BEYOND HER STRENGTH.
TO DEFEND HER OWN.
PERHAPS THERE IS HOPE FOR THIS PLANET YET.
PERHAPS.

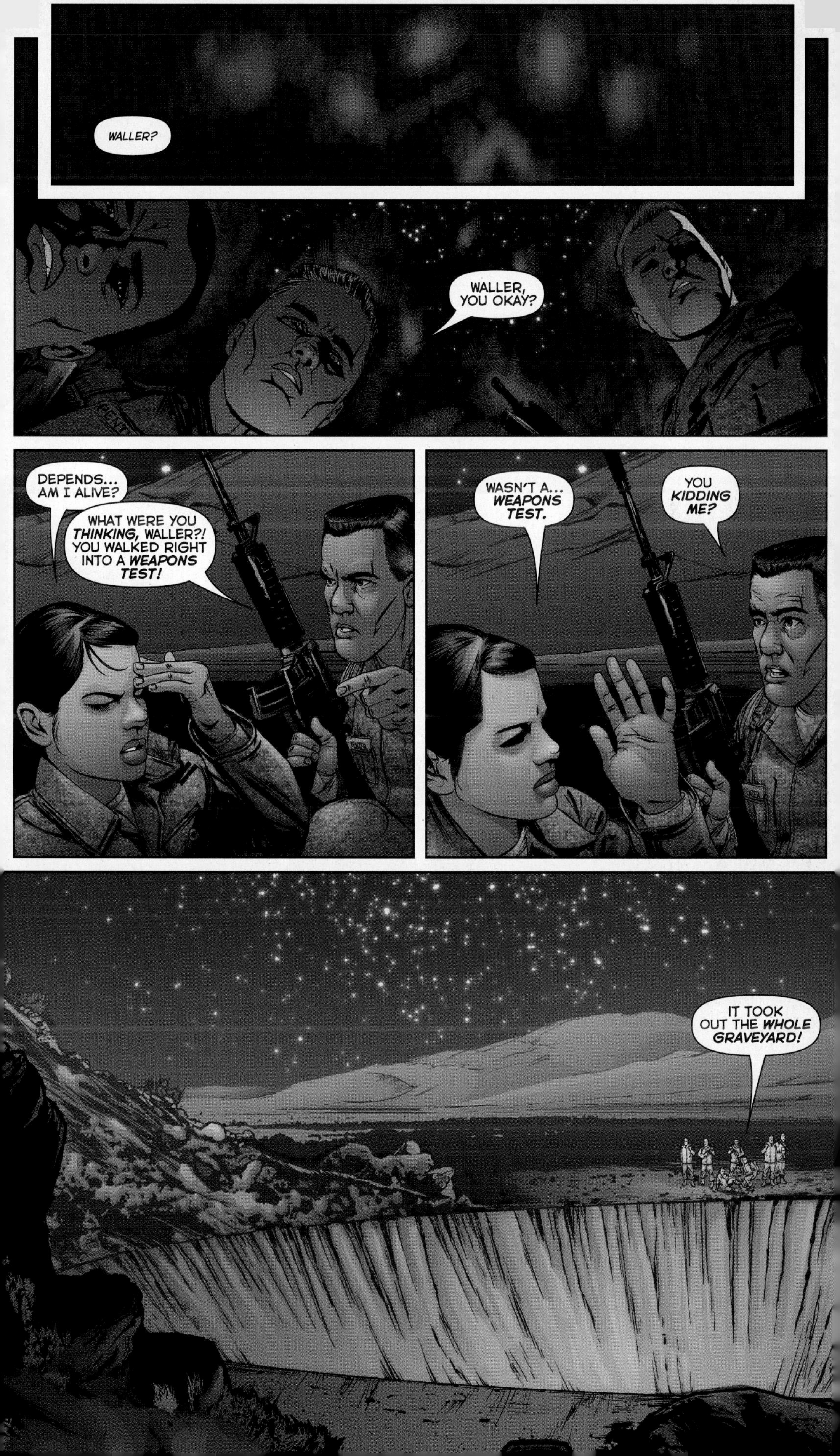
WALLER?
WALLER, YOU OKAY?
DEPENDS... AM I ALIVE?
WHAT WERE YOU *THINKING,* WALLER?! YOU WALKED RIGHT INTO A *WEAPONS TEST!*
WASN'T A... *WEAPONS TEST.*
YOU *KIDDING ME?*
IT TOOK OUT THE *WHOLE GRAVEYARD!*

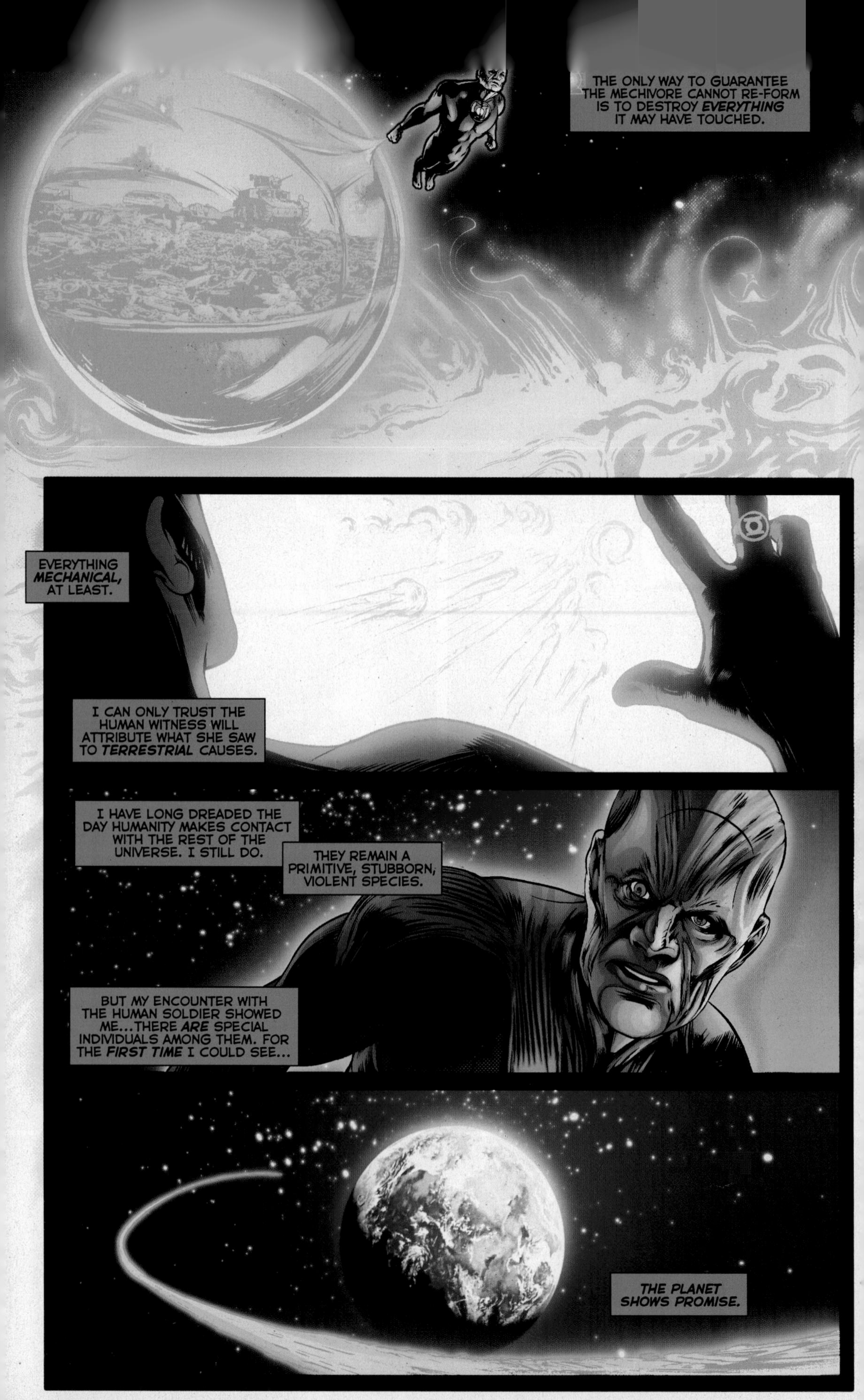
THE ONLY WAY TO GUARANTEE THE MECHIVORE CANNOT RE-FORM IS TO DESTROY *EVERYTHING* IT MAY HAVE TOUCHED.
EVERYTHING *MECHANICAL,* AT LEAST.
I CAN ONLY TRUST THE HUMAN WITNESS WILL ATTRIBUTE WHAT SHE SAW TO *TERRESTRIAL* CAUSES.
I HAVE LONG DREADED THE DAY HUMANITY MAKES CONTACT WITH THE REST OF THE UNIVERSE. I STILL DO.
THEY REMAIN A PRIMITIVE, STUBBORN, VIOLENT SPECIES.
BUT MY ENCOUNTER WITH THE HUMAN SOLDIER SHOWED ME...THERE *ARE* SPECIAL INDIVIDUALS AMONG THEM. FOR THE *FIRST TIME* I COULD SEE...
THE PLANET SHOWS PROMISE.

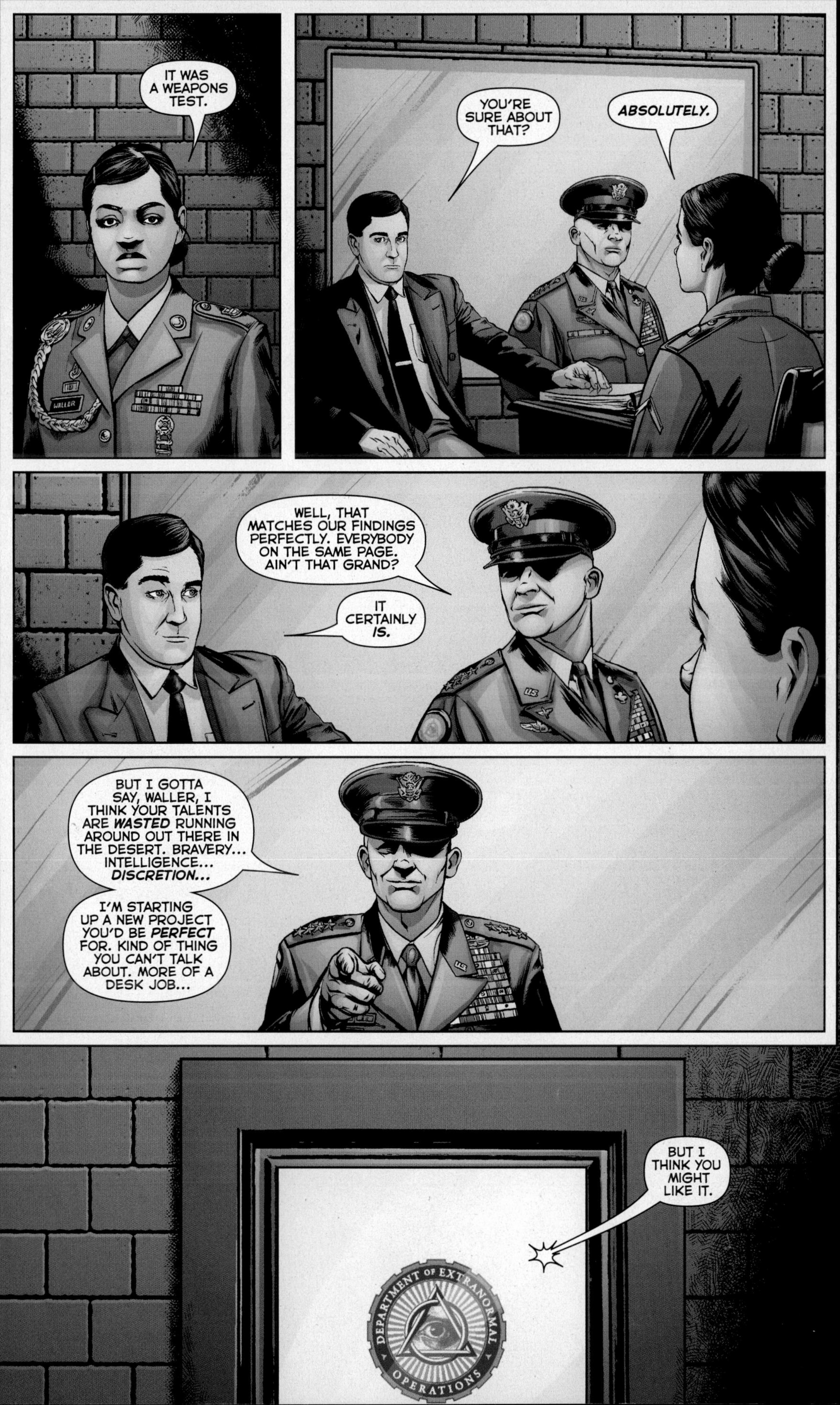
WALLER
IT WAS A WEAPONS TEST.
YOU'RE SURE ABOUT THAT?
ABSOLUTELY.
WELL, THAT MATCHES OUR FINDINGS PERFECTLY. EVERYBODY ON THE SAME PAGE. AIN'T THAT GRAND?
IT CERTAINLY *IS.*
BUT I GOTTA SAY, WALLER, I THINK YOUR TALENTS ARE *WASTED* RUNNING AROUND OUT THERE IN THE DESERT. BRAVERY... INTELLIGENCE... *DISCRETION...*
I'M STARTING UP A NEW PROJECT YOU'D BE *PERFECT* FOR. KIND OF THING YOU CAN'T TALK ABOUT. MORE OF A DESK JOB...
BUT I THINK YOU MIGHT LIKE IT.
DEPARTMENT OF EXTRANORMAL OPERATIONS

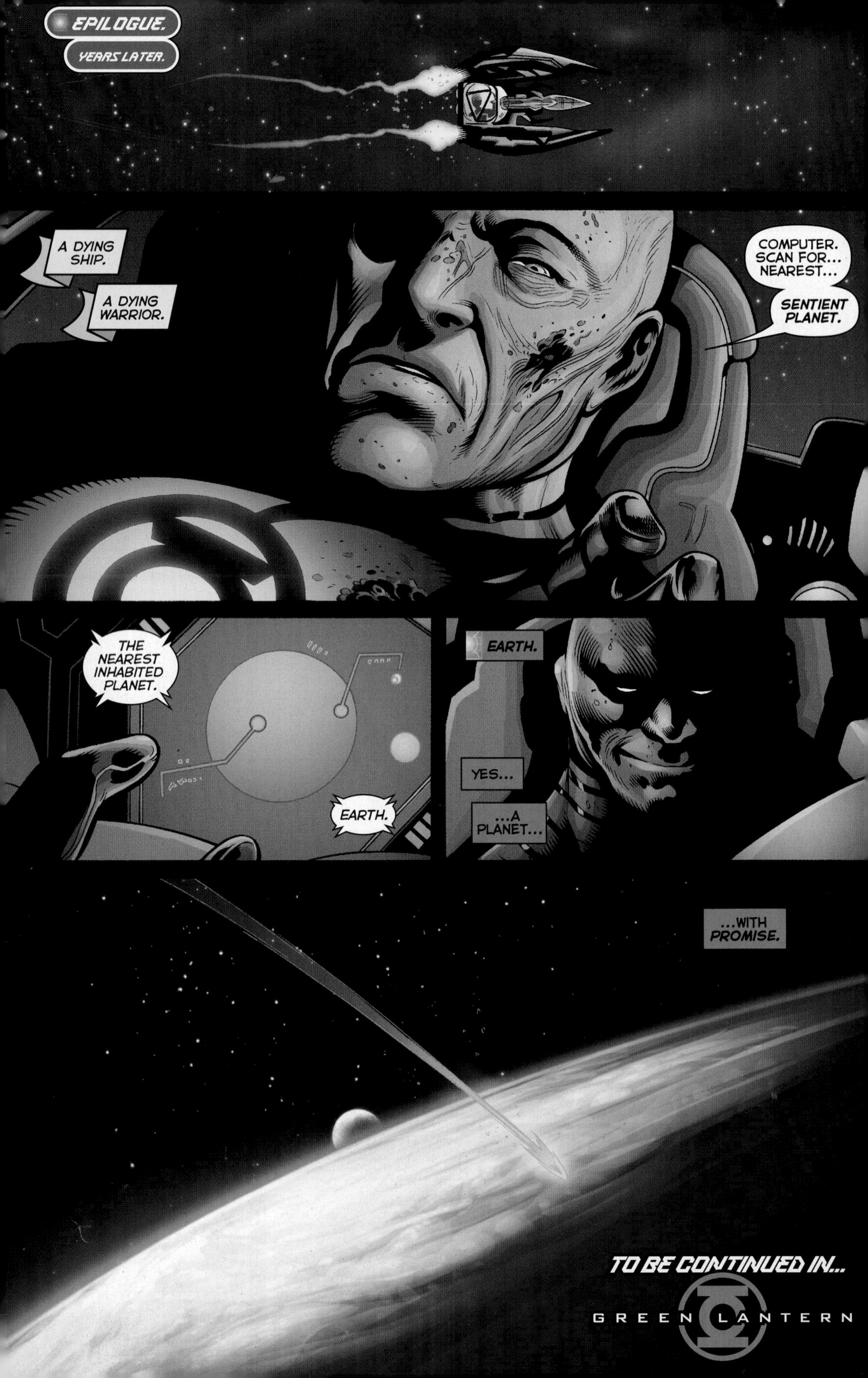

EPILOGUE.
YEARS LATER.
A DYING SHIP.
A DYING WARRIOR.
COMPUTER. SCAN FOR... NEAREST...
SENTIENT PLANET.
THE NEAREST INHABITED PLANET.
EARTH.
EARTH.
YES...
...A PLANET...
...WITH PROMISE.
TO BE CONTINUED IN...
GREEN LANTERN

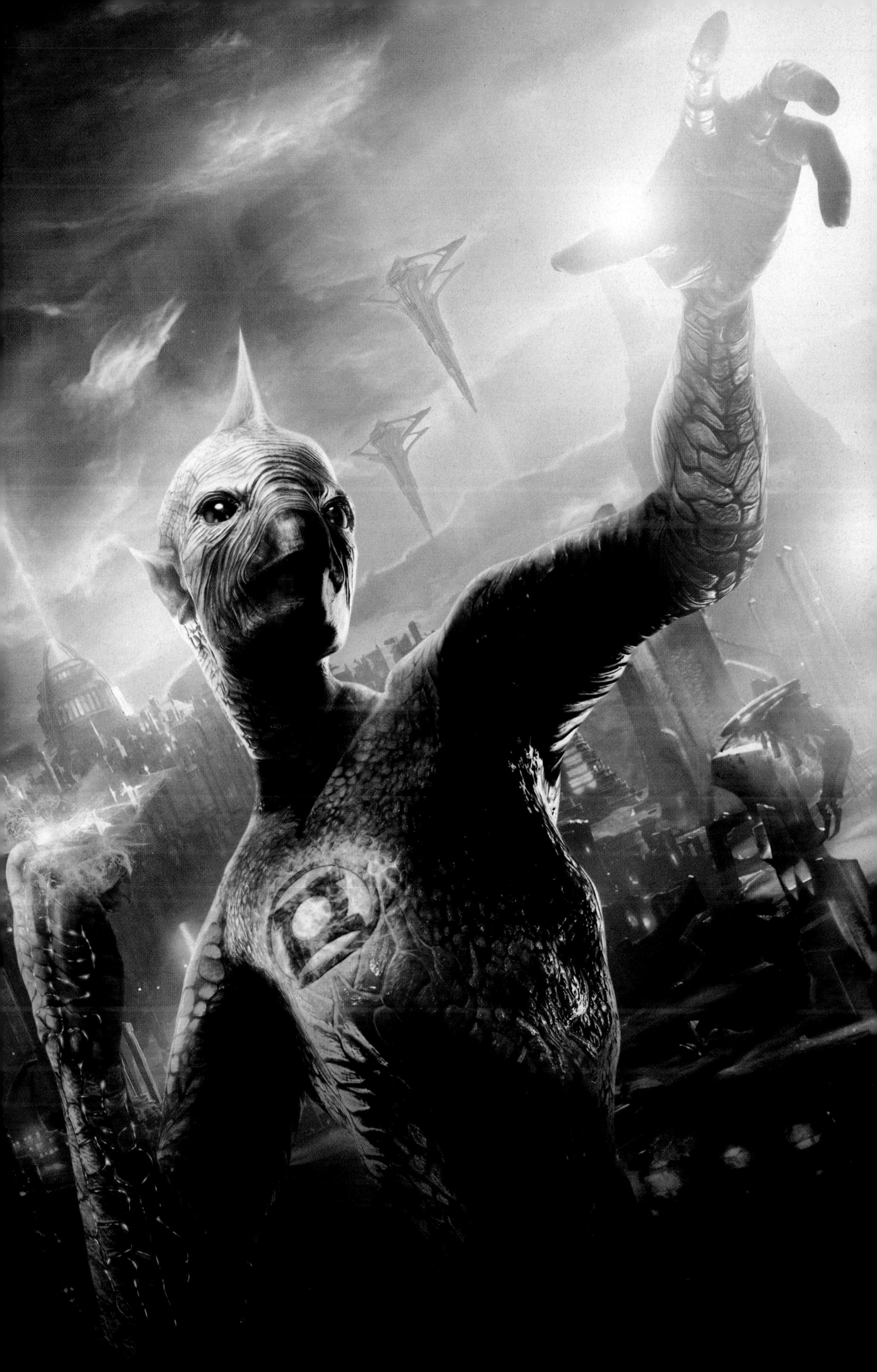

FORBIDDEN PLANET

MARC **GUGGENHEIM** writer

CLIFF **RICHARDS** artist

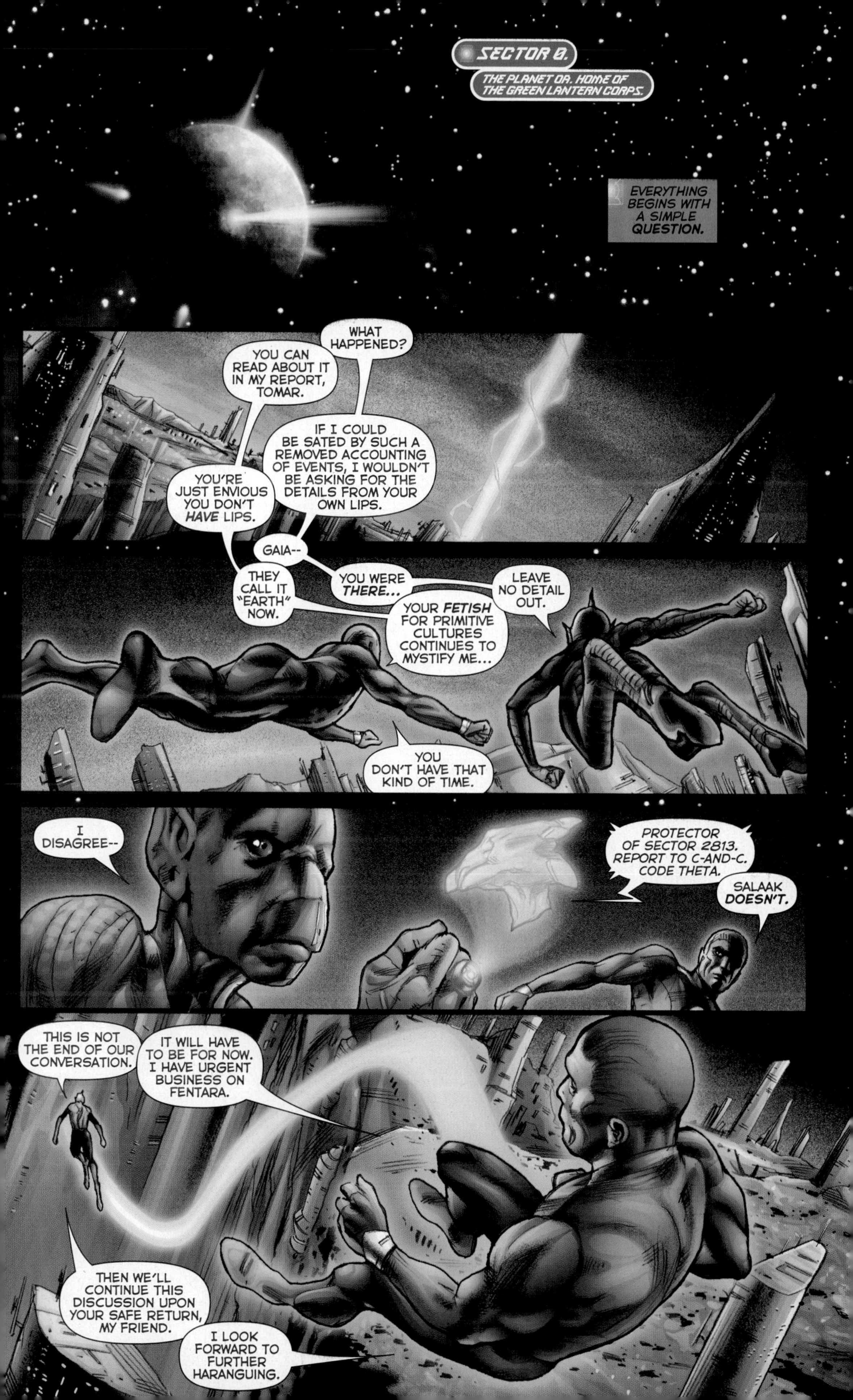
SECTOR 0.
THE PLANET OA. HOME OF THE GREEN LANTERN CORPS.
EVERYTHING BEGINS WITH A SIMPLE QUESTION.
WHAT HAPPENED?
YOU CAN READ ABOUT IT IN MY REPORT, TOMAR.
IF I COULD BE SATED BY SUCH A REMOVED ACCOUNTING OF EVENTS, I WOULDN'T BE ASKING FOR THE DETAILS FROM YOUR OWN LIPS.
YOU'RE JUST ENVIOUS YOU DON'T HAVE LIPS.
GAIA--
THEY CALL IT "EARTH" NOW.
YOU WERE THERE...
YOUR FETISH FOR PRIMITIVE CULTURES CONTINUES TO MYSTIFY ME...
LEAVE NO DETAIL OUT.
YOU DON'T HAVE THAT KIND OF TIME.
I DISAGREE--
PROTECTOR OF SECTOR 2813. REPORT TO C-AND-C. CODE THETA.
SALAAK DOESN'T.
THIS IS NOT THE END OF OUR CONVERSATION.
IT WILL HAVE TO BE FOR NOW. I HAVE URGENT BUSINESS ON FENTARA.
THEN WE'LL CONTINUE THIS DISCUSSION UPON YOUR SAFE RETURN, MY FRIEND.
I LOOK FORWARD TO FURTHER HARANGUING.

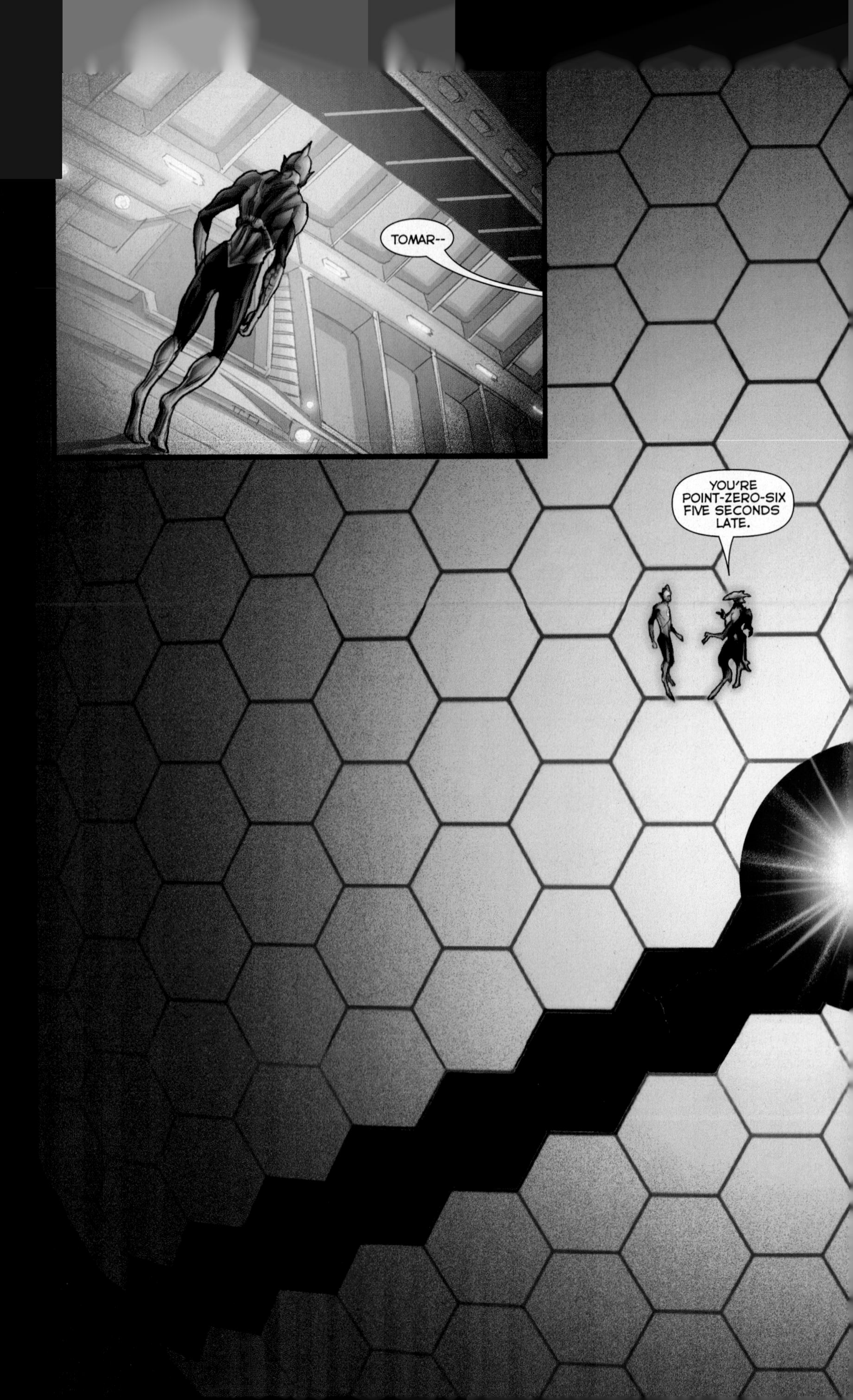
TOMAR--
YOU'RE POINT-ZERO-SIX FIVE SECONDS LATE.

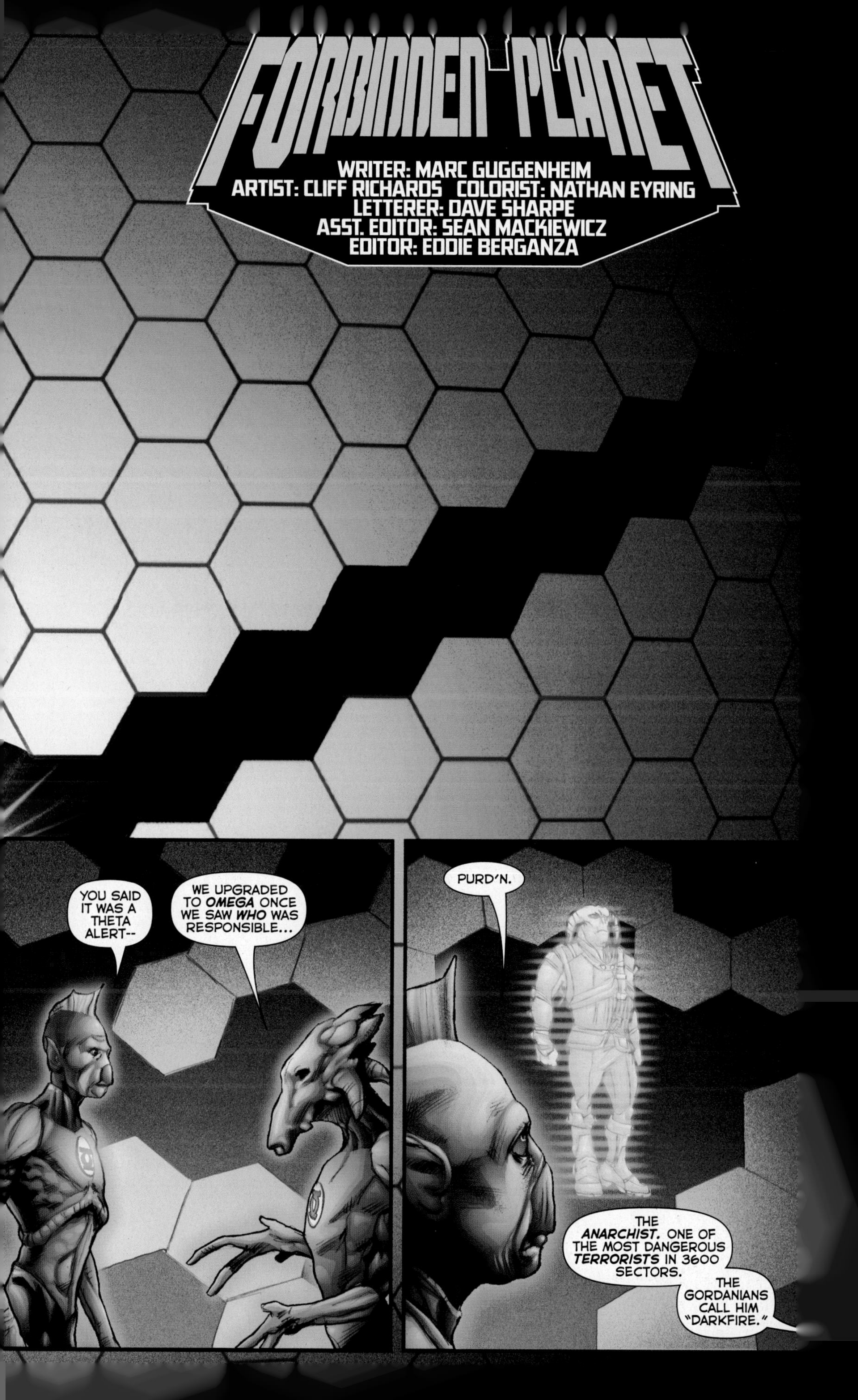
FORBIDDEN PLANET
WRITER: MARC GUGGENHEIM
ARTIST: CLIFF RICHARDS COLORIST: NATHAN EYRING
LETTERER: DAVE SHARPE
ASST. EDITOR: SEAN MACKIEWICZ
EDITOR: EDDIE BERGANZA
YOU SAID IT WAS A THETA ALERT--
WE UPGRADED TO OMEGA ONCE WE SAW WHO WAS RESPONSIBLE...
PURD'N.
THE ANARCHIST. ONE OF THE MOST DANGEROUS TERRORISTS IN 3600 SECTORS.
THE GORDANIANS CALL HIM "DARKFIRE."

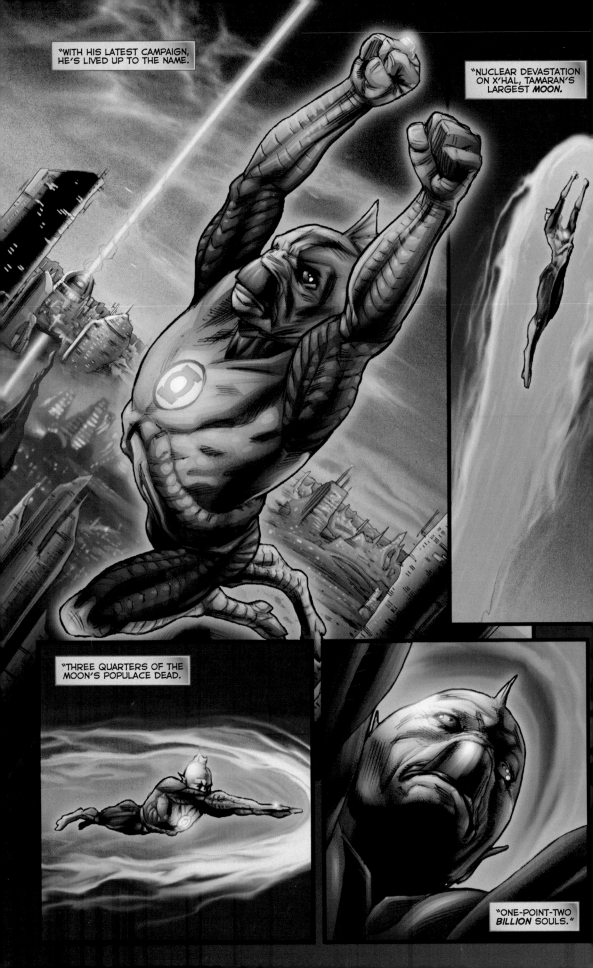

"WITH HIS LATEST CAMPAIGN, HE'S LIVED UP TO THE NAME.

"NUCLEAR DEVASTATION ON X'HAL, TAMARAN'S LARGEST MOON.

"THREE QUARTERS OF THE MOON'S POPULACE DEAD.

"ONE-POINT-TWO BILLION SOULS."

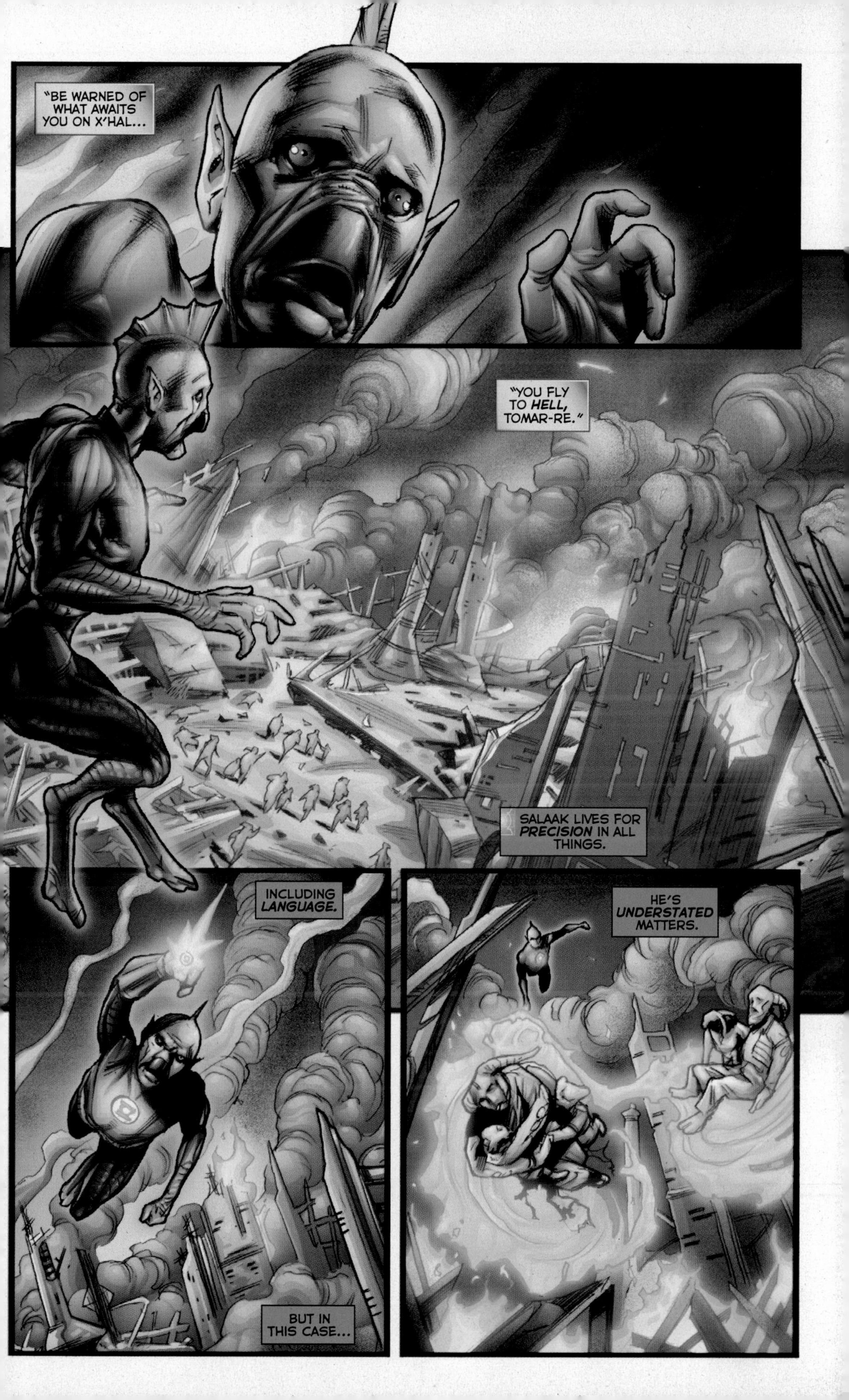
"BE WARNED OF WHAT AWAITS YOU ON X'HAL...
"YOU FLY TO HELL, TOMAR-RE."
SALAAK LIVES FOR PRECISION IN ALL THINGS.
INCLUDING LANGUAGE.
BUT IN THIS CASE...
HE'S UNDERSTATED MATTERS.

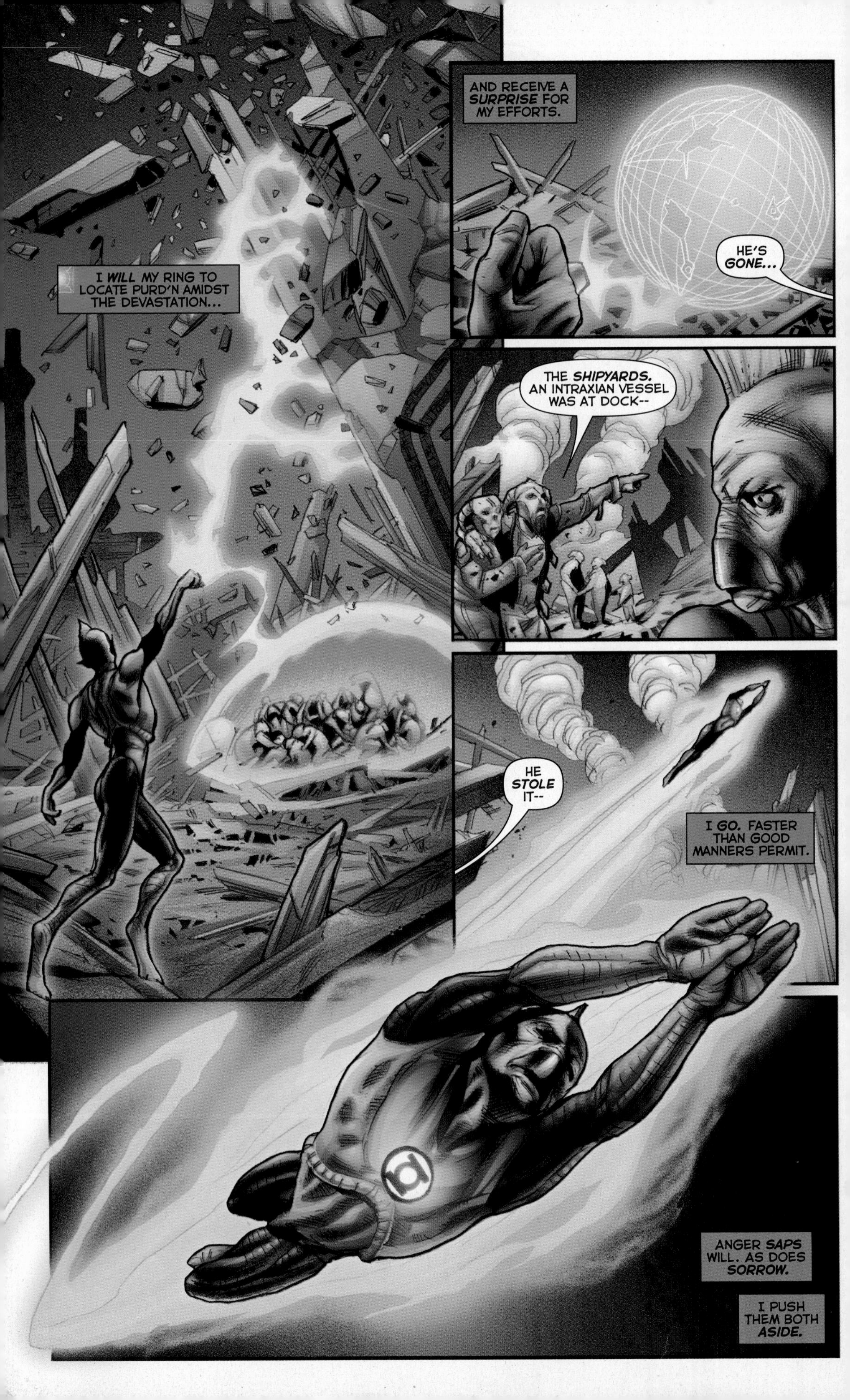
I WILL MY RING TO LOCATE PURD'N AMIDST THE DEVASTATION...
AND RECEIVE A SURPRISE FOR MY EFFORTS.
HE'S GONE...
THE SHIPYARDS. AN INTRAXIAN VESSEL WAS AT DOCK--
HE STOLE IT--
I GO. FASTER THAN GOOD MANNERS PERMIT.
ANGER SAPS WILL. AS DOES SORROW.
I PUSH THEM BOTH ASIDE.

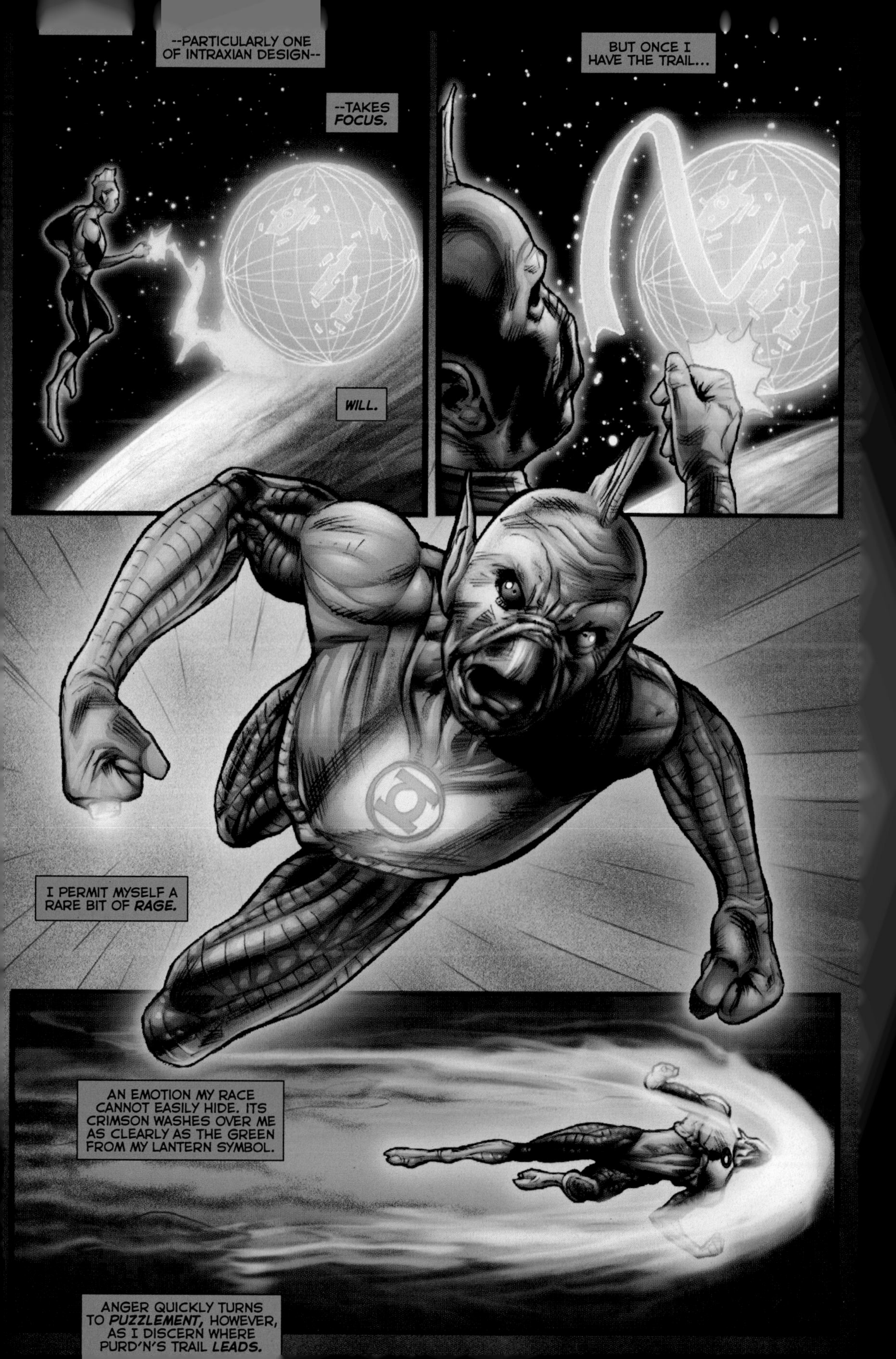
--PARTICULARLY ONE OF INTRAXIAN DESIGN--
--TAKES FOCUS.
WILL.
BUT ONCE I HAVE THE TRAIL...
I PERMIT MYSELF A RARE BIT OF RAGE.
AN EMOTION MY RACE CANNOT EASILY HIDE. ITS CRIMSON WASHES OVER ME AS CLEARLY AS THE GREEN FROM MY LANTERN SYMBOL.
ANGER QUICKLY TURNS TO PUZZLEMENT, HOWEVER, AS I DISCERN WHERE PURD'N'S TRAIL LEADS.

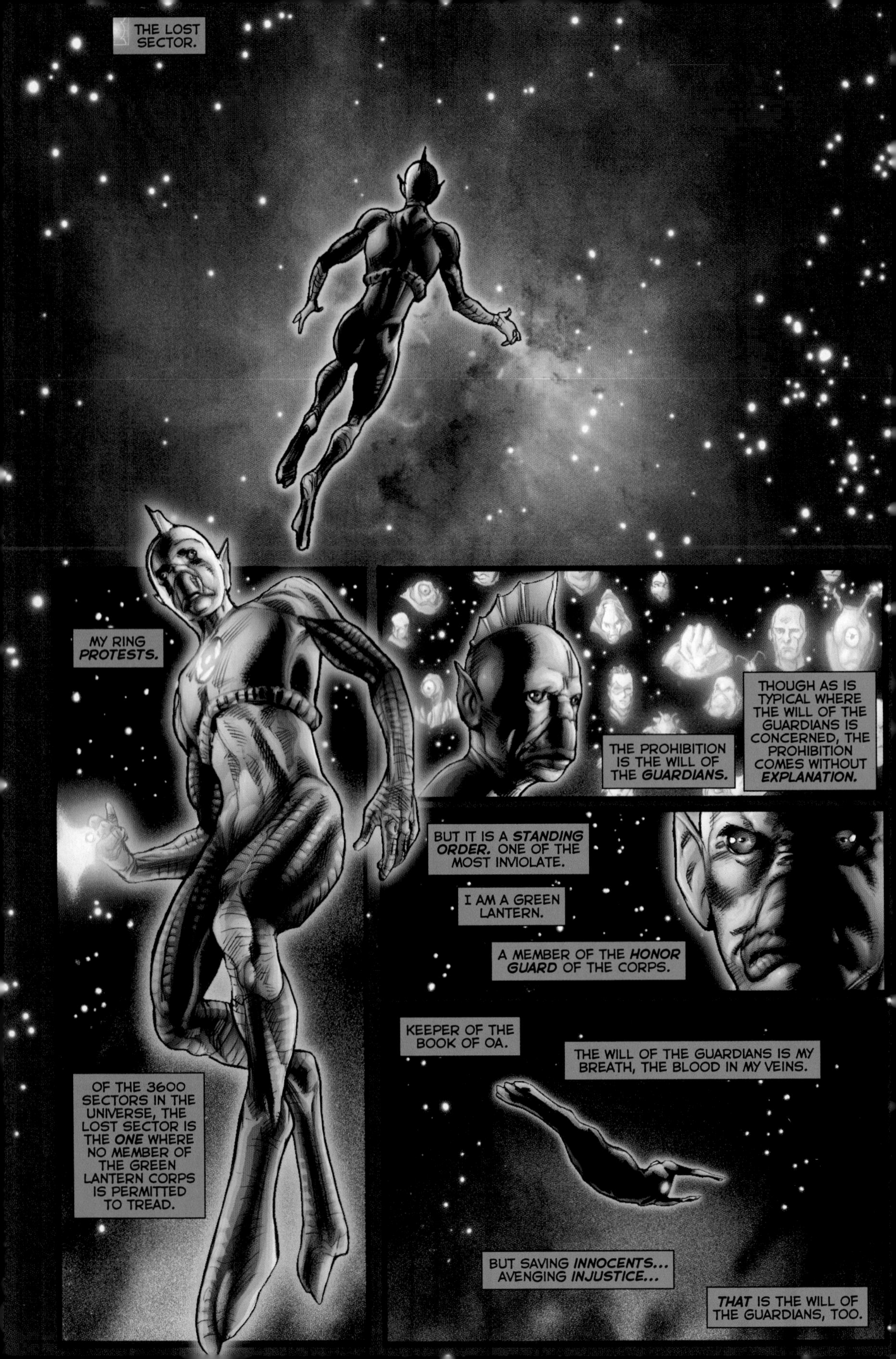
THE LOST SECTOR.
MY RING PROTESTS.
OF THE 3600 SECTORS IN THE UNIVERSE, THE LOST SECTOR IS THE ONE WHERE NO MEMBER OF THE GREEN LANTERN CORPS IS PERMITTED TO TREAD.
THE PROHIBITION IS THE WILL OF THE GUARDIANS.
THOUGH AS IS TYPICAL WHERE THE WILL OF THE GUARDIANS IS CONCERNED, THE PROHIBITION COMES WITHOUT EXPLANATION.
BUT IT IS A STANDING ORDER. ONE OF THE MOST INVIOLATE.
I AM A GREEN LANTERN.
A MEMBER OF THE HONOR GUARD OF THE CORPS.
KEEPER OF THE BOOK OF OA.
THE WILL OF THE GUARDIANS IS MY BREATH, THE BLOOD IN MY VEINS.
BUT SAVING INNOCENTS... AVENGING INJUSTICE...
THAT IS THE WILL OF THE GUARDIANS, TOO.

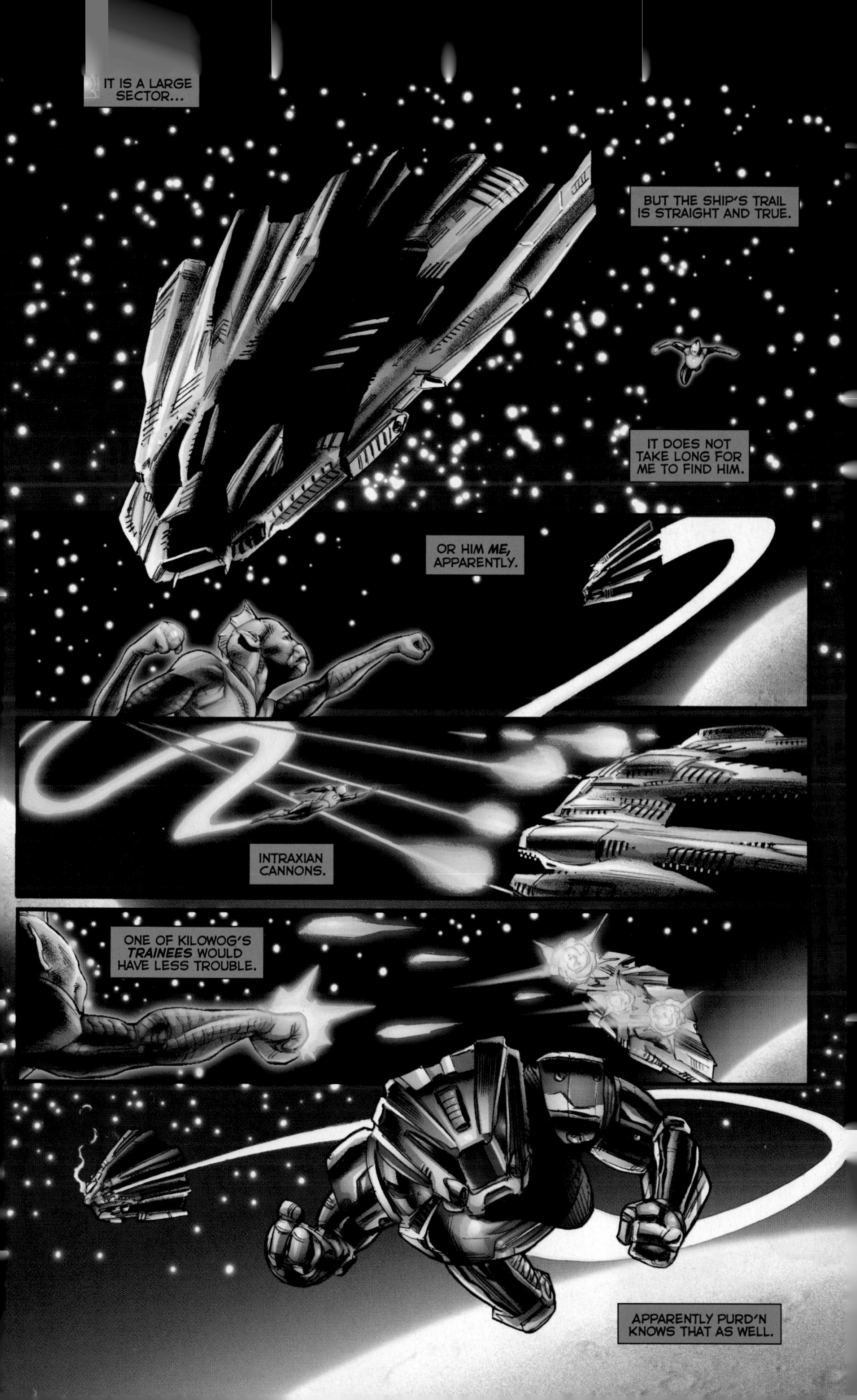
IT IS A LARGE SECTOR...
BUT THE SHIP'S TRAIL IS STRAIGHT AND TRUE.
IT DOES NOT TAKE LONG FOR ME TO FIND HIM.
OR HIM *ME*, APPARENTLY.
INTRAXIAN CANNONS.
ONE OF KILOWOG'S *TRAINEES* WOULD HAVE LESS TROUBLE.
APPARENTLY PURD'N KNOWS THAT AS WELL.

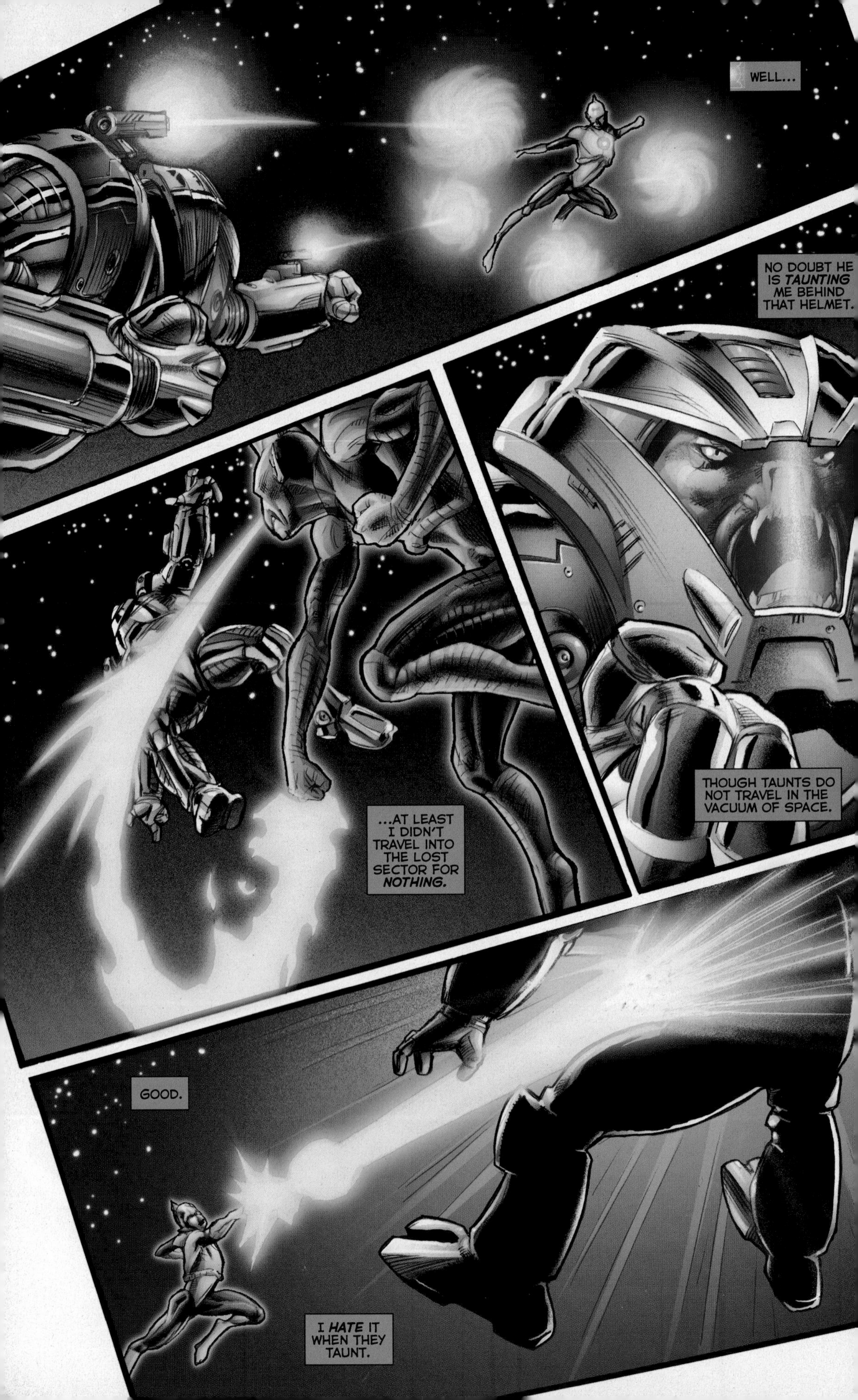
WELL...
NO DOUBT HE IS *TAUNTING* ME BEHIND THAT HELMET.
...AT LEAST I DIDN'T TRAVEL INTO THE LOST SECTOR FOR *NOTHING*.
THOUGH TAUNTS DO NOT TRAVEL IN THE VACUUM OF SPACE.
GOOD.
I *HATE* IT WHEN THEY TAUNT.

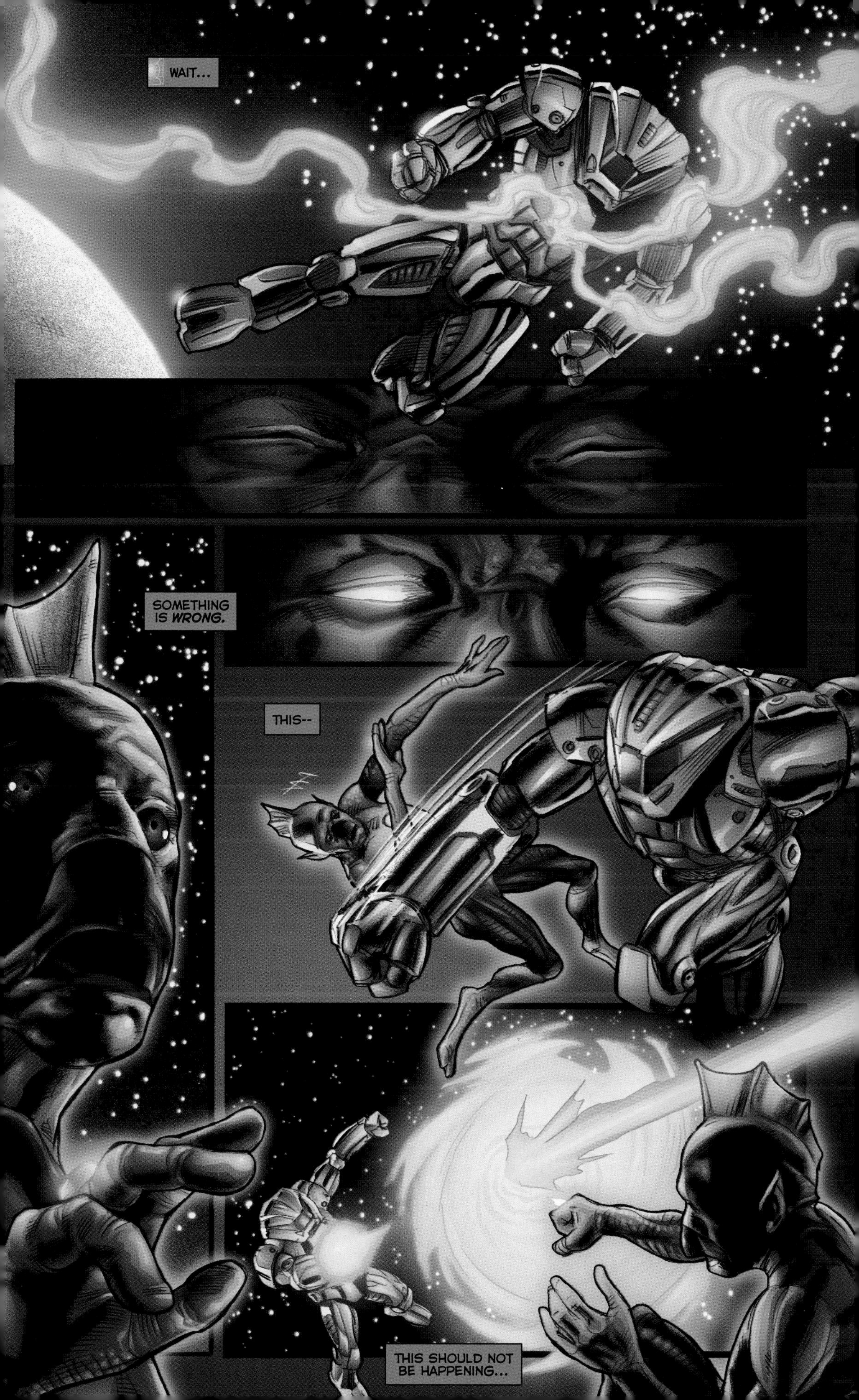
WAIT...
SOMETHING IS *WRONG.*
THIS--
THIS SHOULD NOT BE HAPPENING...

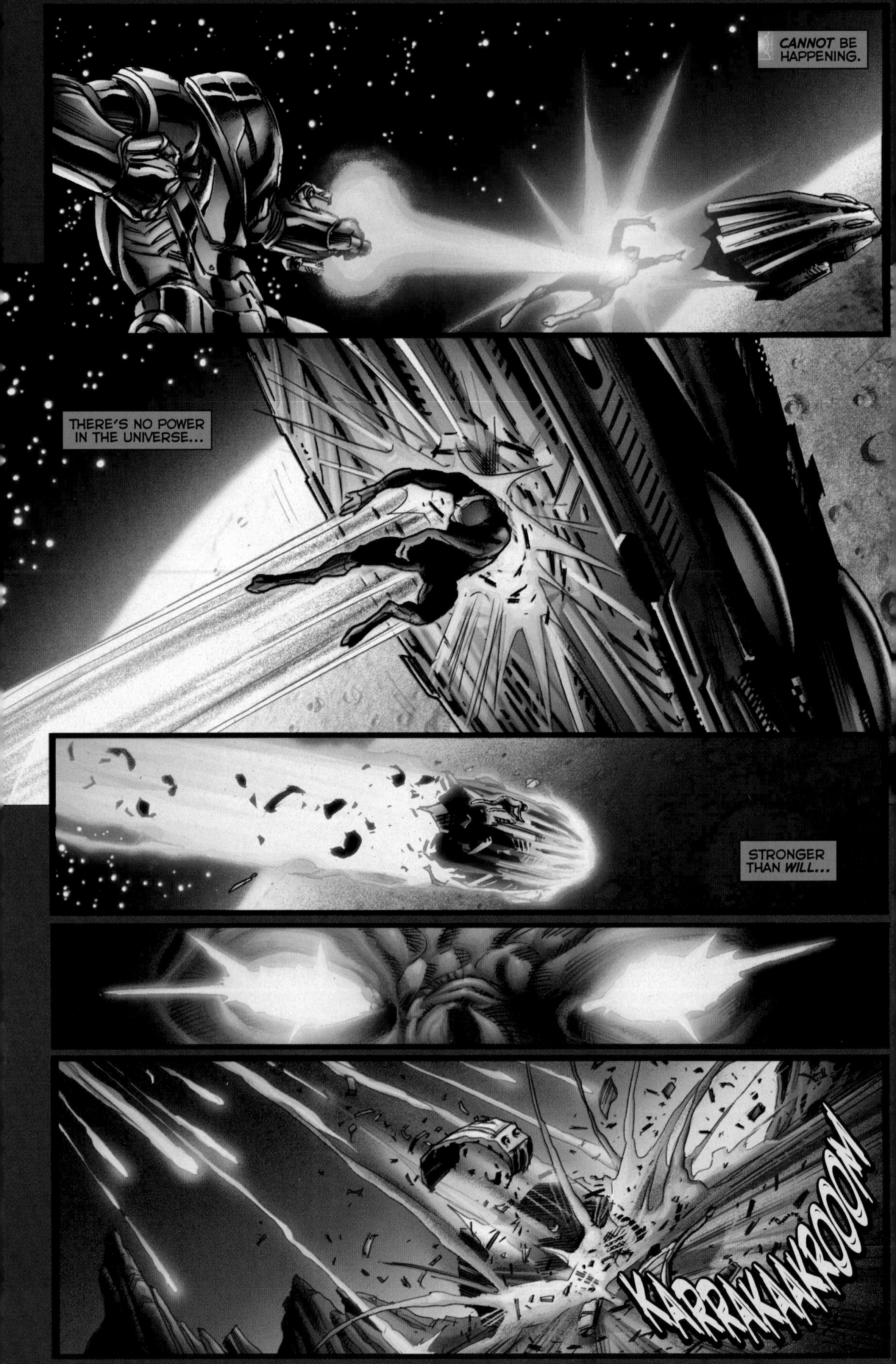

CANNOT BE HAPPENING.
THERE'S NO POWER IN THE UNIVERSE...
STRONGER THAN WILL...
KARRAKAAKROOM

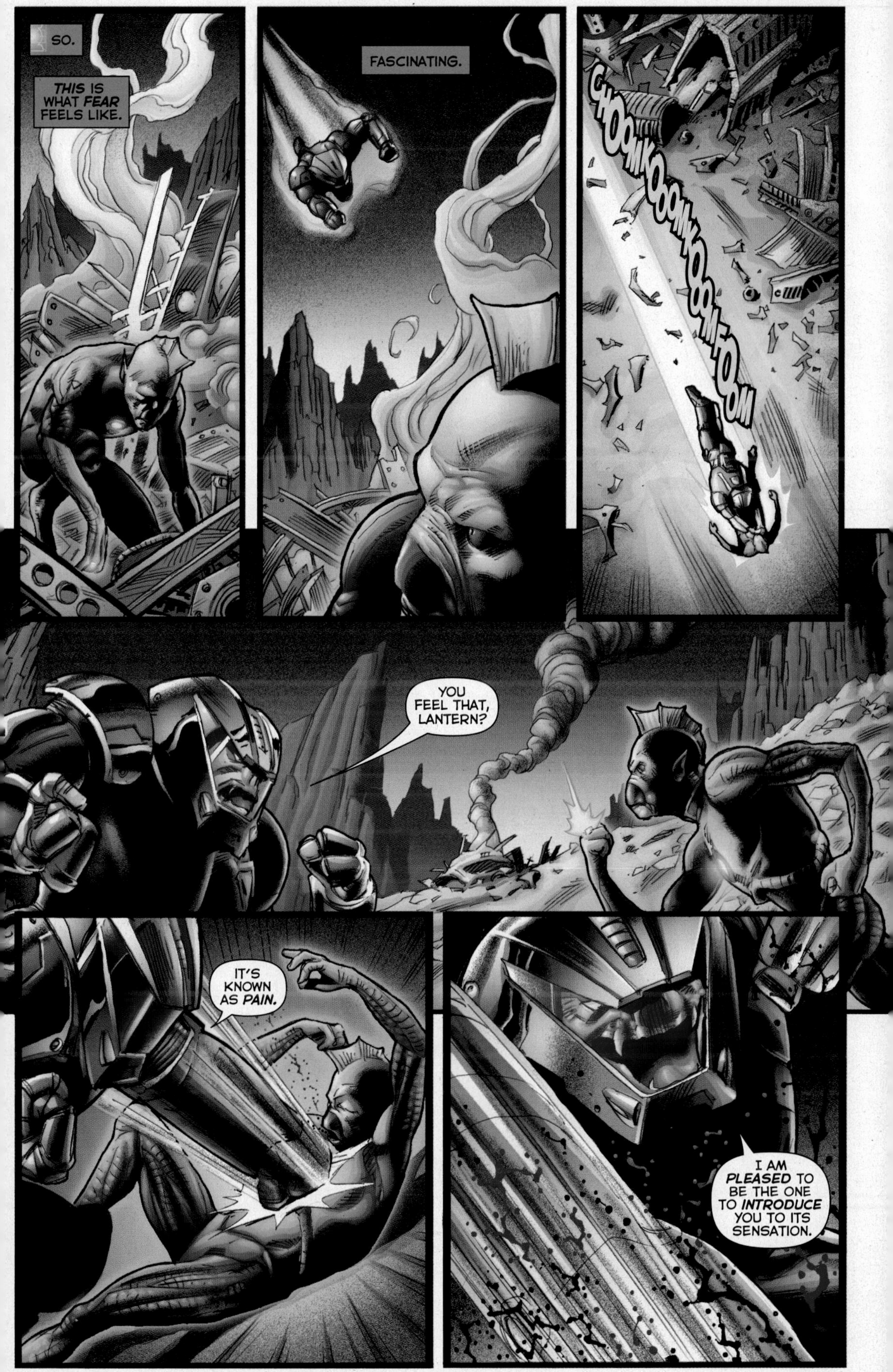
SO.
THIS IS WHAT FEAR FEELS LIKE.
FASCINATING.
CHOOMKOOOMKOOOMFOOOM
YOU FEEL THAT, LANTERN?
IT'S KNOWN AS PAIN.
I AM PLEASED TO BE THE ONE TO INTRODUCE YOU TO ITS SENSATION.

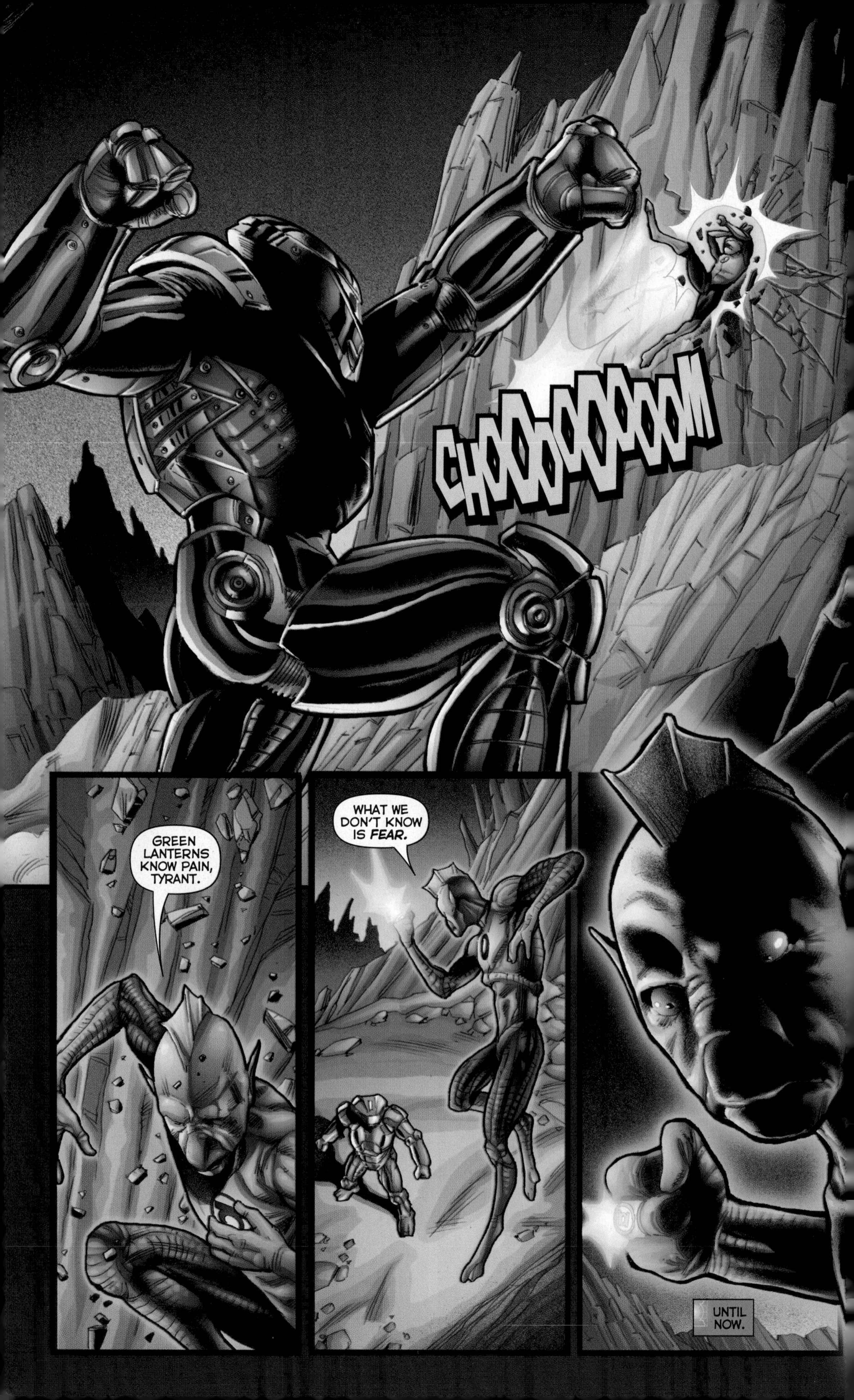
CHOOOOOOOOM
GREEN LANTERNS KNOW PAIN, TYRANT.
WHAT WE DON'T KNOW IS *FEAR.*
UNTIL NOW.

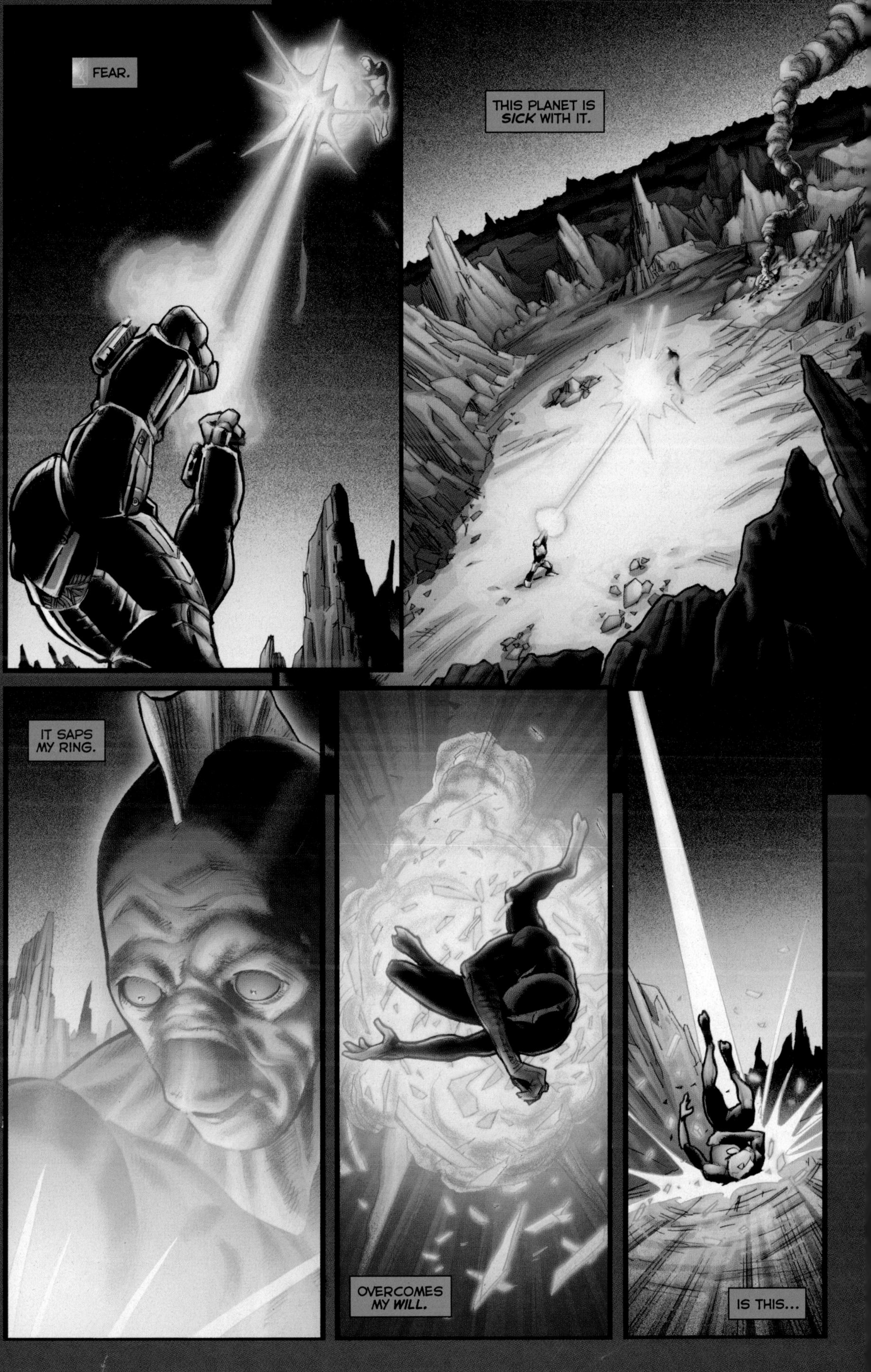
FEAR.
THIS PLANET IS SICK WITH IT.
IT SAPS MY RING.
OVERCOMES MY WILL.
IS THIS...

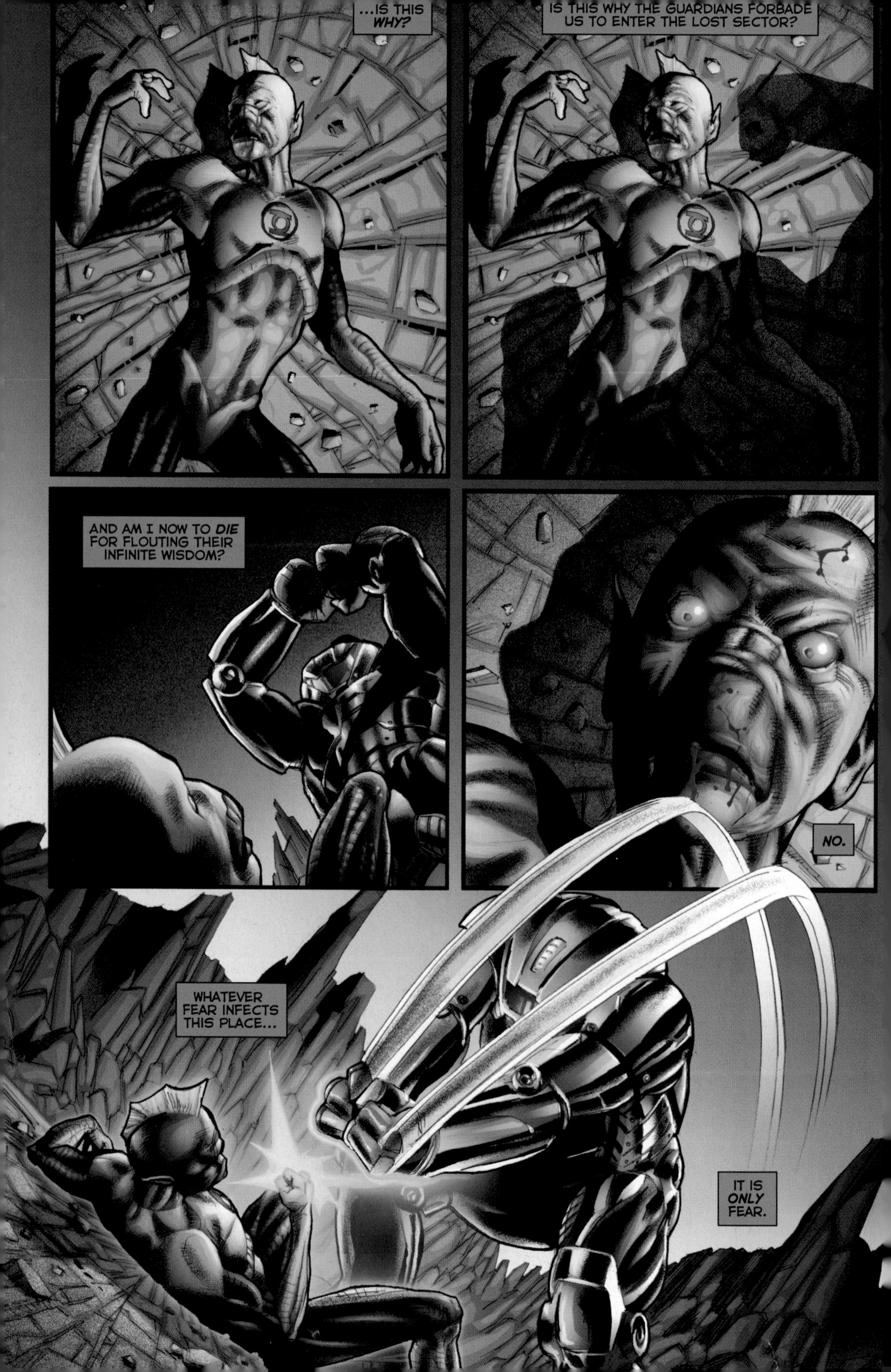
...IS THIS *WHY?*
IS THIS WHY THE GUARDIANS FORBADE US TO ENTER THE LOST SECTOR?
AND AM I NOW TO *DIE* FOR FLOUTING THEIR INFINITE WISDOM?
NO.
WHATEVER FEAR INFECTS THIS PLACE...
IT IS *ONLY* FEAR.

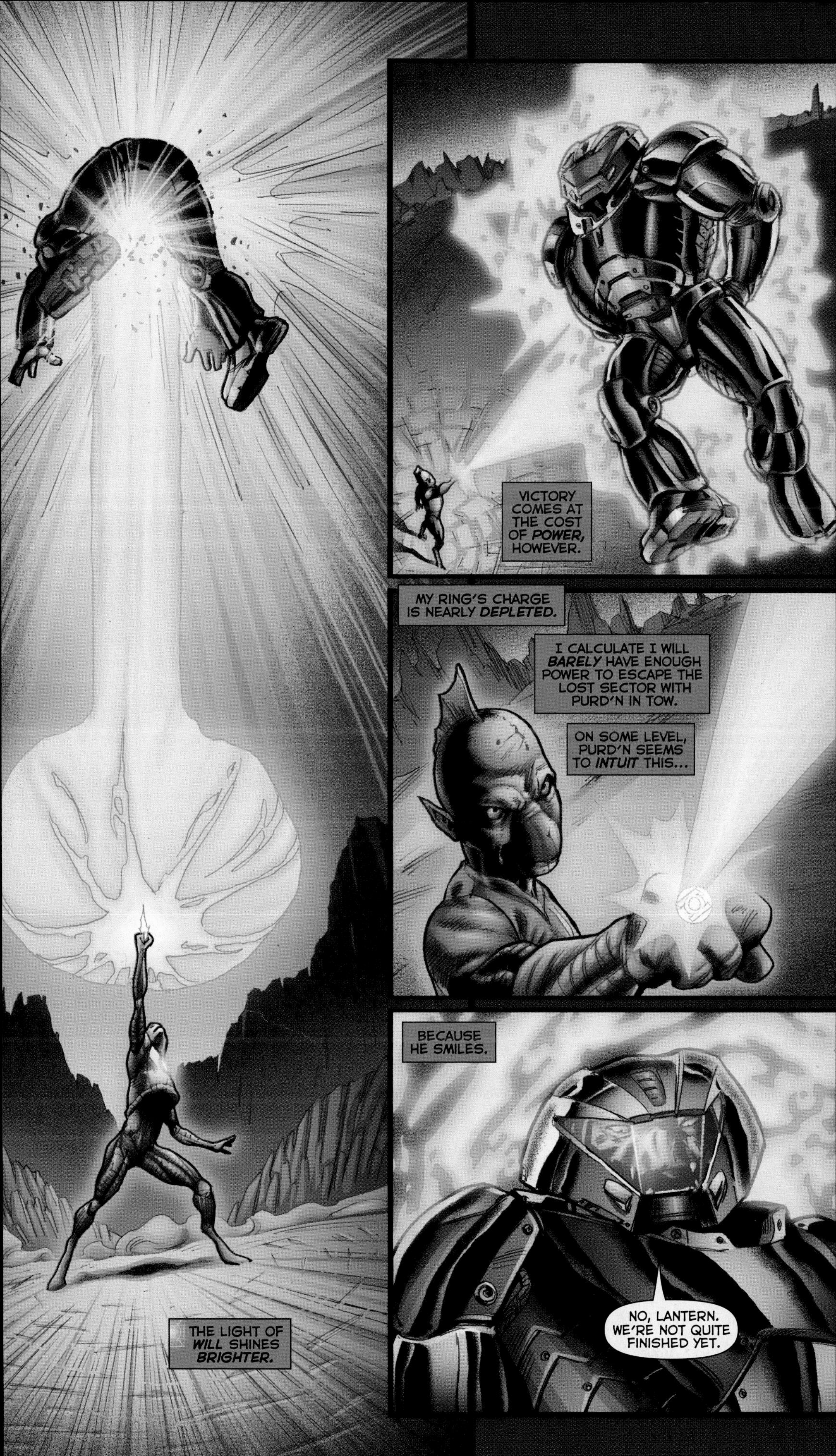
THE LIGHT OF WILL SHINES BRIGHTER.
VICTORY COMES AT THE COST OF POWER, HOWEVER.
MY RING'S CHARGE IS NEARLY DEPLETED.
I CALCULATE I WILL BARELY HAVE ENOUGH POWER TO ESCAPE THE LOST SECTOR WITH PURD'N IN TOW.
ON SOME LEVEL, PURD'N SEEMS TO INTUIT THIS...
BECAUSE HE SMILES.
NO, LANTERN. WE'RE NOT QUITE FINISHED YET.

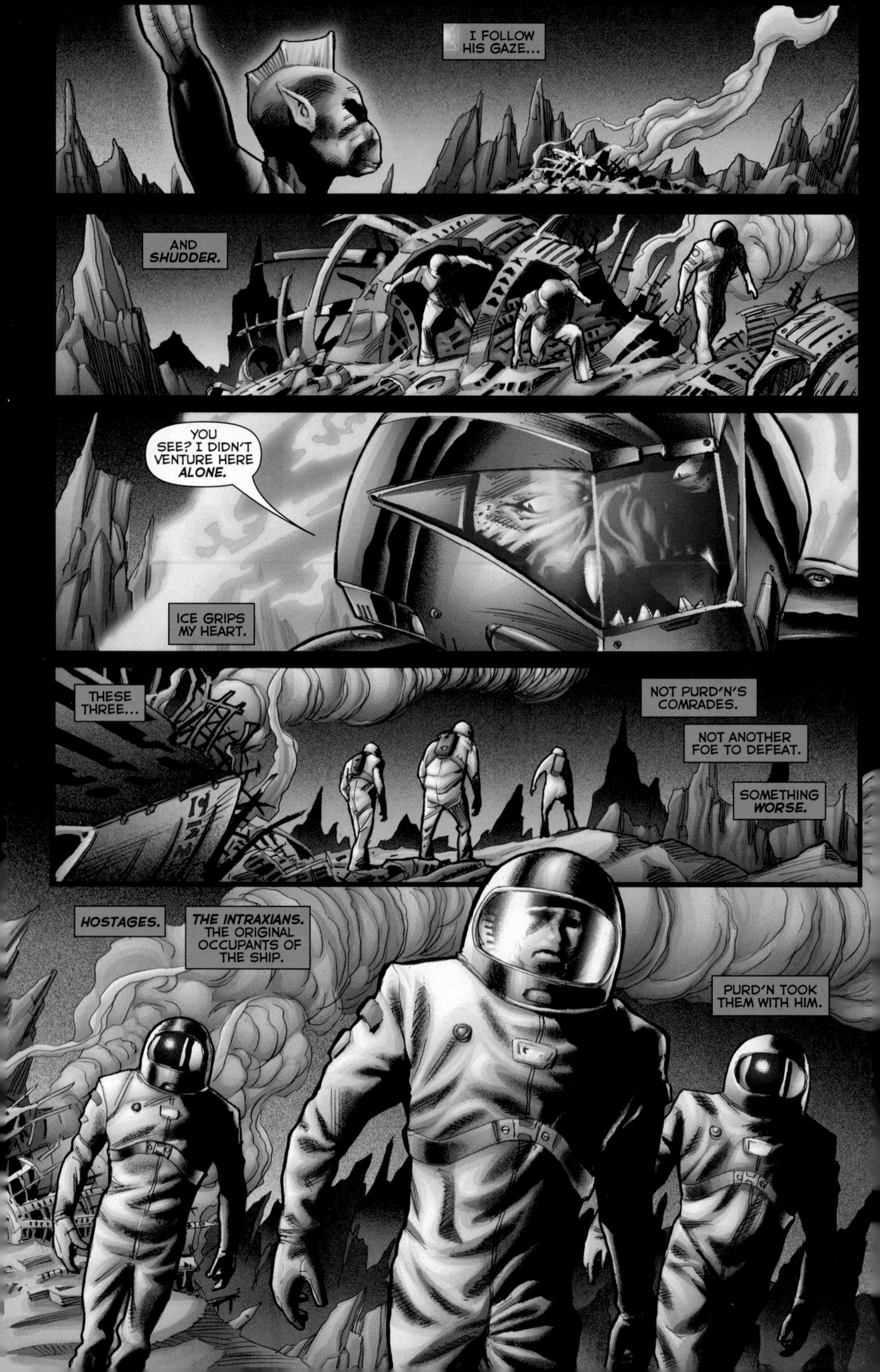
I FOLLOW HIS GAZE...
AND SHUDDER.
YOU SEE? I DIDN'T VENTURE HERE ALONE.
ICE GRIPS MY HEART.
THESE THREE...
NOT PURD'N'S COMRADES.
NOT ANOTHER FOE TO DEFEAT.
SOMETHING WORSE.
HOSTAGES.
THE INTRAXIANS. THE ORIGINAL OCCUPANTS OF THE SHIP.
PURD'N TOOK THEM WITH HIM.

I CAN *SENSE* YOUR *DILEMMA.*

YOU DON'T HAVE ENOUGH POWER.

NOT TO LEAVE HERE WITH ME *AND* THEM.

NOT TO REPAIR THEIR SHIP *AND* KEEP ME FROM ESCAPING OR WORSE.

NOT EVEN ENOUGH TO TAKE *TWO* OF THE THREE.

BUT I OFFER A POTENTIAL SOLUTION. ONE I'M SURE YOU'RE TOO *NOBLE* TO HAVE THOUGHT OF.

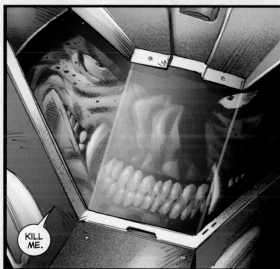

KILL ME.

YOU ONLY HAVE ENOUGH POWER TO TRANSPORT *ONE* PERSON.

WHICH MEANS *MAROONING* ME HERE ISN'T AN OPTION, EITHER. AS YOU KNOW, I WOULD *KILL* WHICHEVER OF THE INTRAXIANS YOU'RE FORCED TO LEAVE BEHIND.

DO WHAT'S *NECESSARY,* LANTERN. YOU CAN *ASSURE* THE SAFETY OF ALL THREE SOULS.

ALL YOU HAVE TO DO... IS BECOME LIKE ME.

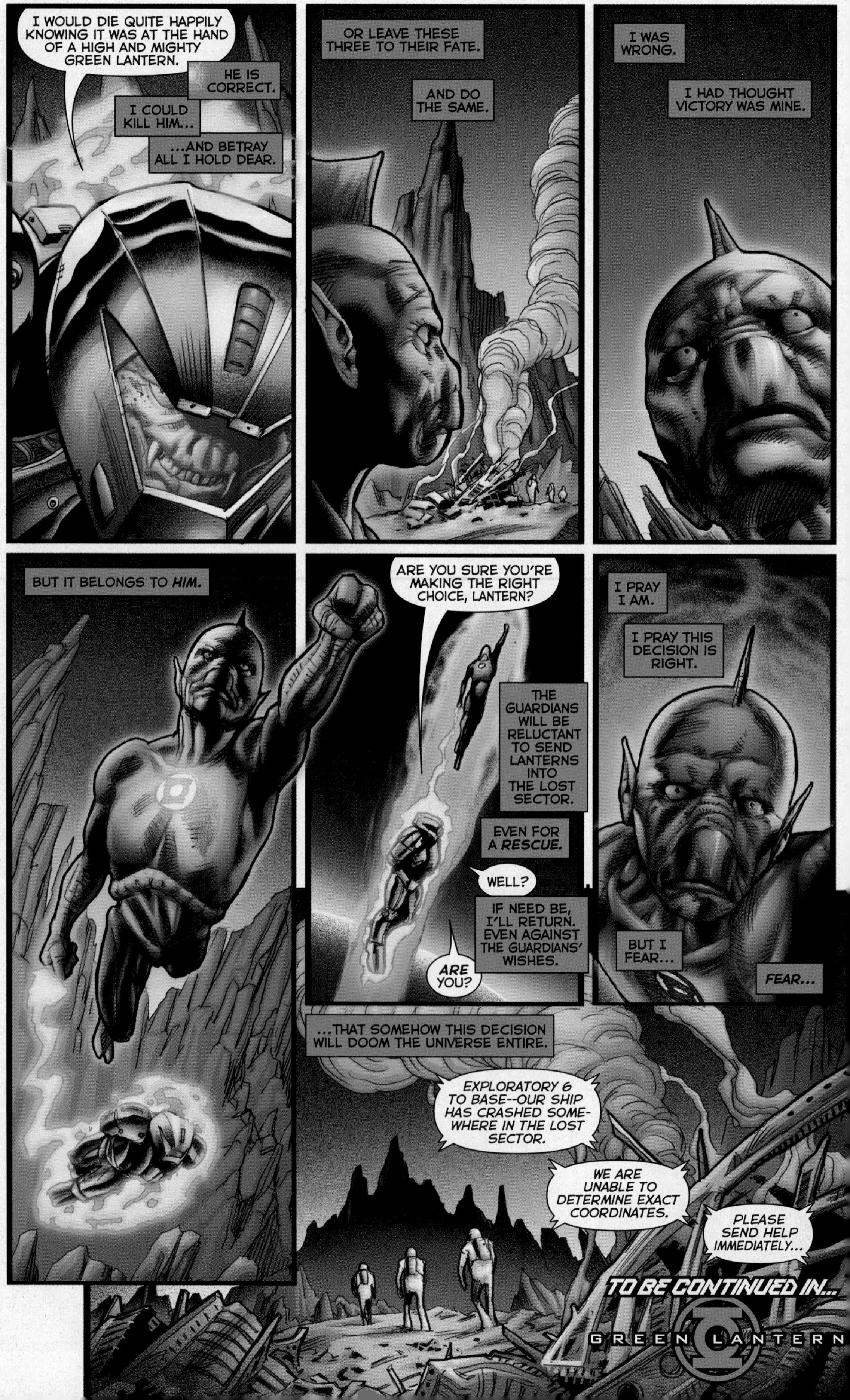

I WOULD DIE QUITE HAPPILY KNOWING IT WAS AT THE HAND OF A HIGH AND MIGHTY GREEN LANTERN.
HE IS CORRECT.
I COULD KILL HIM...
...AND BETRAY ALL I HOLD DEAR.
OR LEAVE THESE THREE TO THEIR FATE.
AND DO THE SAME.
I WAS WRONG.
I HAD THOUGHT VICTORY WAS MINE.
BUT IT BELONGS TO HIM.
ARE YOU SURE YOU'RE MAKING THE RIGHT CHOICE, LANTERN?
THE GUARDIANS WILL BE RELUCTANT TO SEND LANTERNS INTO THE LOST SECTOR.
EVEN FOR A RESCUE.
WELL?
IF NEED BE, I'LL RETURN. EVEN AGAINST THE GUARDIANS' WISHES.
ARE YOU?
I PRAY I AM.
I PRAY THIS DECISION IS RIGHT.
BUT I FEAR...
FEAR...
...THAT SOMEHOW THIS DECISION WILL DOOM THE UNIVERSE ENTIRE.
EXPLORATORY 6 TO BASE--OUR SHIP HAS CRASHED SOME-WHERE IN THE LOST SECTOR.
WE ARE UNABLE TO DETERMINE EXACT COORDINATES.
PLEASE SEND HELP IMMEDIATELY...
TO BE CONTINUED IN...
GREEN LANTERN

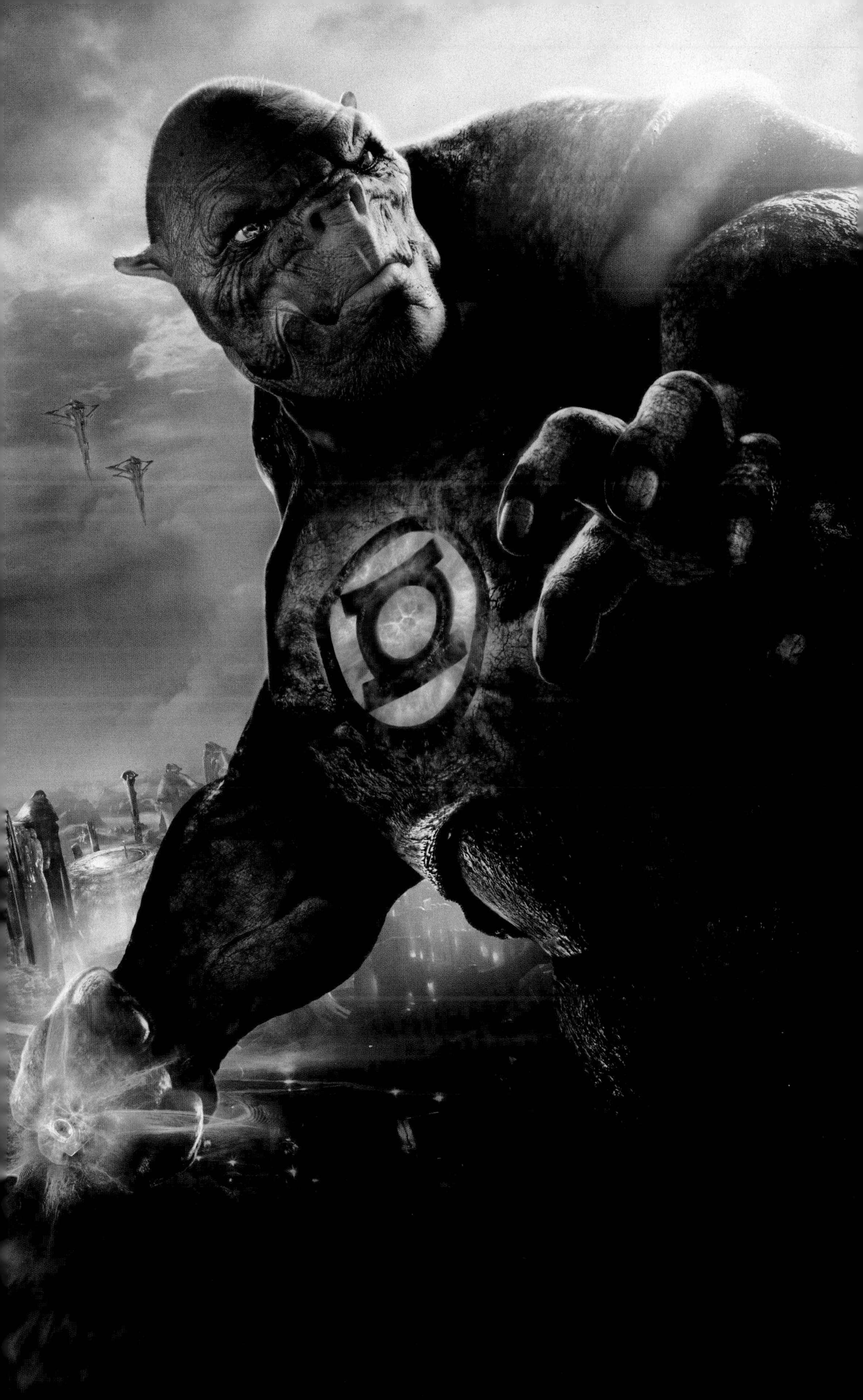

TO BUILD A BETTER LANTERN

PETER J. **TOMASI** writer

CARLOS **FERREIRA** penciller

SILVIO **SPOTTI** inker

Kilowog created by STEVE **ENGLEHART** and JOE **STANTON**

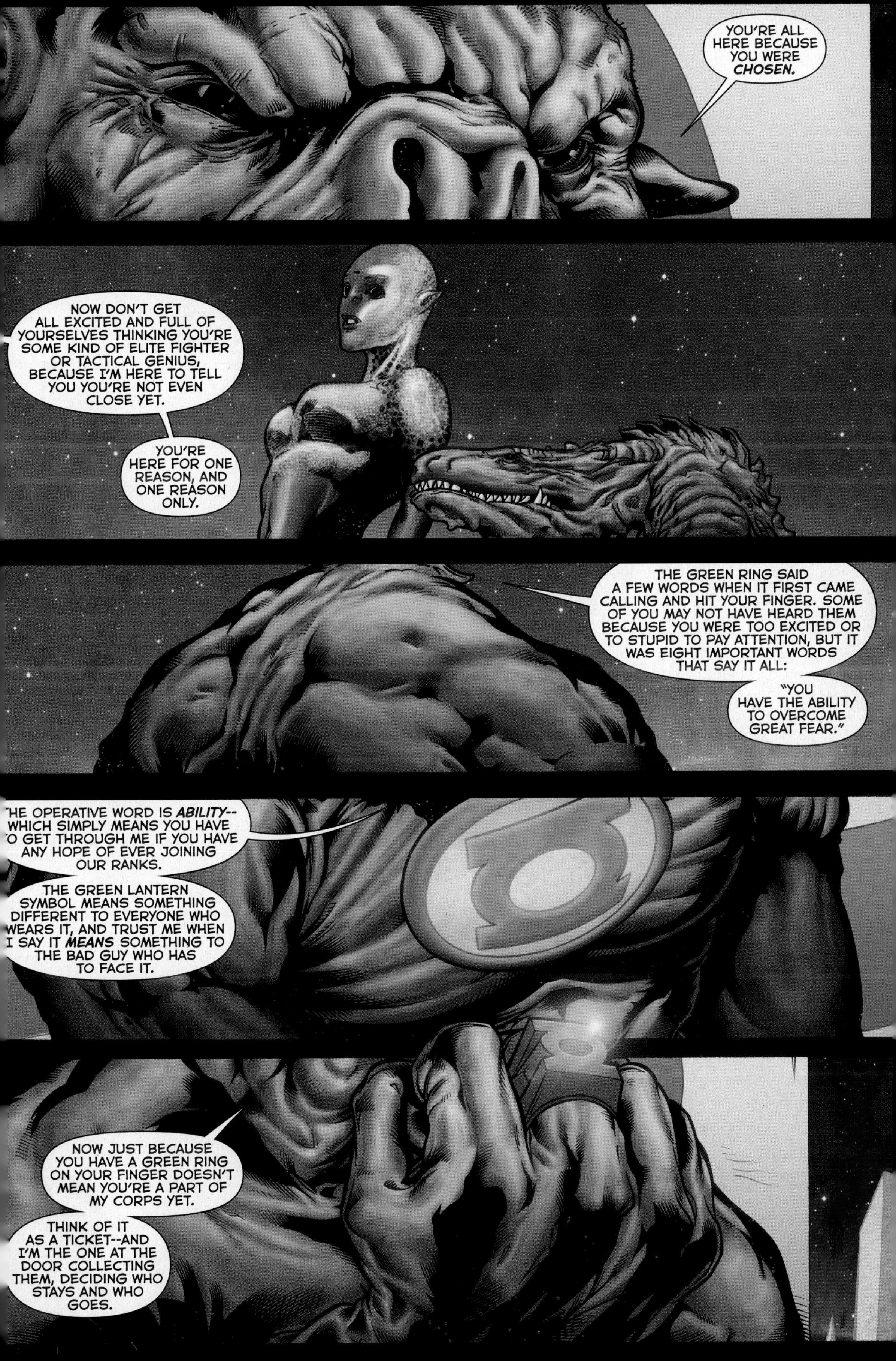
YOU'RE ALL HERE BECAUSE YOU WERE *CHOSEN.*
NOW DON'T GET ALL EXCITED AND FULL OF YOURSELVES THINKING YOU'RE SOME KIND OF ELITE FIGHTER OR TACTICAL GENIUS, BECAUSE I'M HERE TO TELL YOU YOU'RE NOT EVEN CLOSE YET.
YOU'RE HERE FOR ONE REASON, AND ONE REASON ONLY.
THE GREEN RING SAID A FEW WORDS WHEN IT FIRST CAME CALLING AND HIT YOUR FINGER. SOME OF YOU MAY NOT HAVE HEARD THEM BECAUSE YOU WERE TOO EXCITED OR TO STUPID TO PAY ATTENTION, BUT IT WAS EIGHT IMPORTANT WORDS THAT SAY IT ALL:
"YOU HAVE THE ABILITY TO OVERCOME GREAT FEAR."
HE OPERATIVE WORD IS *ABILITY*-- WHICH SIMPLY MEANS YOU HAVE O GET THROUGH ME IF YOU HAVE ANY HOPE OF EVER JOINING OUR RANKS.
THE GREEN LANTERN SYMBOL MEANS SOMETHING DIFFERENT TO EVERYONE WHO WEARS IT, AND TRUST ME WHEN I SAY IT *MEANS* SOMETHING TO THE BAD GUY WHO HAS TO FACE IT.
NOW JUST BECAUSE YOU HAVE A GREEN RING ON YOUR FINGER DOESN'T MEAN YOU'RE A PART OF MY CORPS YET.
THINK OF IT AS A TICKET--AND I'M THE ONE AT THE DOOR COLLECTING THEM, DECIDING WHO STAYS AND WHO GOES.

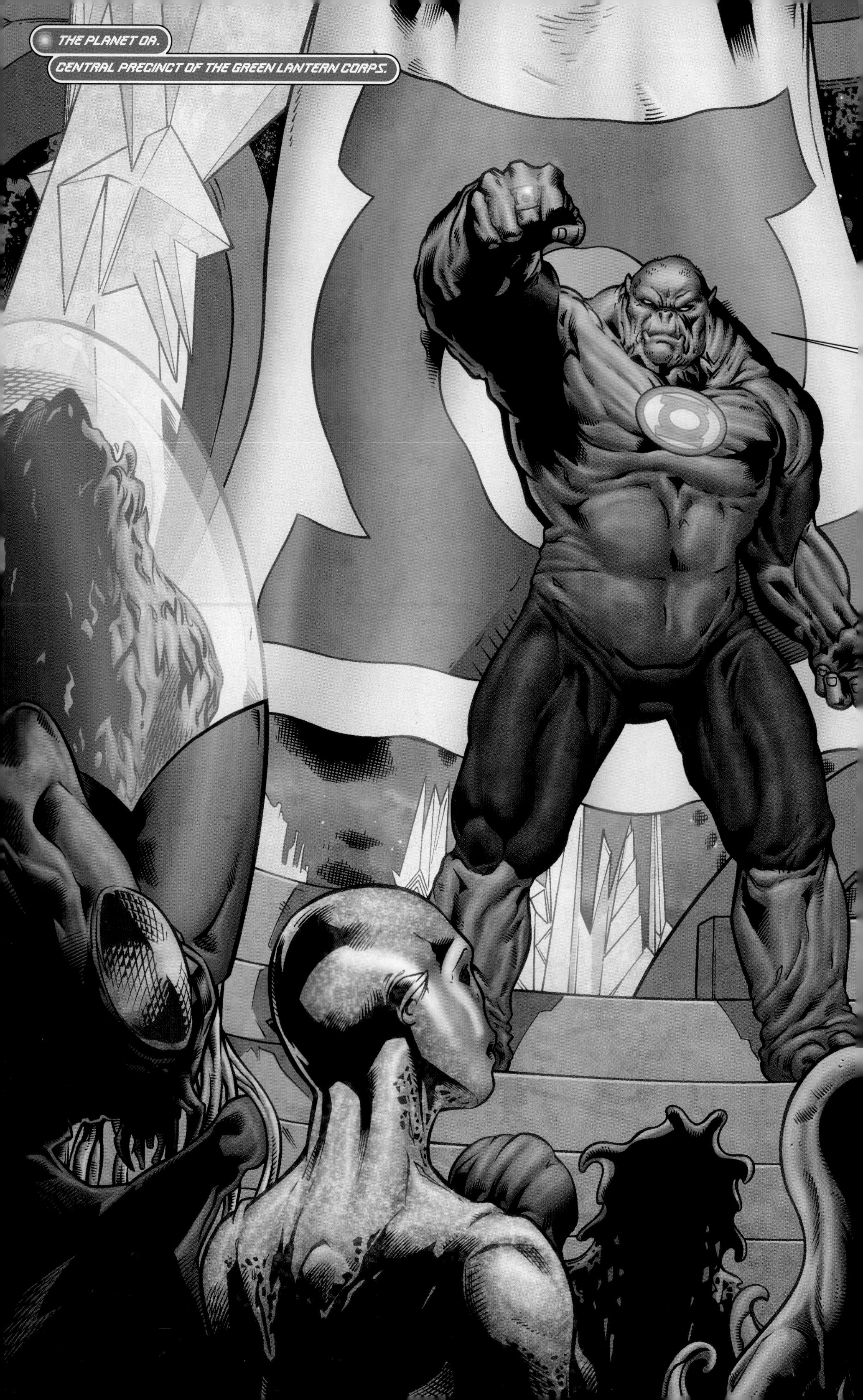
THE PLANET OA.
CENTRAL PRECINCT OF THE GREEN LANTERN CORPS.

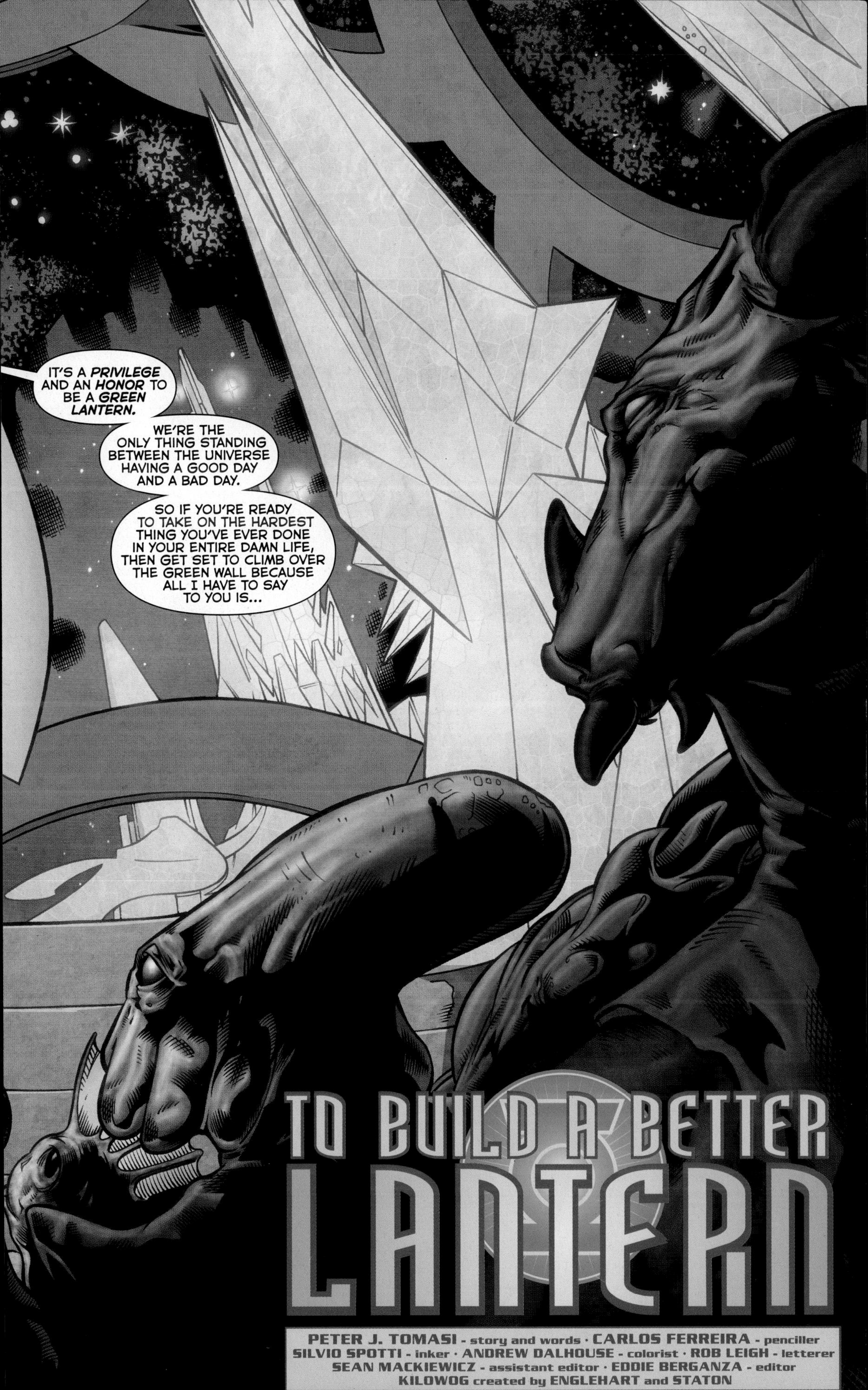

IT'S A PRIVILEGE AND AN HONOR TO BE A GREEN LANTERN.
WE'RE THE ONLY THING STANDING BETWEEN THE UNIVERSE HAVING A GOOD DAY AND A BAD DAY.
SO IF YOU'RE READY TO TAKE ON THE HARDEST THING YOU'VE EVER DONE IN YOUR ENTIRE DAMN LIFE, THEN GET SET TO CLIMB OVER THE GREEN WALL BECAUSE ALL I HAVE TO SAY TO YOU IS...
TO BUILD A BETTER LANTERN
PETER J. TOMASI - story and words · CARLOS FERREIRA - penciller
SILVIO SPOTTI - inker · ANDREW DALHOUSE - colorist · ROB LEIGH - letterer
SEAN MACKIEWICZ - assistant editor · EDDIE BERGANZA - editor
KILOWOG created by ENGLEHART and STATON

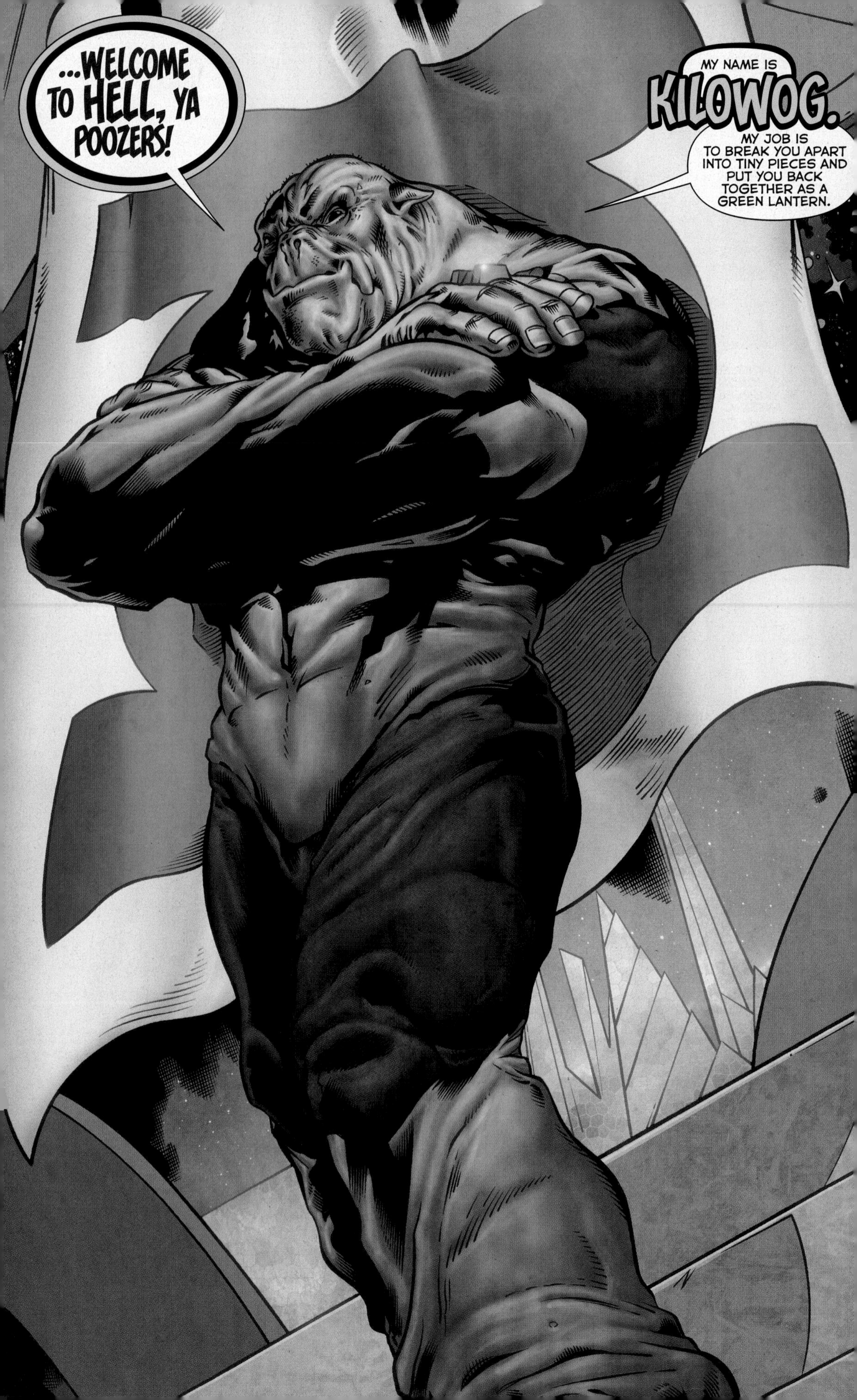
...WELCOME TO HELL, YA POOZERS!
MY NAME IS KILOWOG.
MY JOB IS TO BREAK YOU APART INTO TINY PIECES AND PUT YOU BACK TOGETHER AS A GREEN LANTERN.

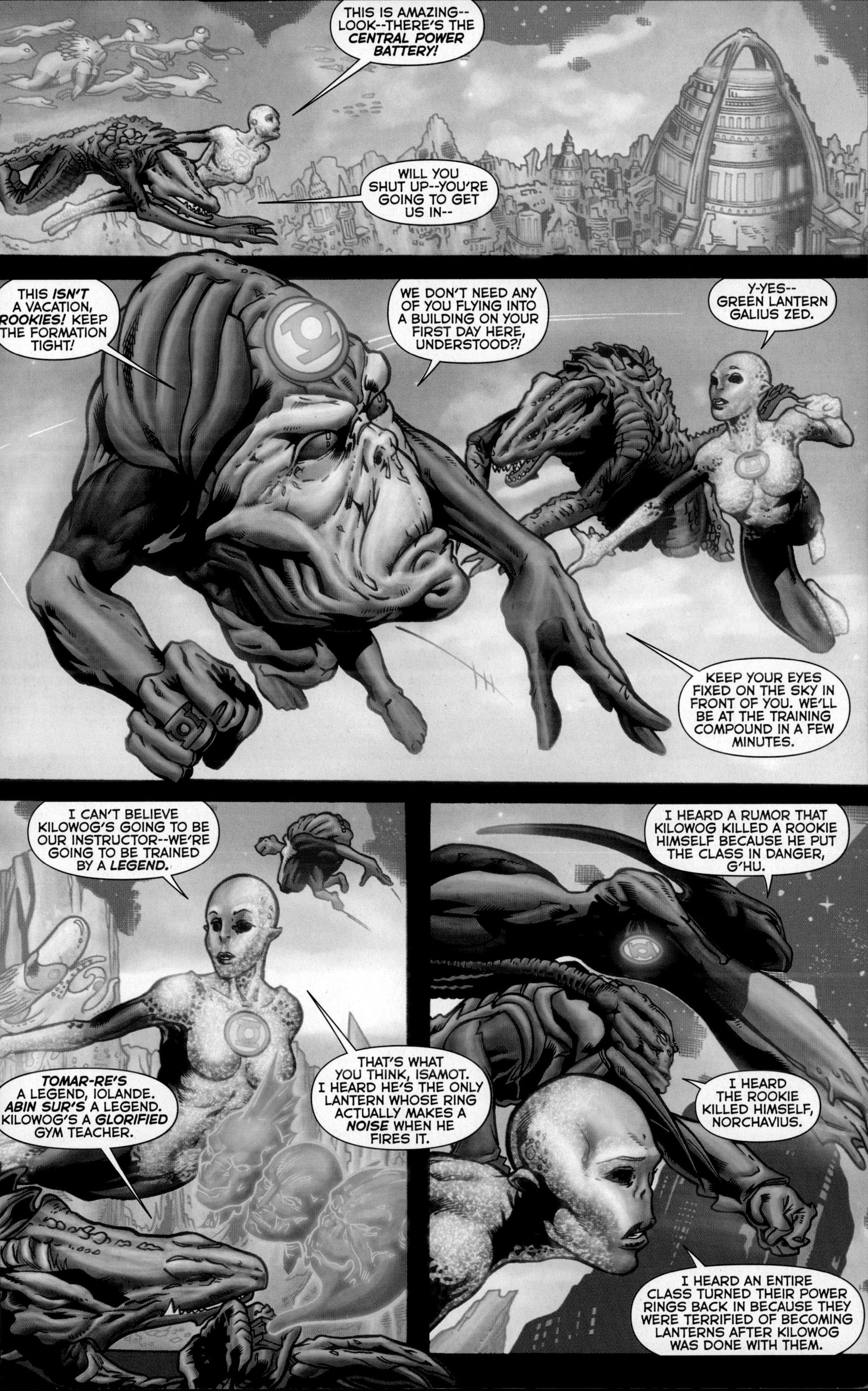
THIS IS AMAZING--LOOK--THERE'S THE CENTRAL POWER BATTERY!
WILL YOU SHUT UP--YOU'RE GOING TO GET US IN--
THIS ISN'T A VACATION, ROOKIES! KEEP THE FORMATION TIGHT!
WE DON'T NEED ANY OF YOU FLYING INTO A BUILDING ON YOUR FIRST DAY HERE, UNDERSTOOD?!
Y-YES--GREEN LANTERN GALIUS ZED.
KEEP YOUR EYES FIXED ON THE SKY IN FRONT OF YOU. WE'LL BE AT THE TRAINING COMPOUND IN A FEW MINUTES.
I CAN'T BELIEVE KILOWOG'S GOING TO BE OUR INSTRUCTOR--WE'RE GOING TO BE TRAINED BY A LEGEND.
TOMAR-RE'S A LEGEND, IOLANDE. ABIN SUR'S A LEGEND. KILOWOG'S A GLORIFIED GYM TEACHER.
THAT'S WHAT YOU THINK, ISAMOT. I HEARD HE'S THE ONLY LANTERN WHOSE RING ACTUALLY MAKES A NOISE WHEN HE FIRES IT.
I HEARD A RUMOR THAT KILOWOG KILLED A ROOKIE HIMSELF BECAUSE HE PUT THE CLASS IN DANGER, G'HU.
I HEARD THE ROOKIE KILLED HIMSELF, NORCHAVIUS.
I HEARD AN ENTIRE CLASS TURNED THEIR POWER RINGS BACK IN BECAUSE THEY WERE TERRIFIED OF BECOMING LANTERNS AFTER KILOWOG WAS DONE WITH THEM.

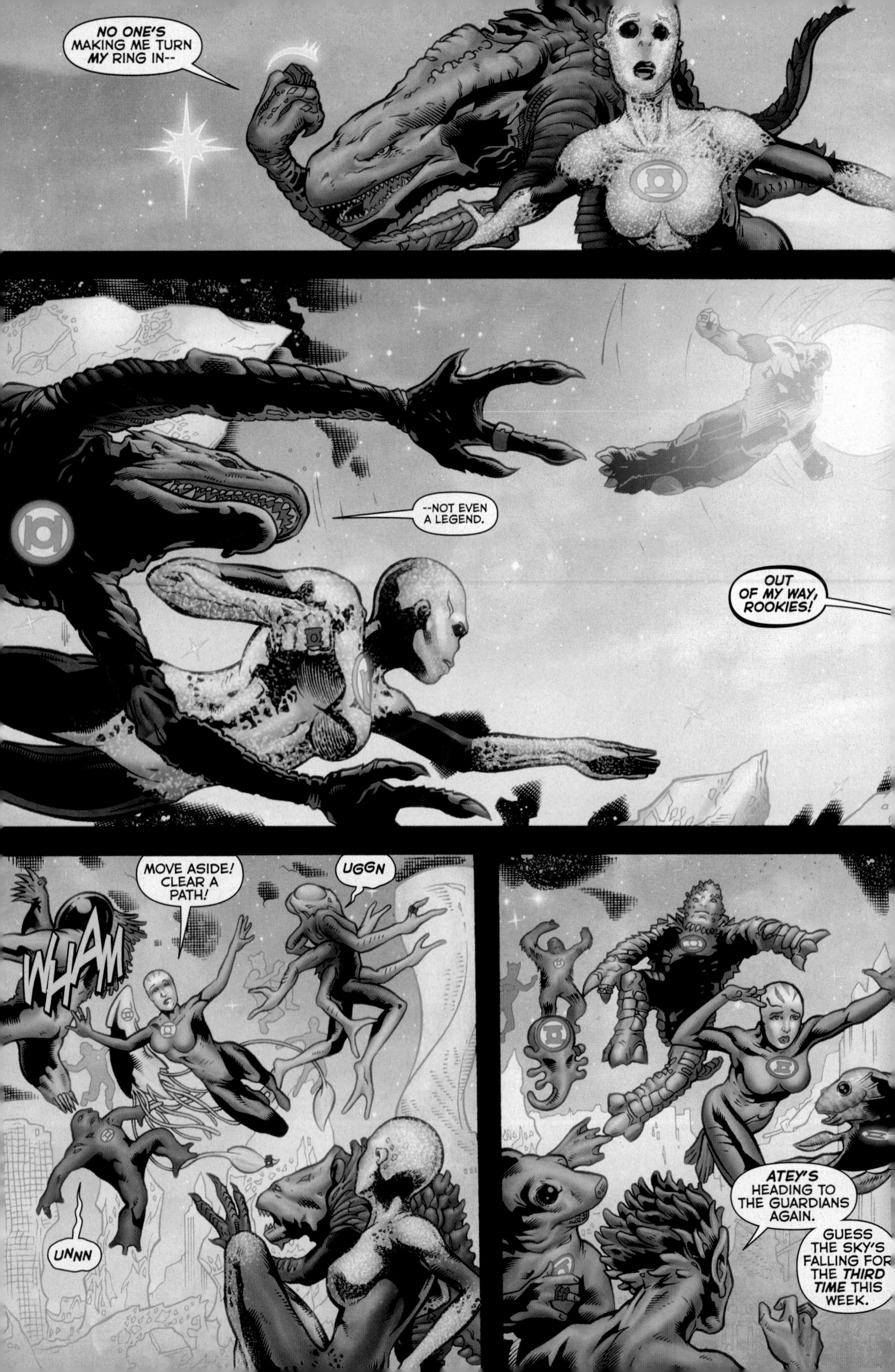

NO ONE'S MAKING ME TURN MY RING IN--
--NOT EVEN A LEGEND.
OUT OF MY WAY, ROOKIES!
WHAM
MOVE ASIDE! CLEAR A PATH!
UGGN
UNNN
ATEY'S HEADING TO THE GUARDIANS AGAIN.
GUESS THE SKY'S FALLING FOR THE THIRD TIME THIS WEEK.

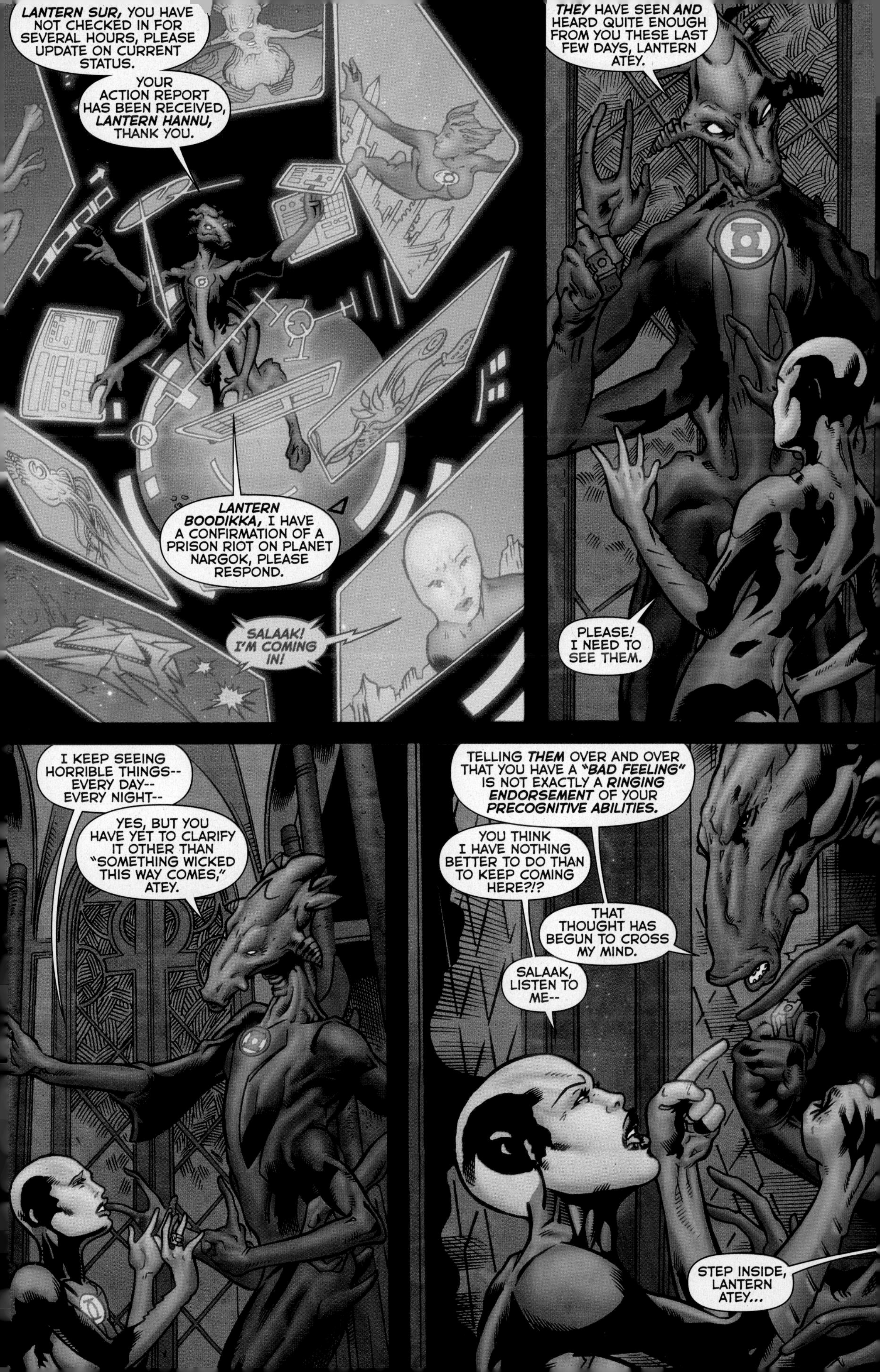
LANTERN SUR, YOU HAVE NOT CHECKED IN FOR SEVERAL HOURS, PLEASE UPDATE ON CURRENT STATUS.
YOUR ACTION REPORT HAS BEEN RECEIVED, LANTERN HANNU, THANK YOU.
LANTERN BOODIKKA, I HAVE A CONFIRMATION OF A PRISON RIOT ON PLANET NARGOK, PLEASE RESPOND.
SALAAK! I'M COMING IN!
THEY HAVE SEEN AND HEARD QUITE ENOUGH FROM YOU THESE LAST FEW DAYS, LANTERN ATEY.
PLEASE! I NEED TO SEE THEM.
I KEEP SEEING HORRIBLE THINGS-- EVERY DAY-- EVERY NIGHT--
YES, BUT YOU HAVE YET TO CLARIFY IT OTHER THAN "SOMETHING WICKED THIS WAY COMES," ATEY.
TELLING THEM OVER AND OVER THAT YOU HAVE A "BAD FEELING" IS NOT EXACTLY A RINGING ENDORSEMENT OF YOUR PRECOGNITIVE ABILITIES.
YOU THINK I HAVE NOTHING BETTER TO DO THAN TO KEEP COMING HERE?!?
THAT THOUGHT HAS BEGUN TO CROSS MY MIND.
SALAAK, LISTEN TO ME--
STEP INSIDE, LANTERN ATEY...

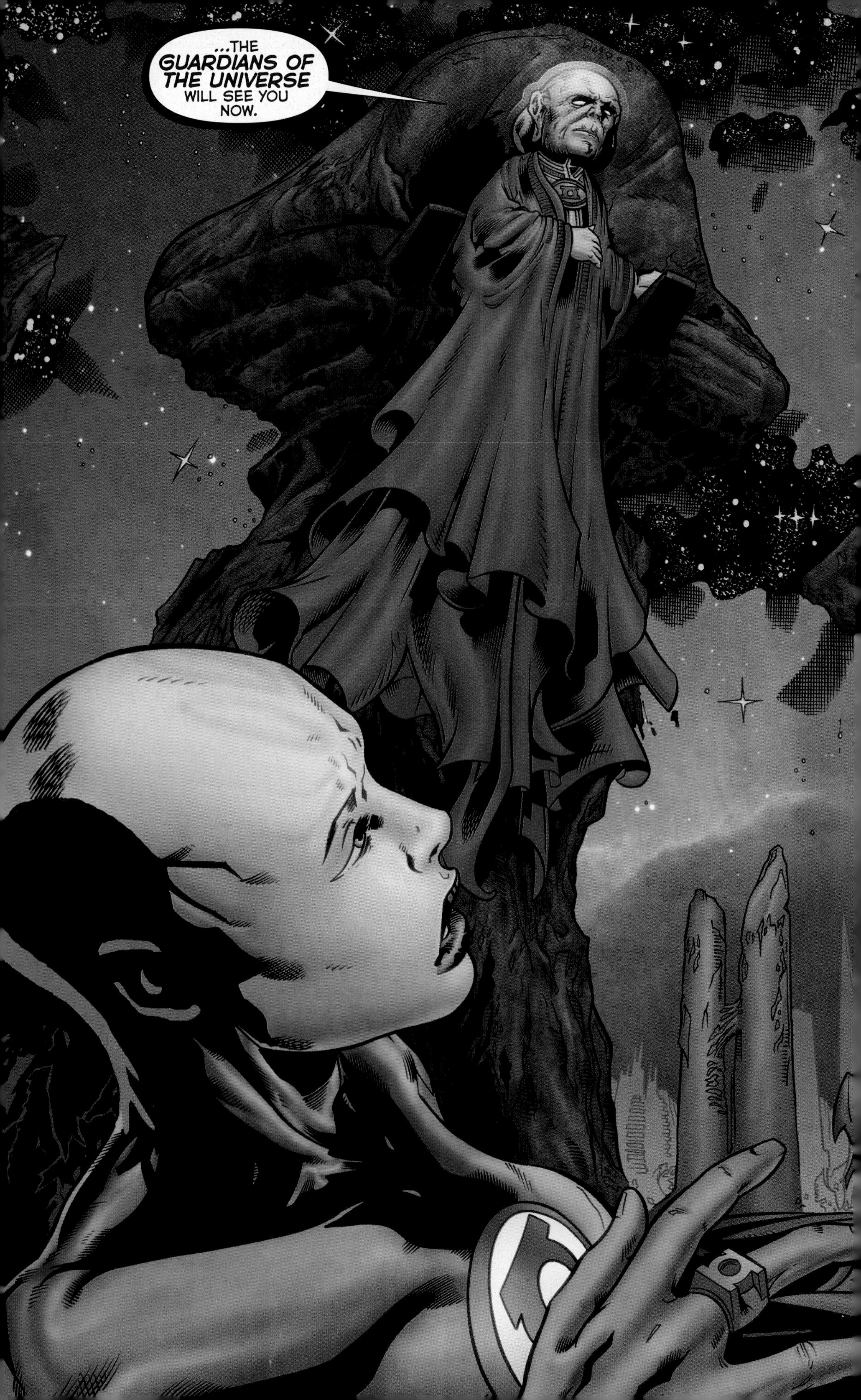
...THE GUARDIANS OF THE UNIVERSE WILL SEE YOU NOW.

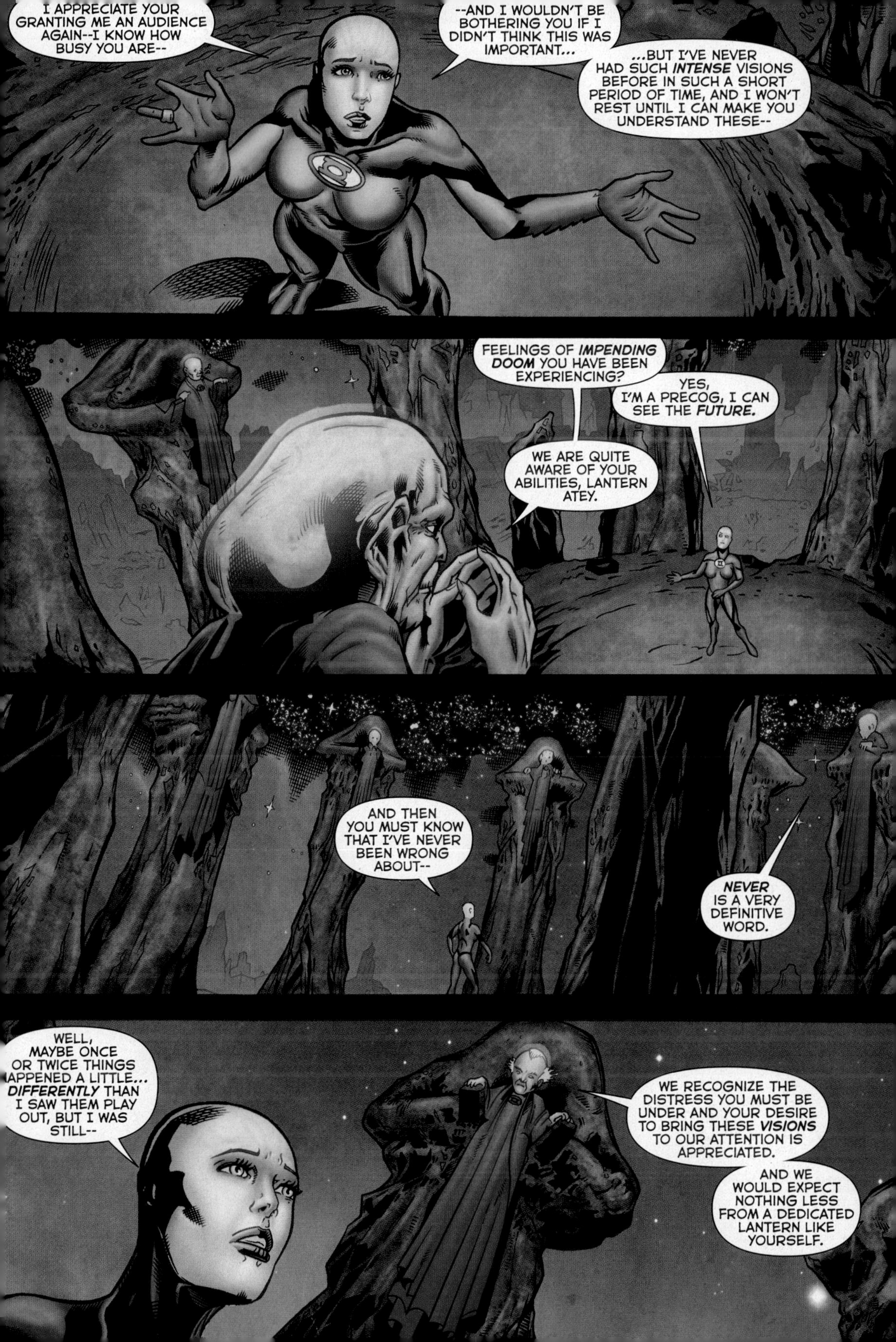
I APPRECIATE YOUR GRANTING ME AN AUDIENCE AGAIN--I KNOW HOW BUSY YOU ARE--
--AND I WOULDN'T BE BOTHERING YOU IF I DIDN'T THINK THIS WAS IMPORTANT...
...BUT I'VE NEVER HAD SUCH INTENSE VISIONS BEFORE IN SUCH A SHORT PERIOD OF TIME, AND I WON'T REST UNTIL I CAN MAKE YOU UNDERSTAND THESE--
FEELINGS OF IMPENDING DOOM YOU HAVE BEEN EXPERIENCING?
YES, I'M A PRECOG, I CAN SEE THE FUTURE.
WE ARE QUITE AWARE OF YOUR ABILITIES, LANTERN ATEY.
AND THEN YOU MUST KNOW THAT I'VE NEVER BEEN WRONG ABOUT--
NEVER IS A VERY DEFINITIVE WORD.
WELL, MAYBE ONCE OR TWICE THINGS APPENED A LITTLE... DIFFERENTLY THAN I SAW THEM PLAY OUT, BUT I WAS STILL--
WE RECOGNIZE THE DISTRESS YOU MUST BE UNDER AND YOUR DESIRE TO BRING THESE VISIONS TO OUR ATTENTION IS APPRECIATED.
AND WE WOULD EXPECT NOTHING LESS FROM A DEDICATED LANTERN LIKE YOURSELF.

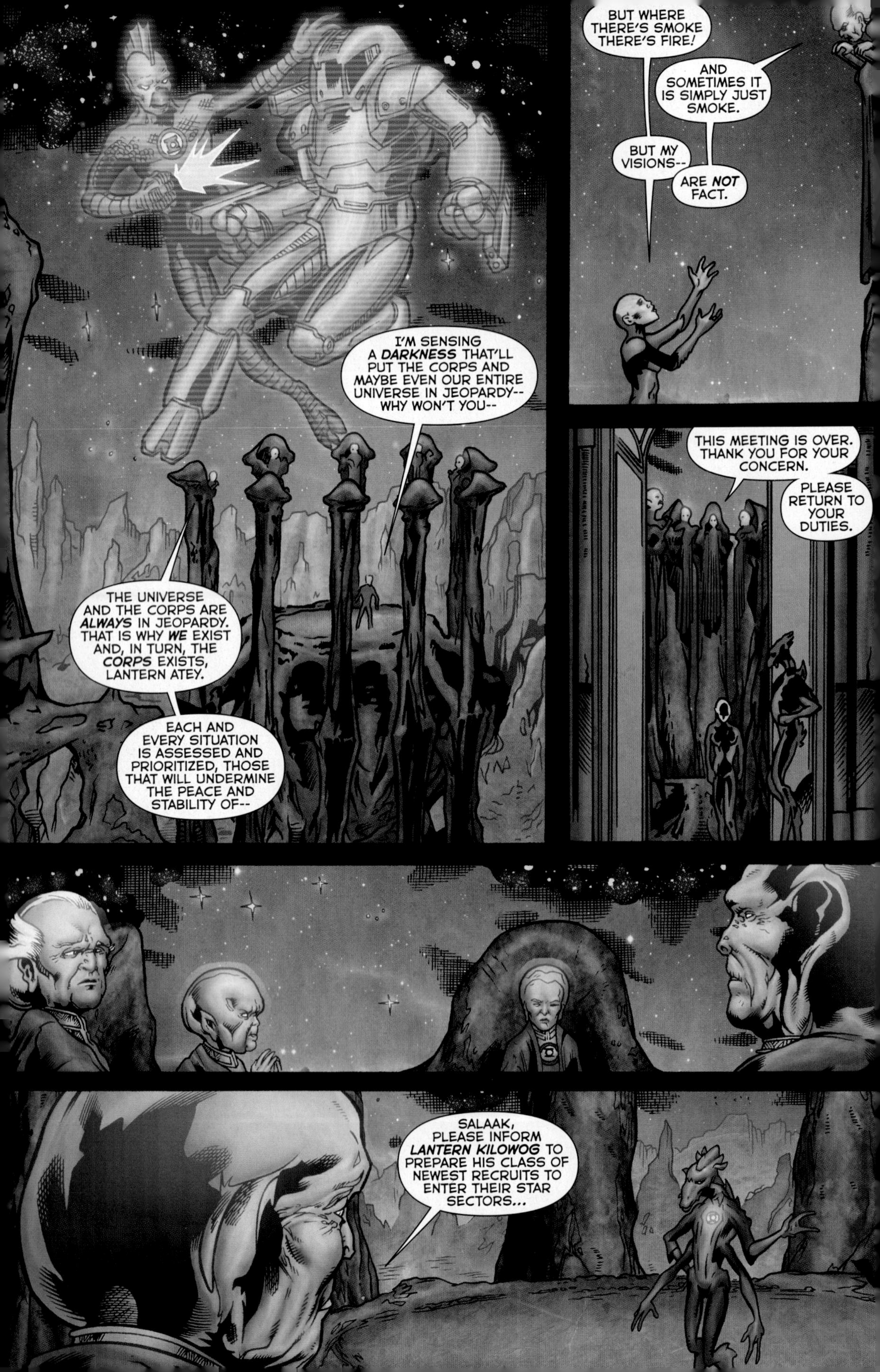
I'M SENSING A DARKNESS THAT'LL PUT THE CORPS AND MAYBE EVEN OUR ENTIRE UNIVERSE IN JEOPARDY-- WHY WON'T YOU--
THE UNIVERSE AND THE CORPS ARE ALWAYS IN JEOPARDY. THAT IS WHY WE EXIST AND, IN TURN, THE CORPS EXISTS, LANTERN ATEY.
EACH AND EVERY SITUATION IS ASSESSED AND PRIORITIZED, THOSE THAT WILL UNDERMINE THE PEACE AND STABILITY OF--
BUT WHERE THERE'S SMOKE THERE'S FIRE!
AND SOMETIMES IT IS SIMPLY JUST SMOKE.
BUT MY VISIONS--
ARE NOT FACT.
THIS MEETING IS OVER. THANK YOU FOR YOUR CONCERN.
PLEASE RETURN TO YOUR DUTIES.
SALAAK, PLEASE INFORM LANTERN KILOWOG TO PREPARE HIS CLASS OF NEWEST RECRUITS TO ENTER THEIR STAR SECTORS...

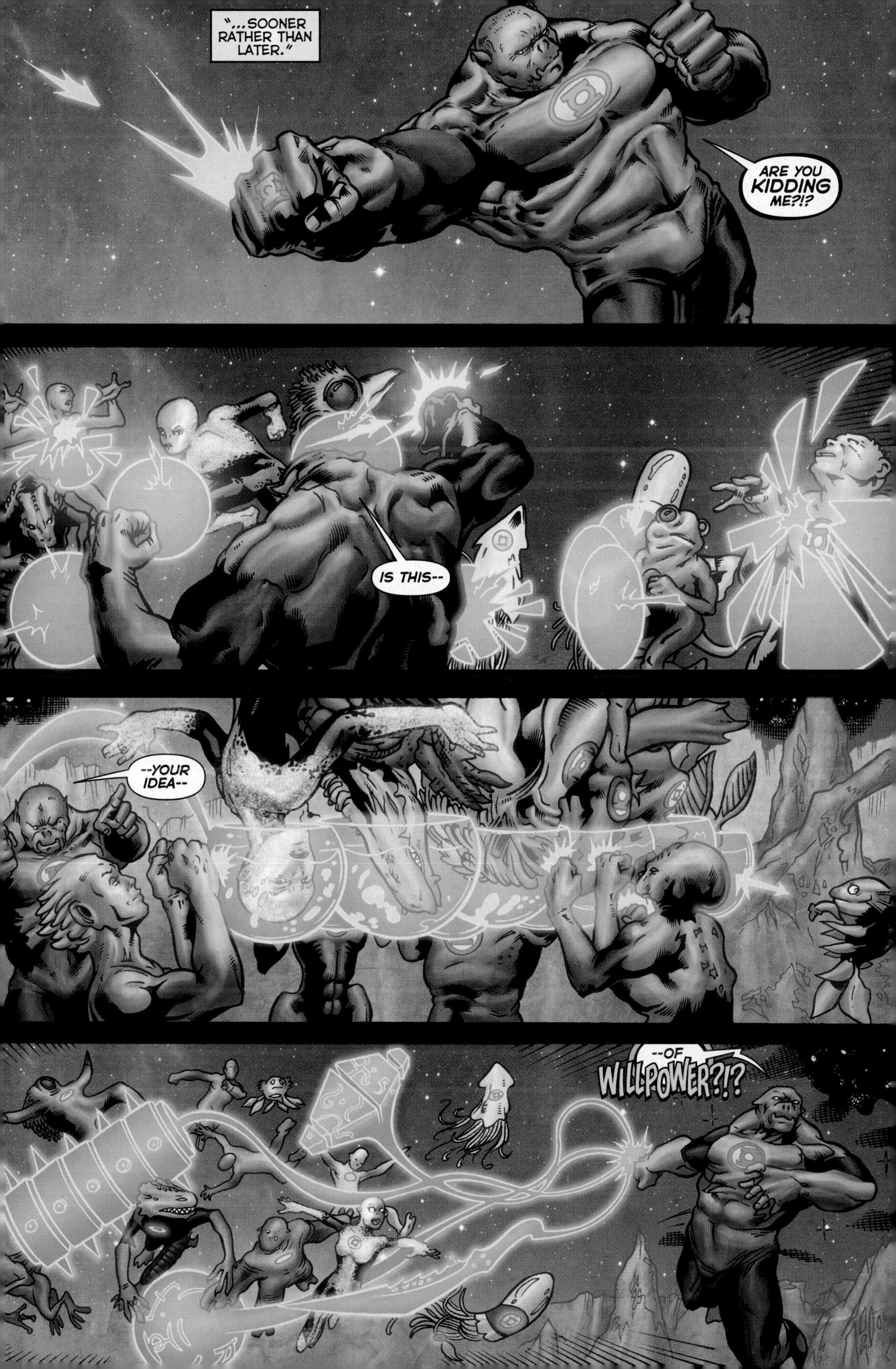
"...SOONER RATHER THAN LATER."
ARE YOU KIDDING ME?!?
IS THIS--
--YOUR IDEA--
--OF
WILLPOWER?!?

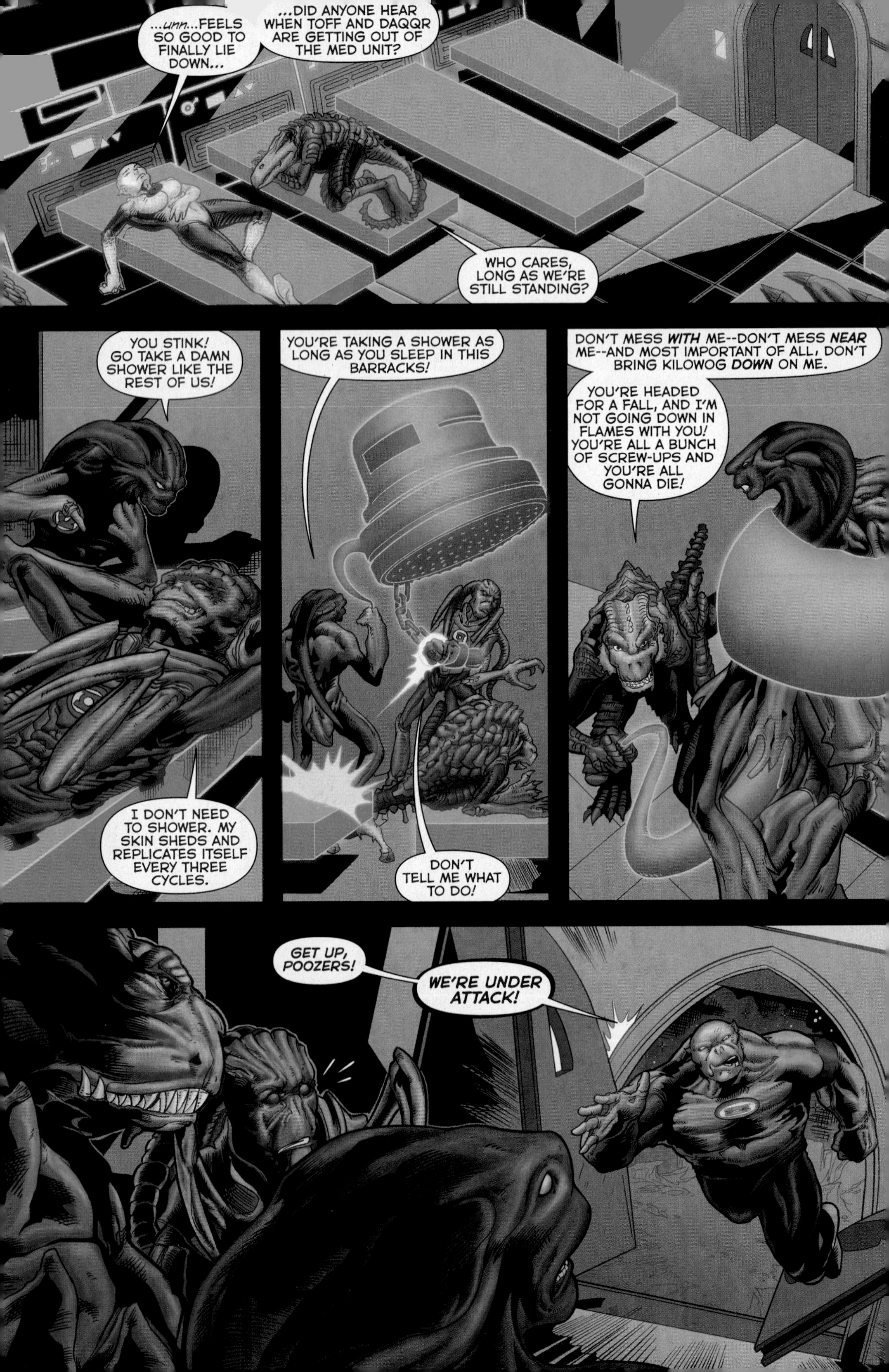
...unn...FEELS SO GOOD TO FINALLY LIE DOWN...
...DID ANYONE HEAR WHEN TOFF AND DAQQR ARE GETTING OUT OF THE MED UNIT?
WHO CARES, LONG AS WE'RE STILL STANDING?
YOU STINK! GO TAKE A DAMN SHOWER LIKE THE REST OF US!
I DON'T NEED TO SHOWER. MY SKIN SHEDS AND REPLICATES ITSELF EVERY THREE CYCLES.
YOU'RE TAKING A SHOWER AS LONG AS YOU SLEEP IN THIS BARRACKS!
DON'T TELL ME WHAT TO DO!
DON'T MESS WITH ME--DON'T MESS NEAR ME--AND MOST IMPORTANT OF ALL, DON'T BRING KILOWOG DOWN ON ME.
YOU'RE HEADED FOR A FALL, AND I'M NOT GOING DOWN IN FLAMES WITH YOU! YOU'RE ALL A BUNCH OF SCREW-UPS AND YOU'RE ALL GONNA DIE!
GET UP, POOZERS!
WE'RE UNDER ATTACK!

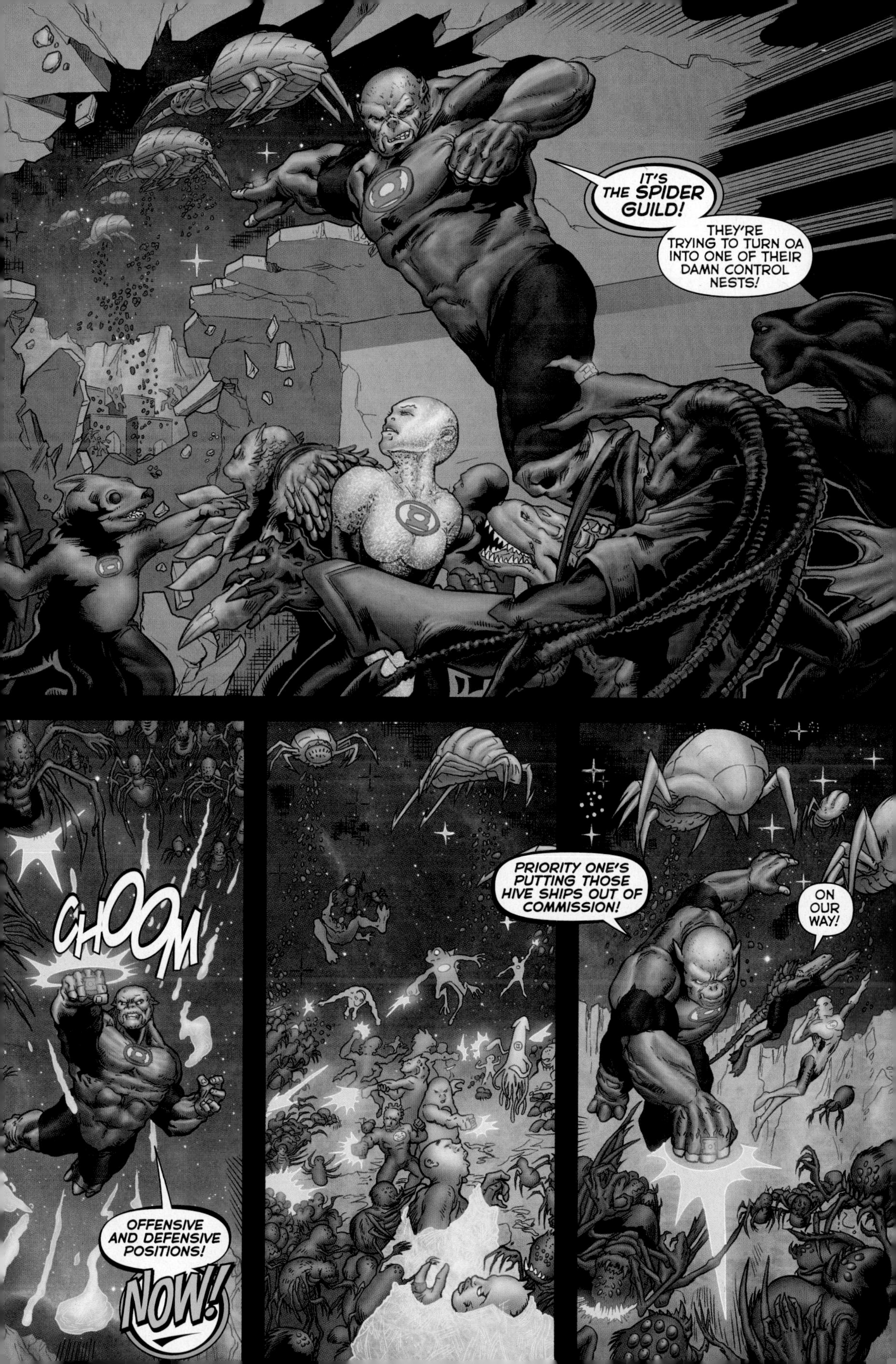
IT'S THE SPIDER GUILD!
THEY'RE TRYING TO TURN OA INTO ONE OF THEIR DAMN CONTROL NESTS!
CHOOM
OFFENSIVE AND DEFENSIVE POSITIONS!
NOW!
PRIORITY ONE'S PUTTING THOSE HIVE SHIPS OUT OF COMMISSION!
ON OUR WAY!

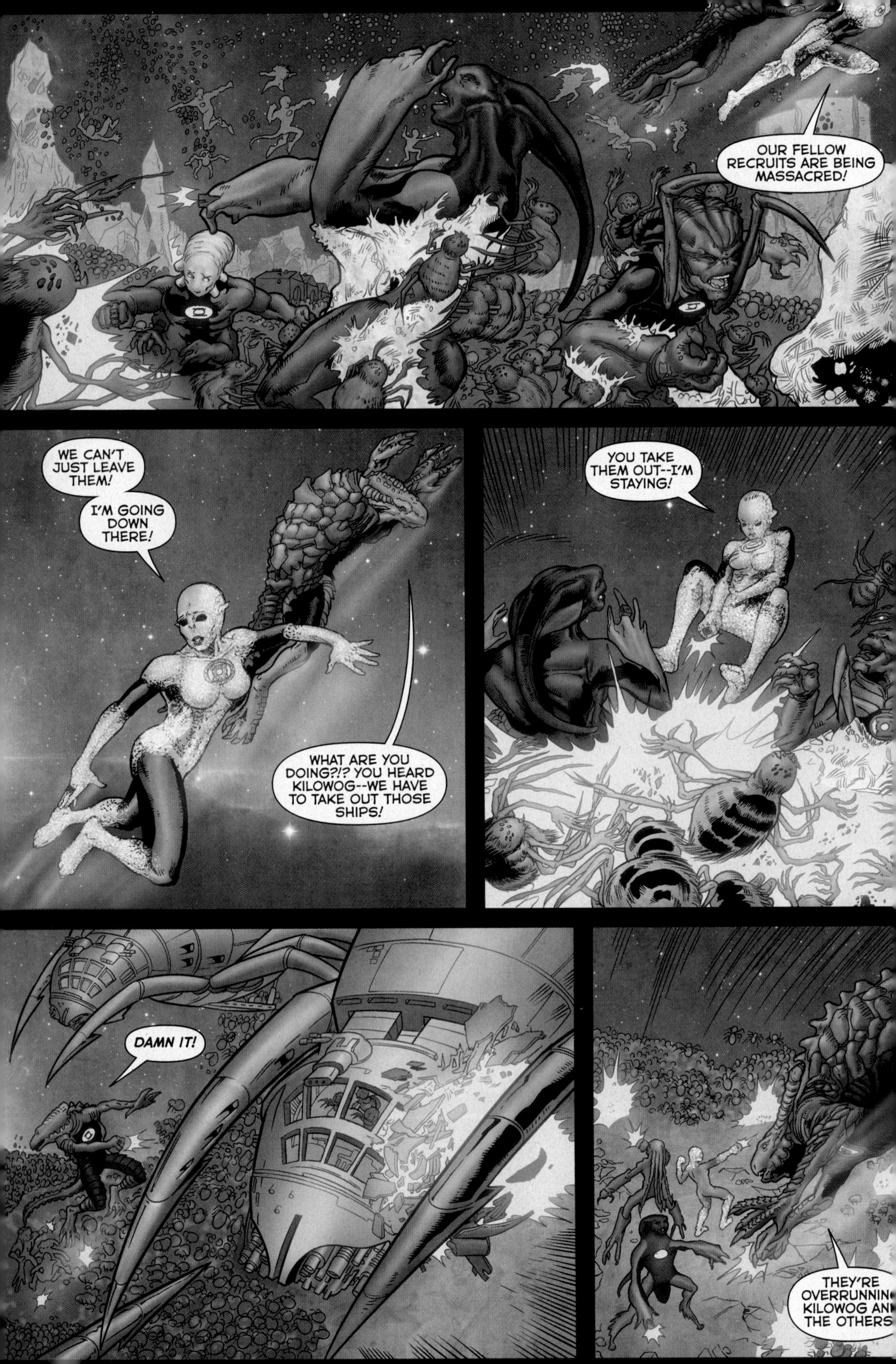
OUR FELLOW RECRUITS ARE BEING MASSACRED!
WE CAN'T JUST LEAVE THEM!
I'M GOING DOWN THERE!
WHAT ARE YOU DOING?!? YOU HEARD KILOWOG--WE HAVE TO TAKE OUT THOSE SHIPS!
YOU TAKE THEM OUT--I'M STAYING!
DAMN IT!
THEY'RE OVERRUNNIN KILOWOG AN THE OTHERS

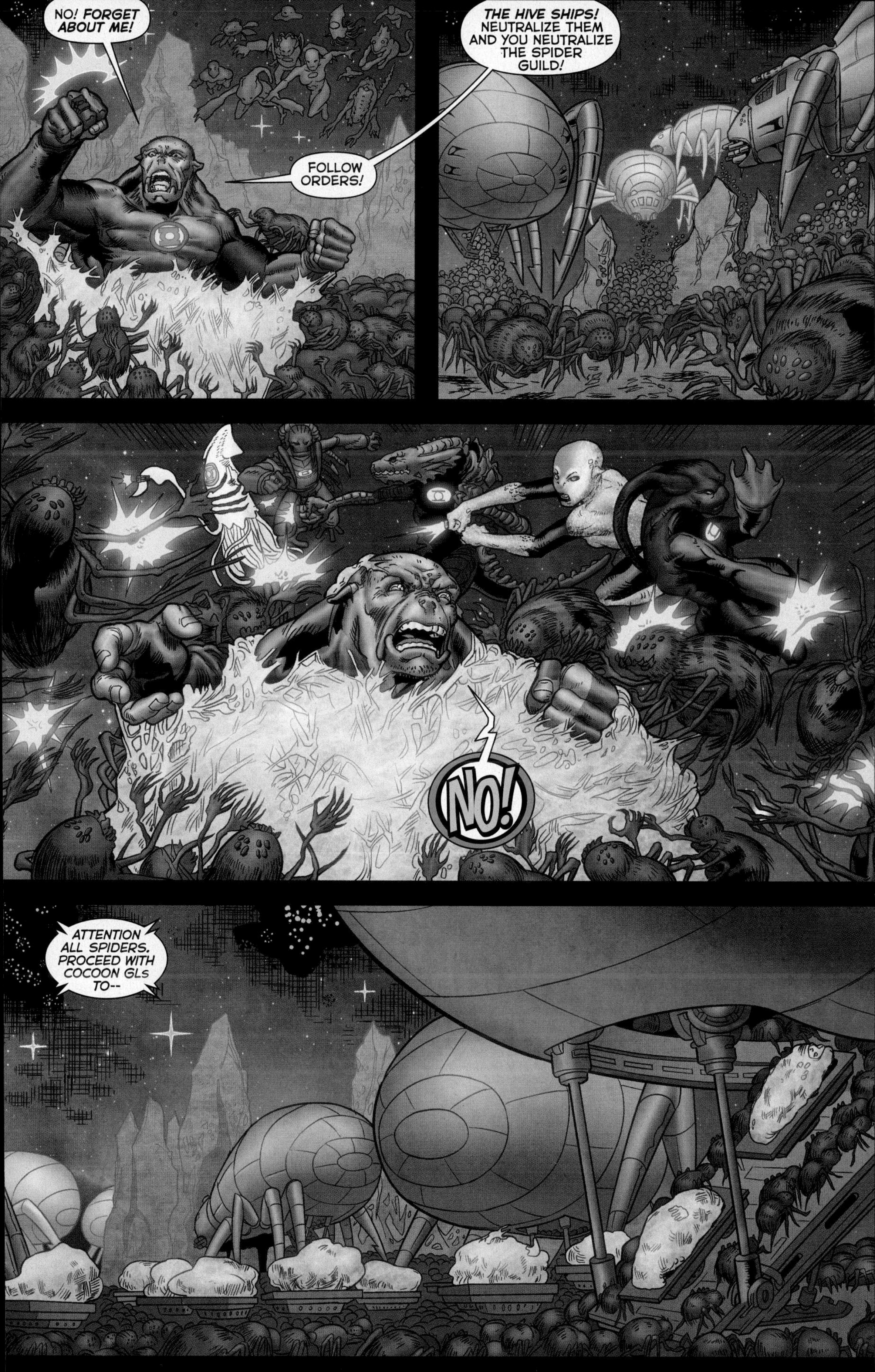
NO! FORGET ABOUT ME!
THE HIVE SHIPS! NEUTRALIZE THEM AND YOU NEUTRALIZE THE SPIDER GUILD!
FOLLOW ORDERS!
NO!
ATTENTION ALL SPIDERS. PROCEED WITH COCOON GLs TO--

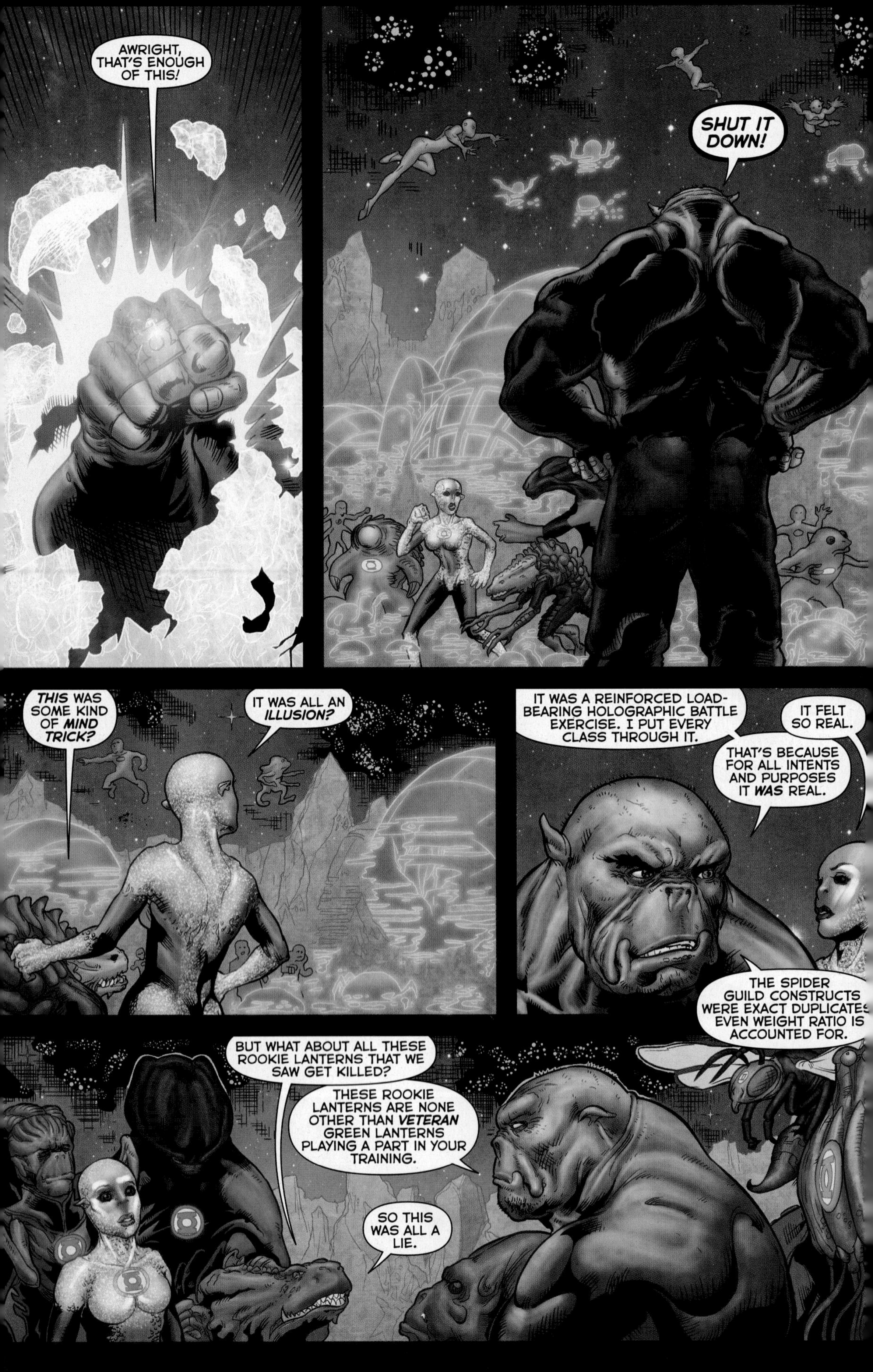
AWRIGHT, THAT'S ENOUGH OF THIS!
SHUT IT DOWN!
THIS WAS SOME KIND OF MIND TRICK?
IT WAS ALL AN ILLUSION?
IT WAS A REINFORCED LOAD-BEARING HOLOGRAPHIC BATTLE EXERCISE. I PUT EVERY CLASS THROUGH IT.
IT FELT SO REAL.
THAT'S BECAUSE FOR ALL INTENTS AND PURPOSES IT WAS REAL.
THE SPIDER GUILD CONSTRUCTS WERE EXACT DUPLICATES. EVEN WEIGHT RATIO IS ACCOUNTED FOR.
BUT WHAT ABOUT ALL THESE ROOKIE LANTERNS THAT WE SAW GET KILLED?
THESE ROOKIE LANTERNS ARE NONE OTHER THAN VETERAN GREEN LANTERNS PLAYING A PART IN YOUR TRAINING.
SO THIS WAS ALL A LIE.

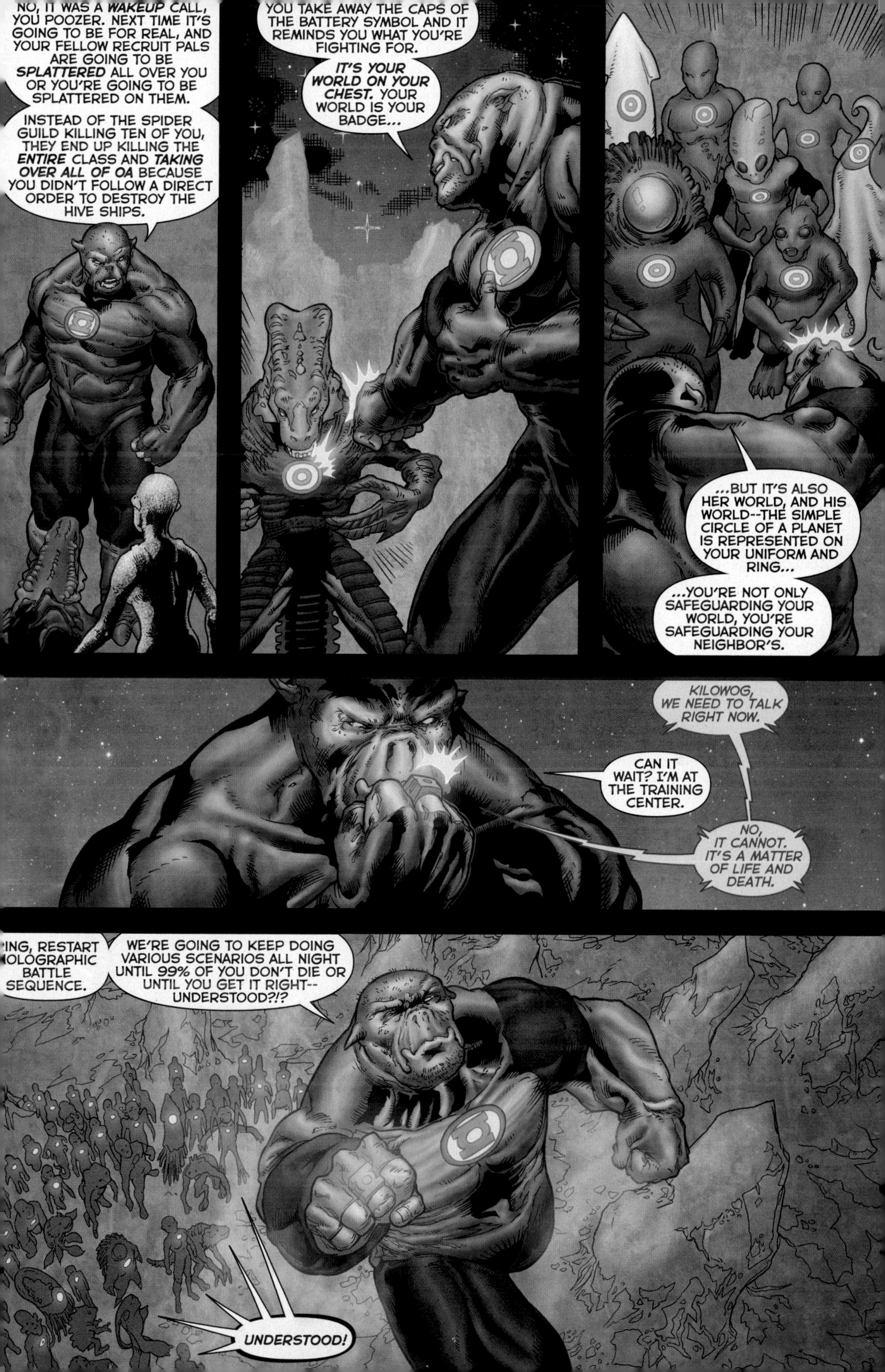
NO, IT WAS A WAKEUP CALL, YOU POOZER. NEXT TIME IT'S GOING TO BE FOR REAL, AND YOUR FELLOW RECRUIT PALS ARE GOING TO BE SPLATTERED ALL OVER YOU OR YOU'RE GOING TO BE SPLATTERED ON THEM.
INSTEAD OF THE SPIDER GUILD KILLING TEN OF YOU, THEY END UP KILLING THE ENTIRE CLASS AND TAKING OVER ALL OF OA BECAUSE YOU DIDN'T FOLLOW A DIRECT ORDER TO DESTROY THE HIVE SHIPS.
YOU TAKE AWAY THE CAPS OF THE BATTERY SYMBOL AND IT REMINDS YOU WHAT YOU'RE FIGHTING FOR.
IT'S YOUR WORLD ON YOUR CHEST. YOUR WORLD IS YOUR BADGE...
...BUT IT'S ALSO HER WORLD, AND HIS WORLD--THE SIMPLE CIRCLE OF A PLANET IS REPRESENTED ON YOUR UNIFORM AND RING...
...YOU'RE NOT ONLY SAFEGUARDING YOUR WORLD, YOU'RE SAFEGUARDING YOUR NEIGHBOR'S.
KILOWOG, WE NEED TO TALK RIGHT NOW.
CAN IT WAIT? I'M AT THE TRAINING CENTER.
NO, IT CANNOT. IT'S A MATTER OF LIFE AND DEATH.
BATTLE SEQUENCE.
WE'RE GOING TO KEEP DOING VARIOUS SCENARIOS ALL NIGHT UNTIL 99% OF YOU DON'T DIE OR UNTIL YOU GET IT RIGHT--UNDERSTOOD?!?
UNDERSTOOD!

BLEAK NEWS FROM SECTOR 2814, KILOWOG.

WHAT IS IT, TOMAR-RE?

WE JUST RECEIVED WORD FROM THE GUARDIANS.

A GREEN LANTERN HAS *PASSED* THIS DAY.

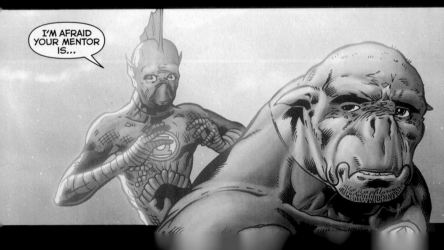

I'M AFRAID YOUR MENTOR IS...

NO-- IT CAN'T BE--

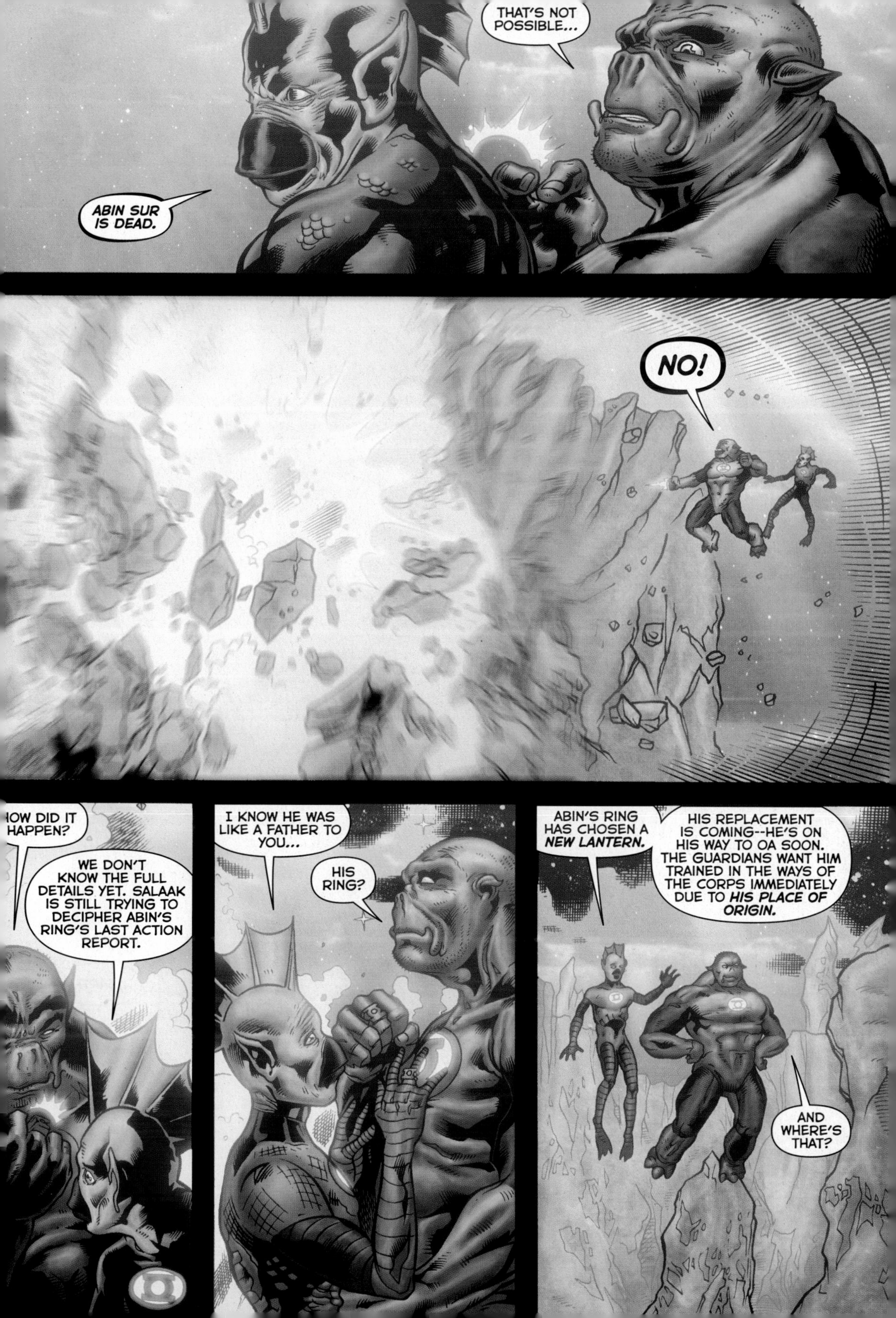

THAT'S NOT POSSIBLE...
ABIN SUR IS DEAD.
NO!
HOW DID IT HAPPEN?
WE DON'T KNOW THE FULL DETAILS YET. SALAAK IS STILL TRYING TO DECIPHER ABIN'S RING'S LAST ACTION REPORT.
I KNOW HE WAS LIKE A FATHER TO YOU...
HIS RING?
ABIN'S RING HAS CHOSEN A *NEW LANTERN.*
HIS REPLACEMENT IS COMING--HE'S ON HIS WAY TO OA SOON. THE GUARDIANS WANT HIM TRAINED IN THE WAYS OF THE CORPS IMMEDIATELY DUE TO *HIS PLACE OF ORIGIN.*
AND WHERE'S THAT?

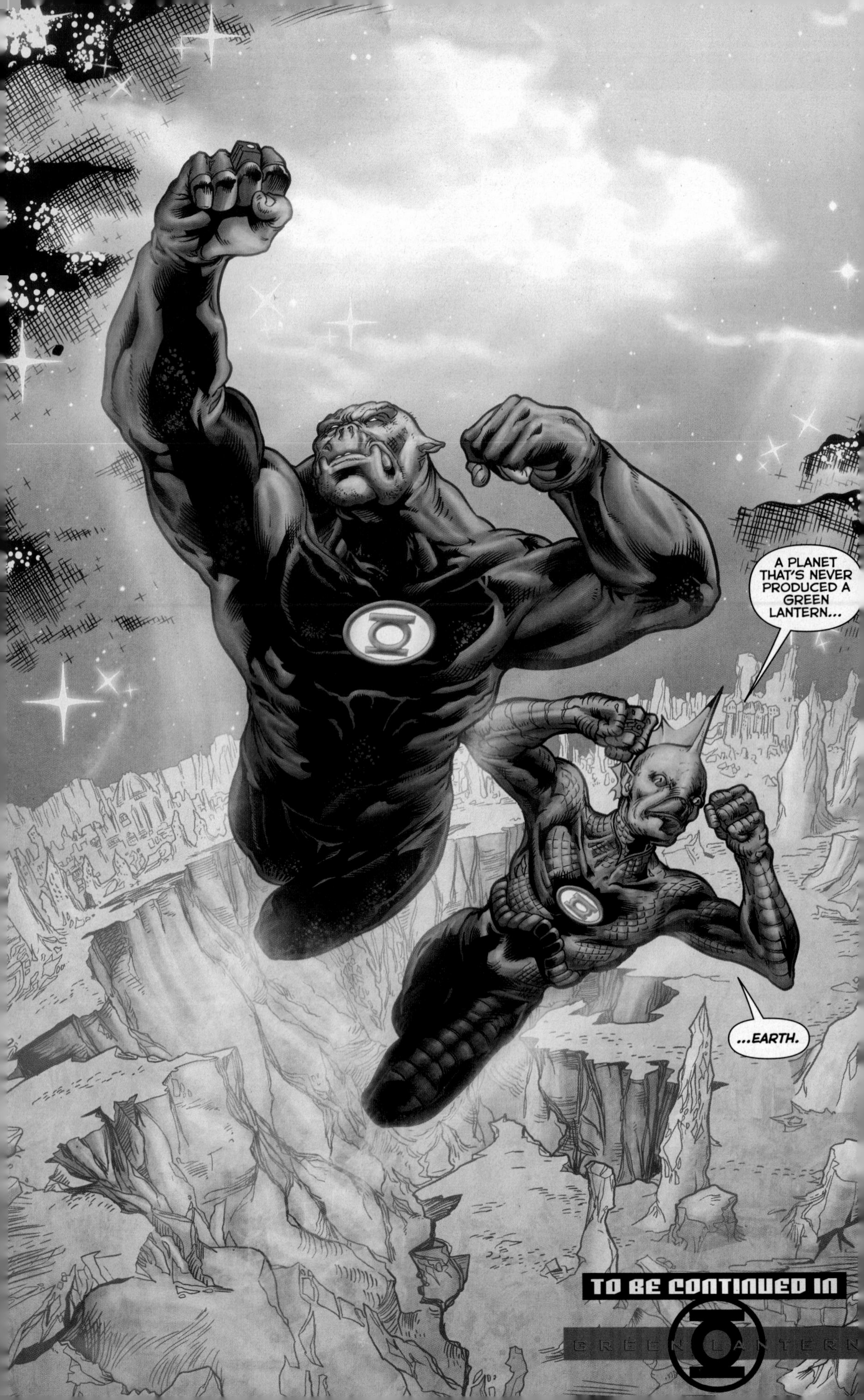
A PLANET THAT'S NEVER PRODUCED A GREEN LANTERN...
...EARTH.
TO BE CONTINUED IN
GREEN LANTERN

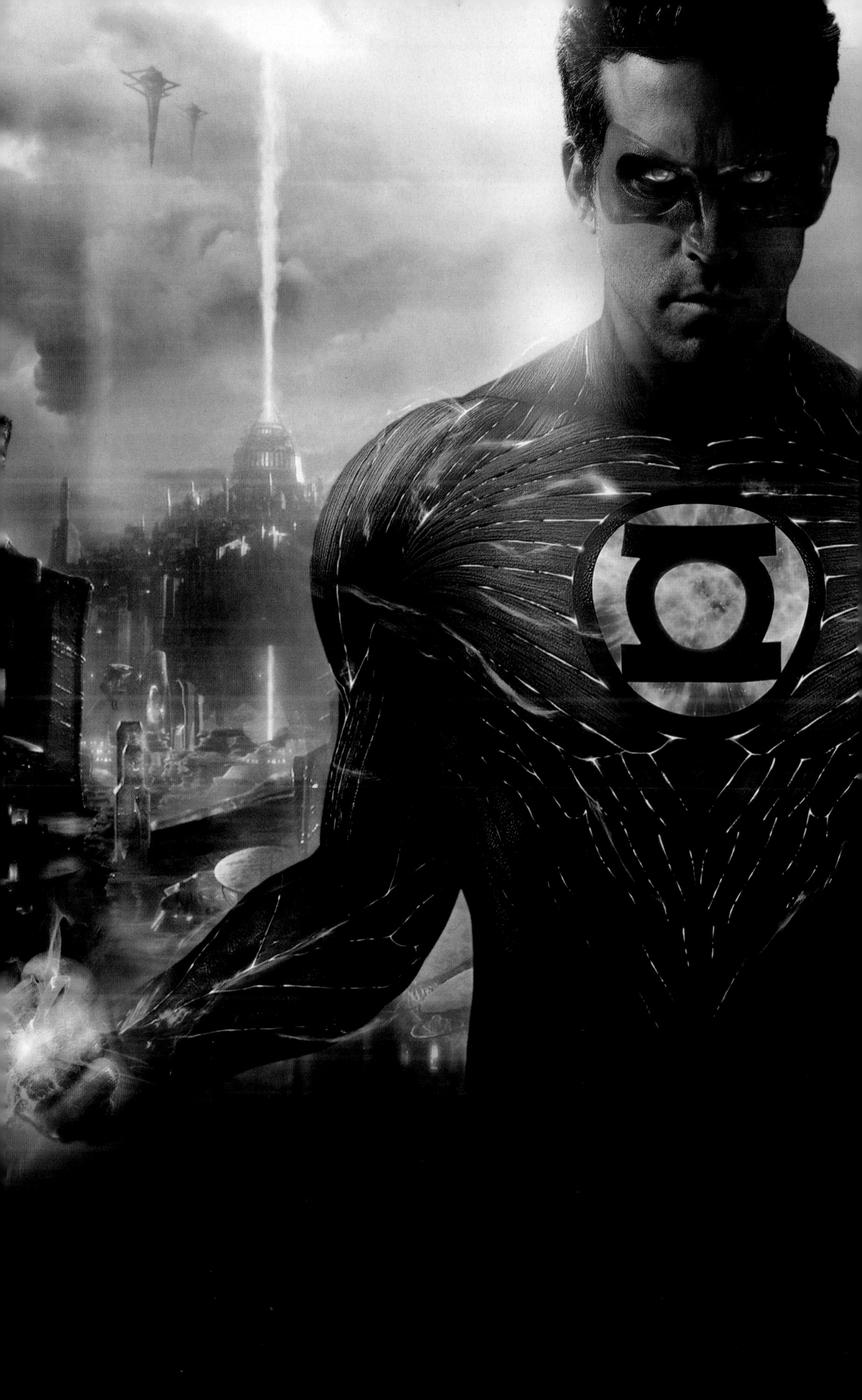

BEING HUMAN

GEOFF **JOHNS** & GREG **BERLANTI** writers

JERRY **ORDWAY** artist

EMERALD CITY

DONALD **DE LINE** & ADAM **SCHLAGMAN** writers

TYLER **KIRKHAM** penciller

BATT inker

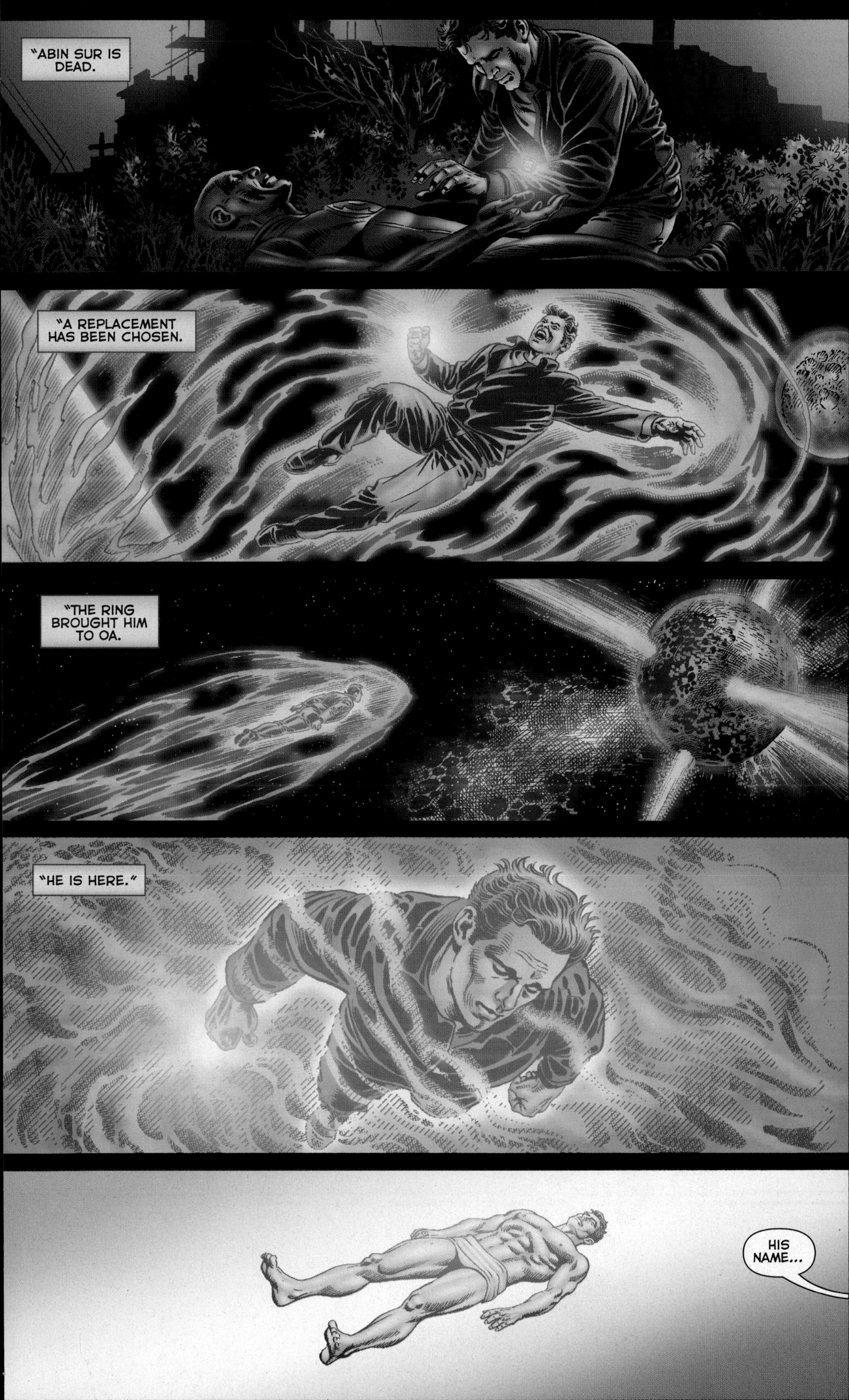
"ABIN SUR IS DEAD.
"A REPLACEMENT HAS BEEN CHOSEN.
"THE RING BROUGHT HIM TO OA.
"HE IS HERE."
HIS NAME...

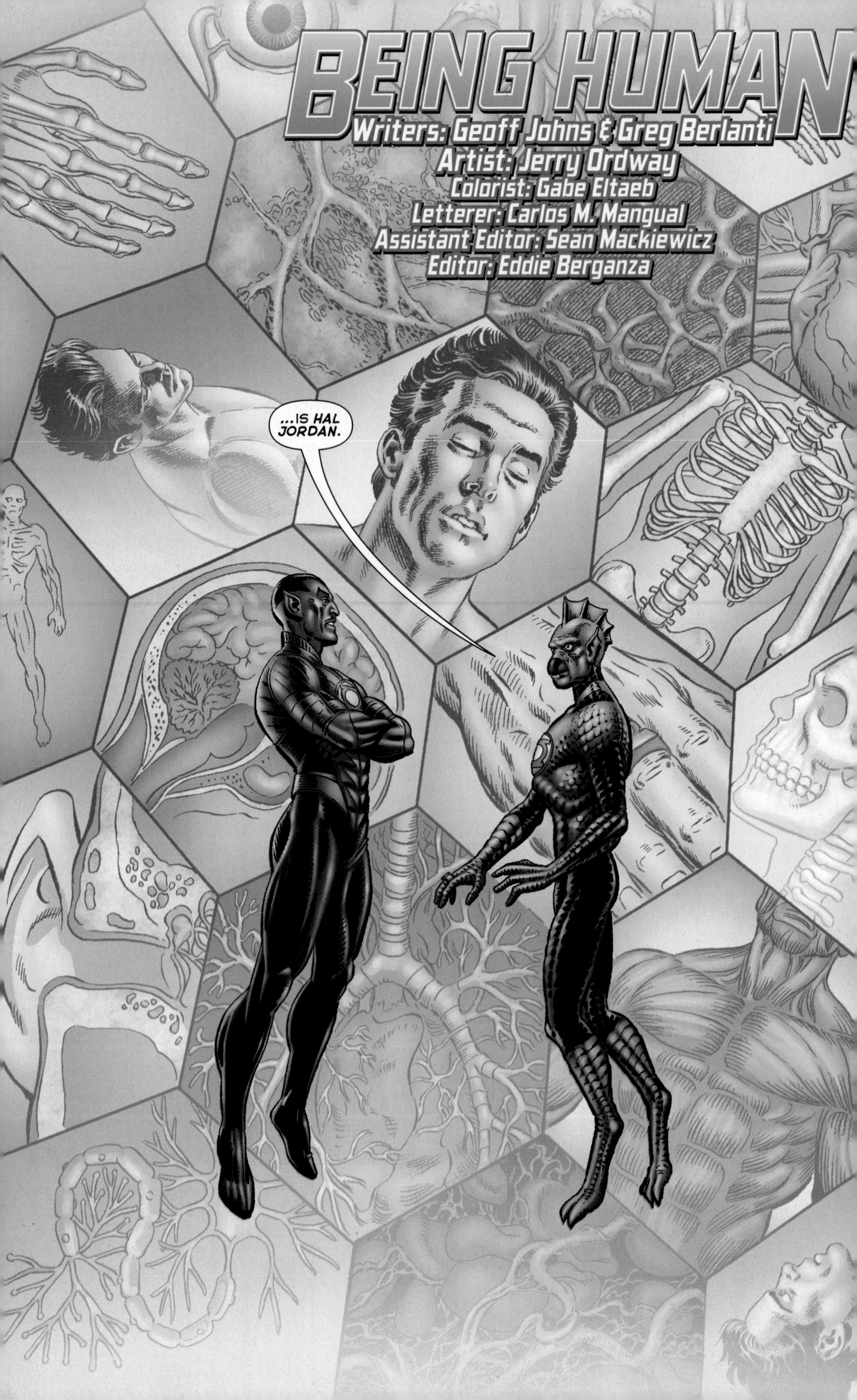
BEING HUMAN
Writers: Geoff Johns & Greg Berlanti
Artist: Jerry Ordway
Colorist: Gabe Eltaeb
Letterer: Carlos M. Mangual
Assistant Editor: Sean Mackiewicz
Editor: Eddie Berganza
...IS HAL JORDAN.

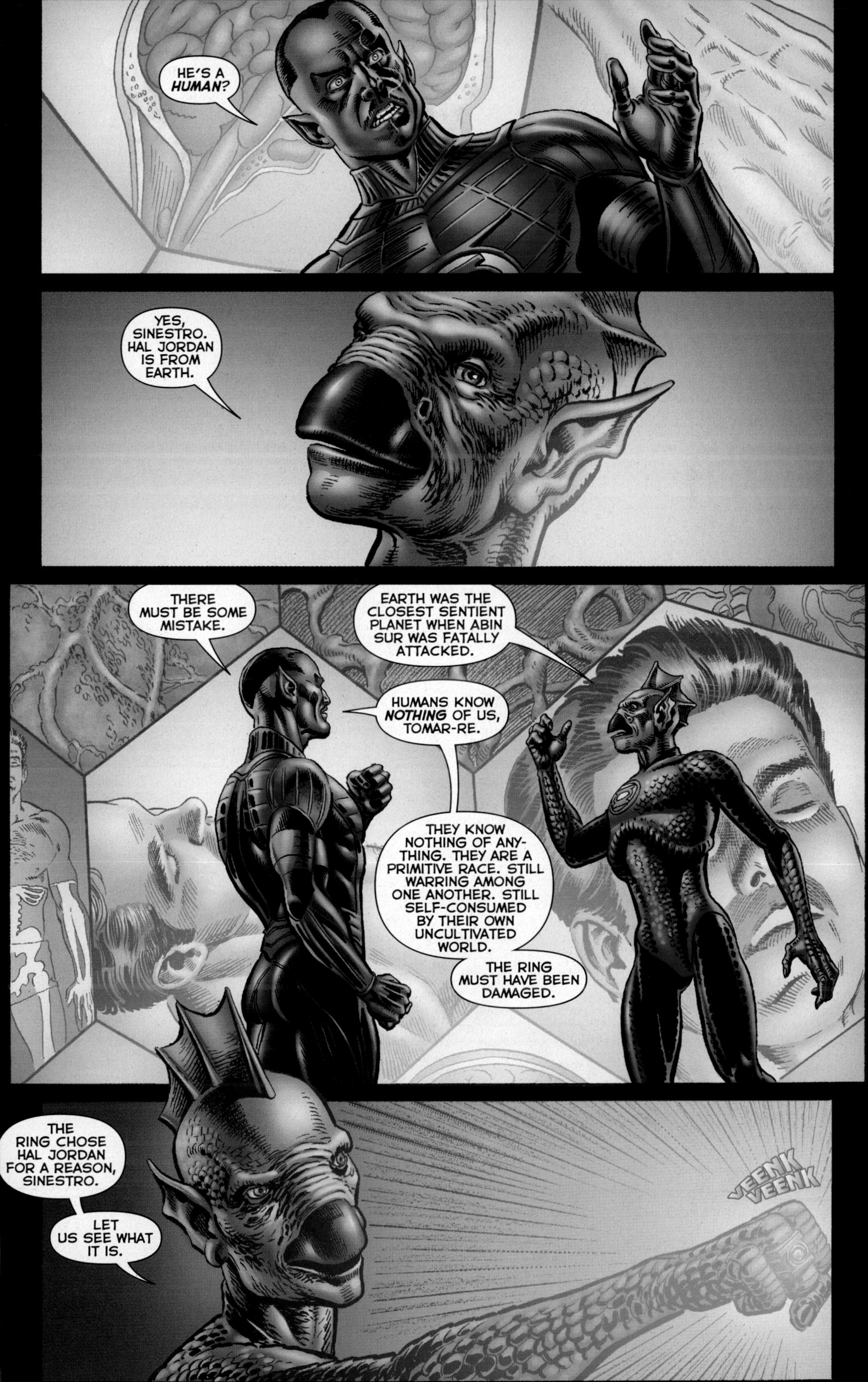
HE'S A *HUMAN*?
YES, SINESTRO. HAL JORDAN IS FROM EARTH.
THERE MUST BE SOME MISTAKE.
EARTH WAS THE CLOSEST SENTIENT PLANET WHEN ABIN SUR WAS FATALLY ATTACKED.
HUMANS KNOW *NOTHING* OF US, TOMAR-RE.
THEY KNOW NOTHING OF ANY-THING. THEY ARE A PRIMITIVE RACE. STILL WARRING AMONG ONE ANOTHER. STILL SELF-CONSUMED BY THEIR OWN UNCULTIVATED WORLD.
THE RING MUST HAVE BEEN DAMAGED.
THE RING CHOSE HAL JORDAN FOR A REASON, SINESTRO.
LET US SEE WHAT IT IS.
VEENK VEENK

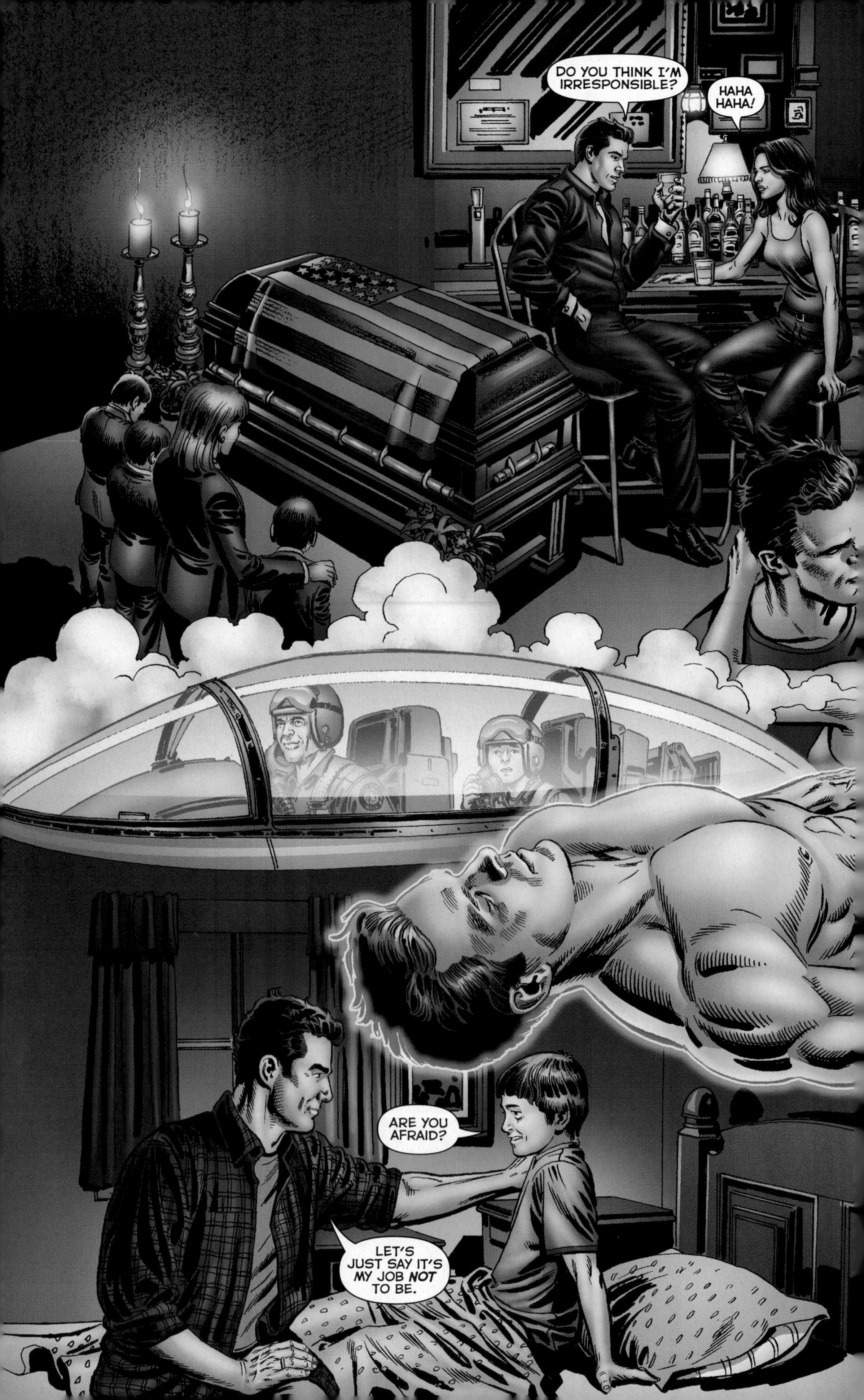
DO YOU THINK I'M IRRESPONSIBLE?
HAHA HAHA!
ARE YOU AFRAID?
LET'S JUST SAY IT'S MY JOB NOT TO BE.

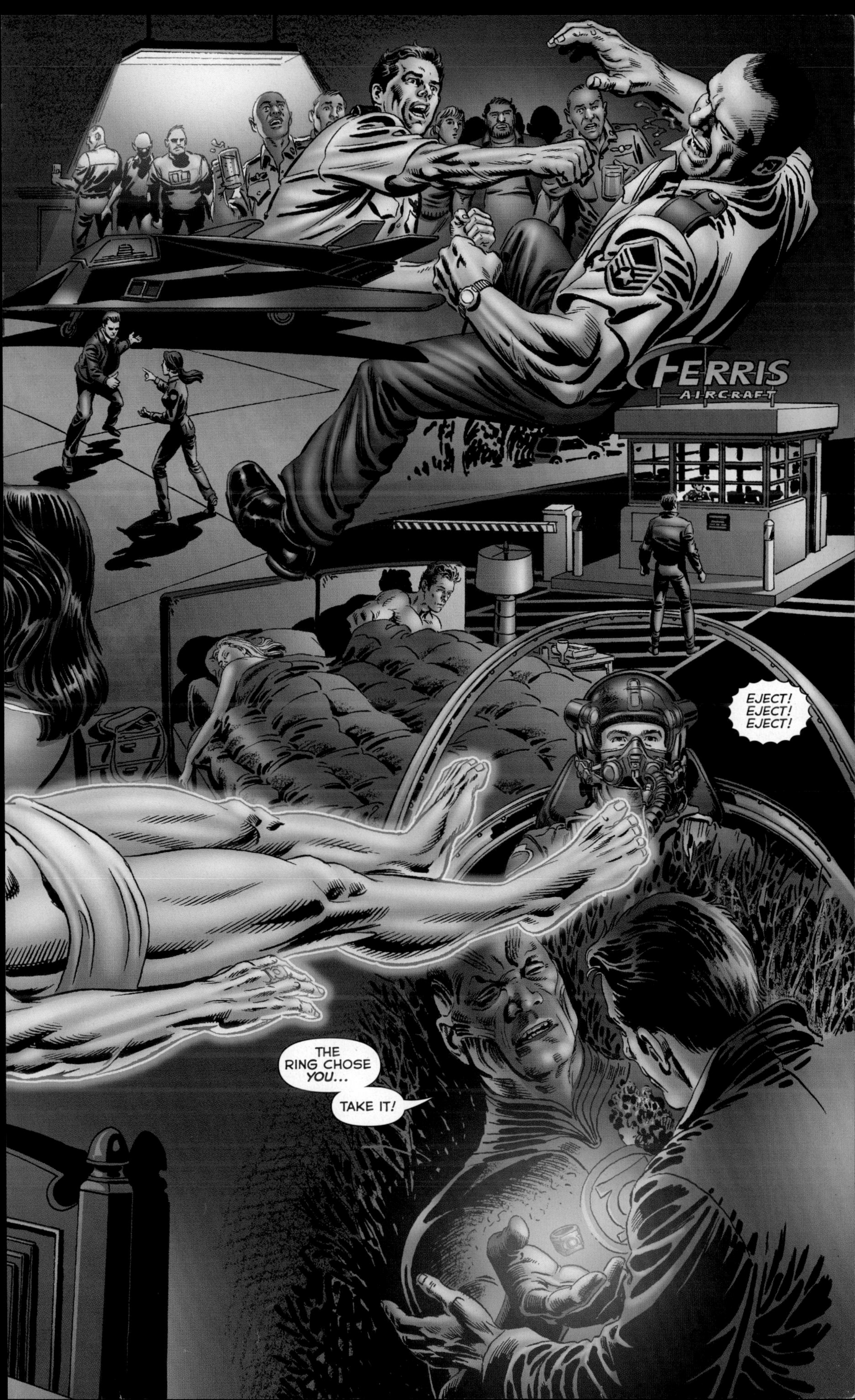
FERRIS
AIRCRAFT
EJECT! EJECT! EJECT!
THE RING CHOSE YOU...
TAKE IT!

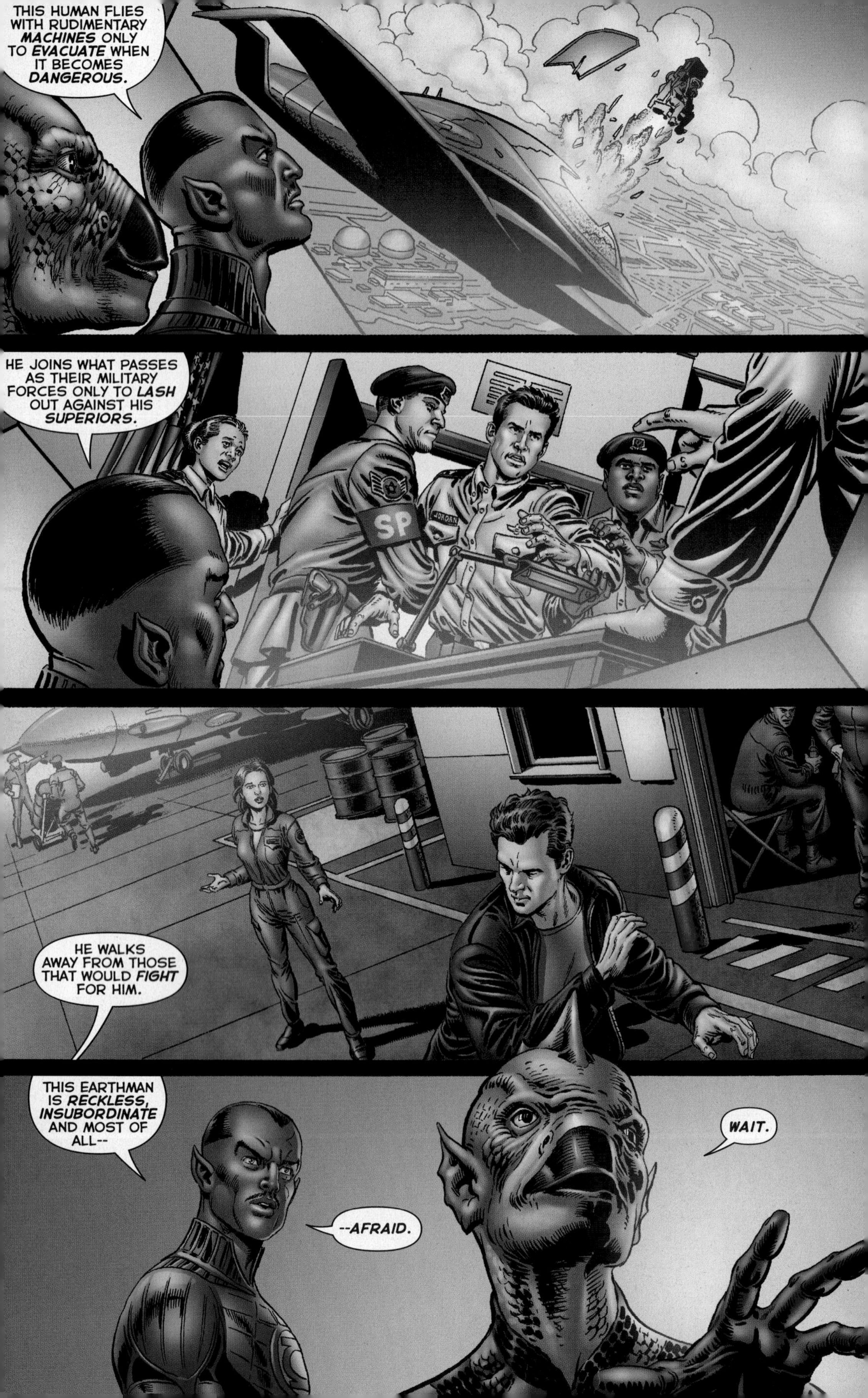
THIS HUMAN FLIES WITH RUDIMENTARY MACHINES ONLY TO EVACUATE WHEN IT BECOMES DANGEROUS.
HE JOINS WHAT PASSES AS THEIR MILITARY FORCES ONLY TO LASH OUT AGAINST HIS SUPERIORS.
SP
JORDAN
HE WALKS AWAY FROM THOSE THAT WOULD FIGHT FOR HIM.
THIS EARTHMAN IS RECKLESS, INSUBORDINATE AND MOST OF ALL--
WAIT.
--AFRAID.

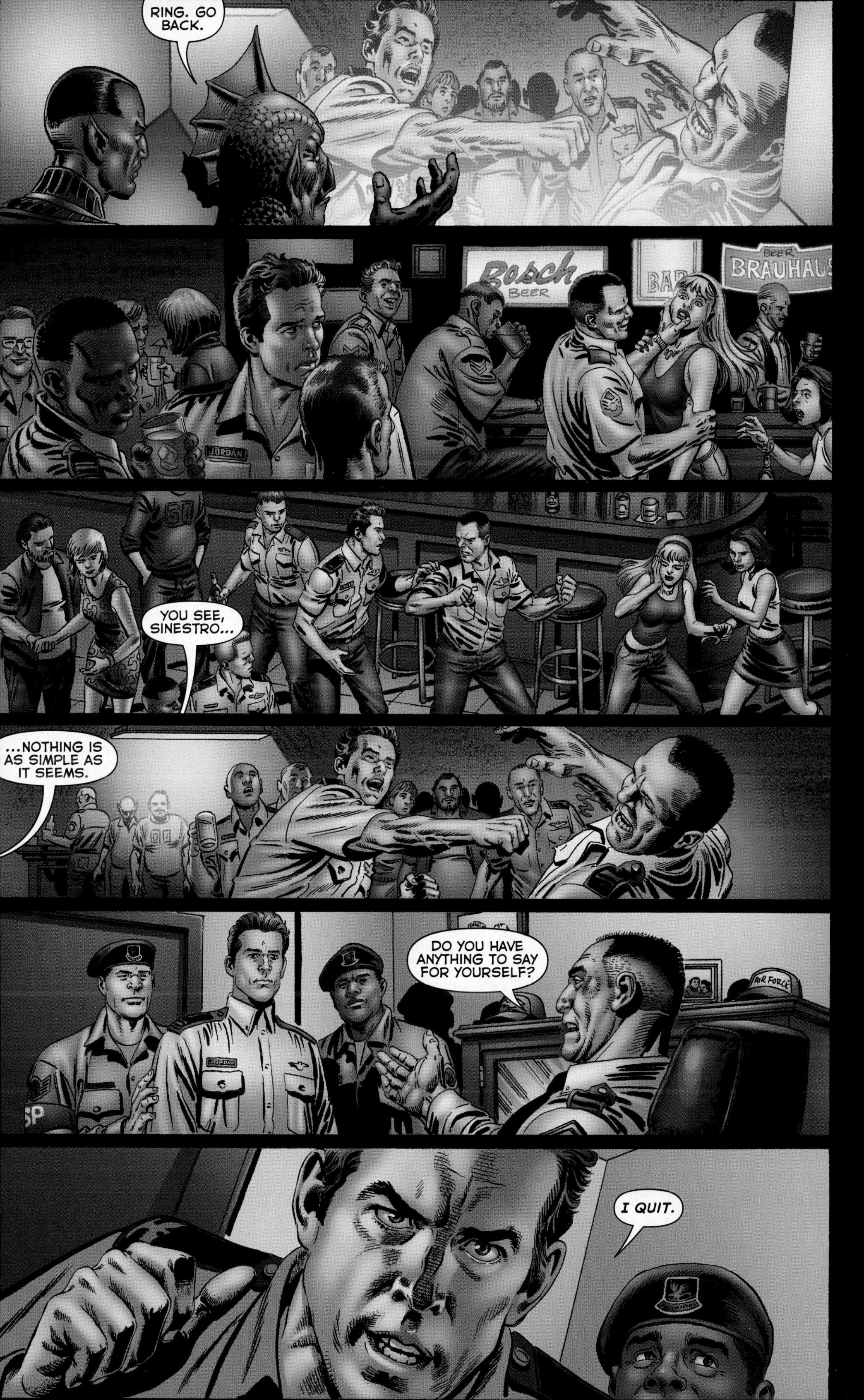
RING. GO BACK.
BOSCH BEER
BAR
BEER BRAUHAUS
JORDAN
YOU SEE, SINESTRO...
...NOTHING IS AS SIMPLE AS IT SEEMS.
JORDAN
DO YOU HAVE ANYTHING TO SAY FOR YOURSELF?
AIR FORCE
SP
I QUIT.

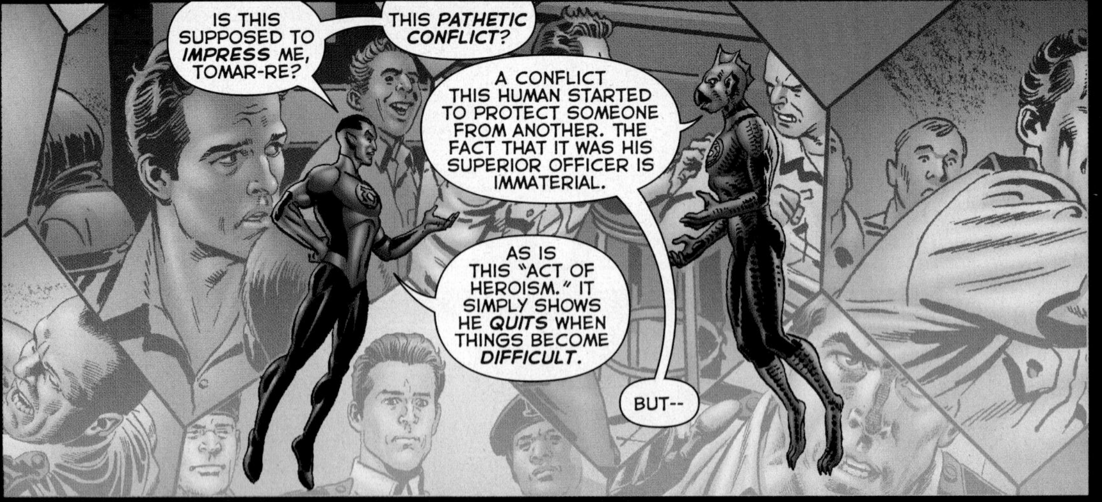
IS THIS SUPPOSED TO *IMPRESS* ME, TOMAR-RE?
THIS *PATHETIC CONFLICT?*
A CONFLICT THIS HUMAN STARTED TO PROTECT SOMEONE FROM ANOTHER. THE FACT THAT IT WAS HIS SUPERIOR OFFICER IS IMMATERIAL.
AS IS THIS "ACT OF HEROISM." IT SIMPLY SHOWS HE *QUITS* WHEN THINGS BECOME *DIFFICULT*.
BUT--

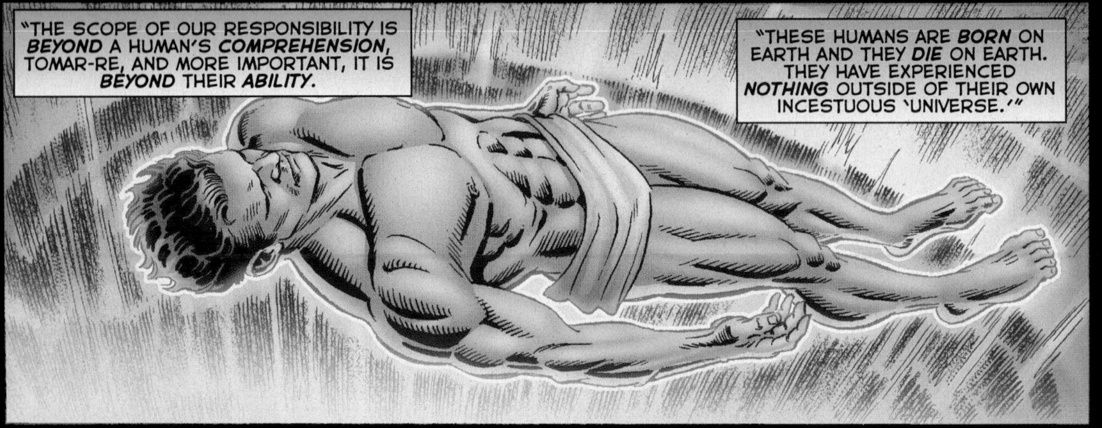
"THE SCOPE OF OUR RESPONSIBILITY IS *BEYOND* A HUMAN'S *COMPREHENSION*, TOMAR-RE, AND MORE IMPORTANT, IT IS *BEYOND* THEIR *ABILITY*.
"THESE HUMANS ARE *BORN* ON EARTH AND THEY *DIE* ON EARTH. THEY HAVE EXPERIENCED *NOTHING* OUTSIDE OF THEIR OWN INCESTUOUS 'UNIVERSE.'"

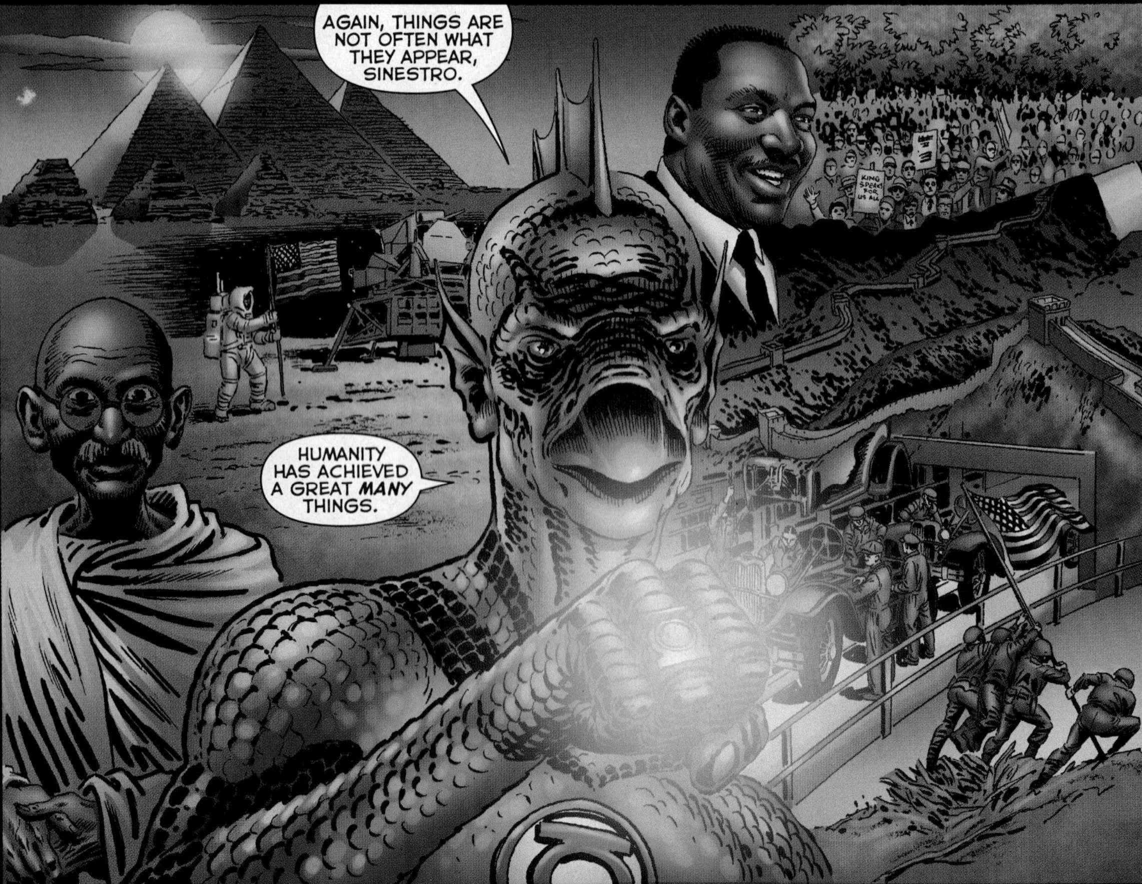
AGAIN, THINGS ARE NOT OFTEN WHAT THEY APPEAR, SINESTRO.
KING SPEAKS FOR US ALL
HUMANITY HAS ACHIEVED A GREAT *MANY* THINGS.

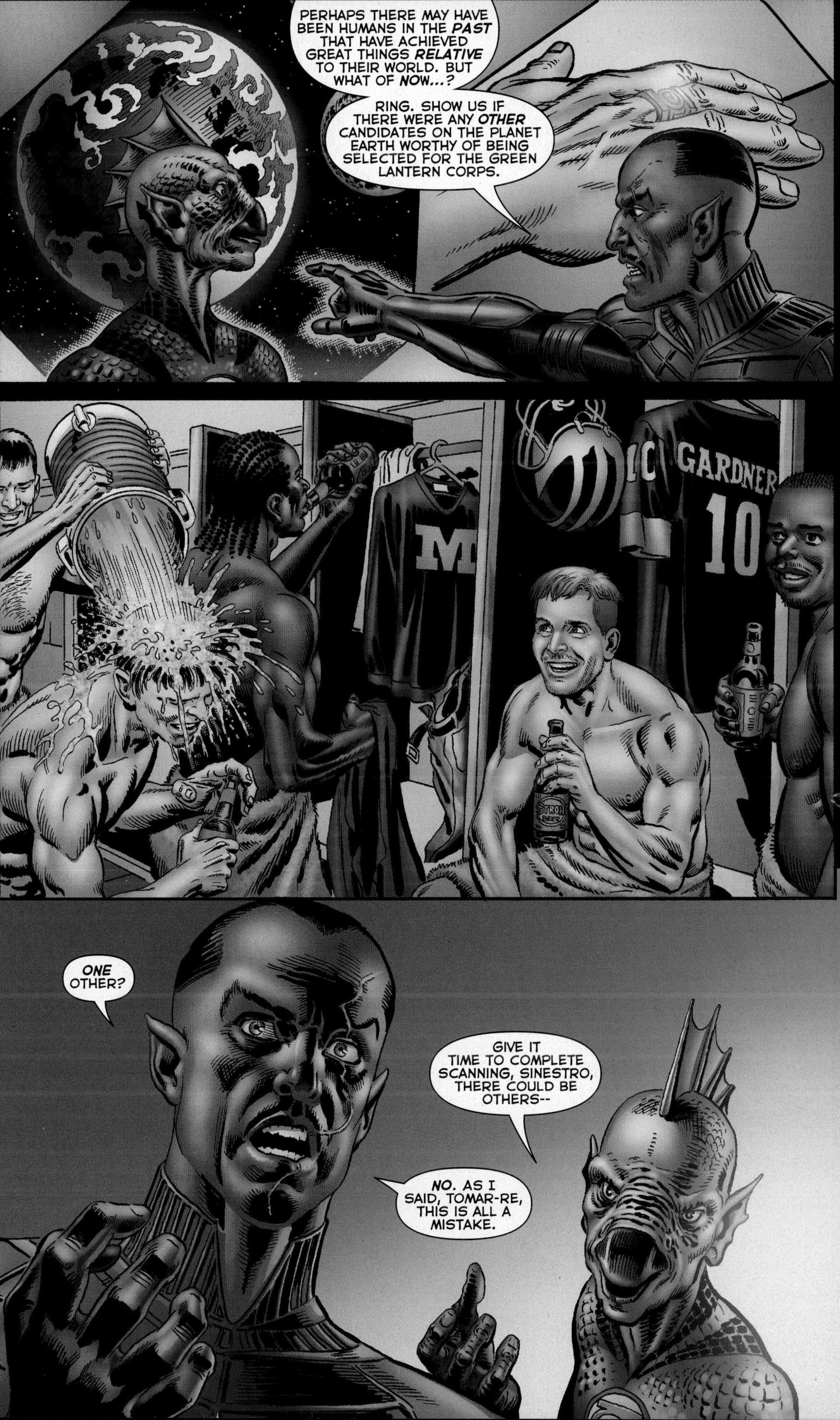
PERHAPS THERE MAY HAVE BEEN HUMANS IN THE PAST THAT HAVE ACHIEVED GREAT THINGS RELATIVE TO THEIR WORLD. BUT WHAT OF NOW...?
RING. SHOW US IF THERE WERE ANY OTHER CANDIDATES ON THE PLANET EARTH WORTHY OF BEING SELECTED FOR THE GREEN LANTERN CORPS.
M
GARDNER
10
ONE OTHER?
GIVE IT TIME TO COMPLETE SCANNING, SINESTRO, THERE COULD BE OTHERS--
NO. AS I SAID, TOMAR-RE, THIS IS ALL A MISTAKE.

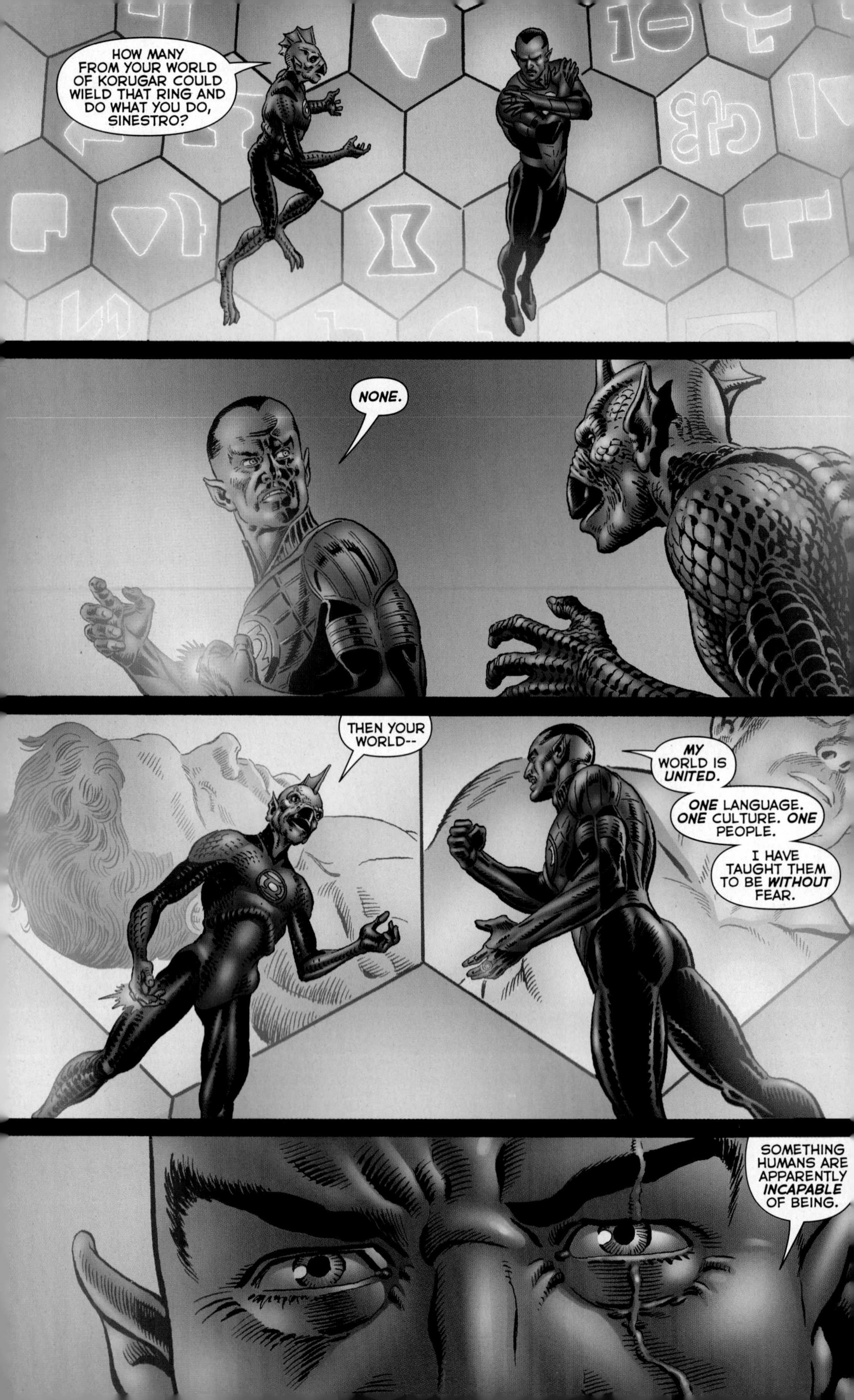

HOW MANY FROM YOUR WORLD OF KORUGAR COULD WIELD THAT RING AND DO WHAT YOU DO, SINESTRO?
NONE.
THEN YOUR WORLD--
MY WORLD IS UNITED.
ONE LANGUAGE. ONE CULTURE. ONE PEOPLE.
I HAVE TAUGHT THEM TO BE WITHOUT FEAR.
SOMETHING HUMANS ARE APPARENTLY INCAPABLE OF BEING.

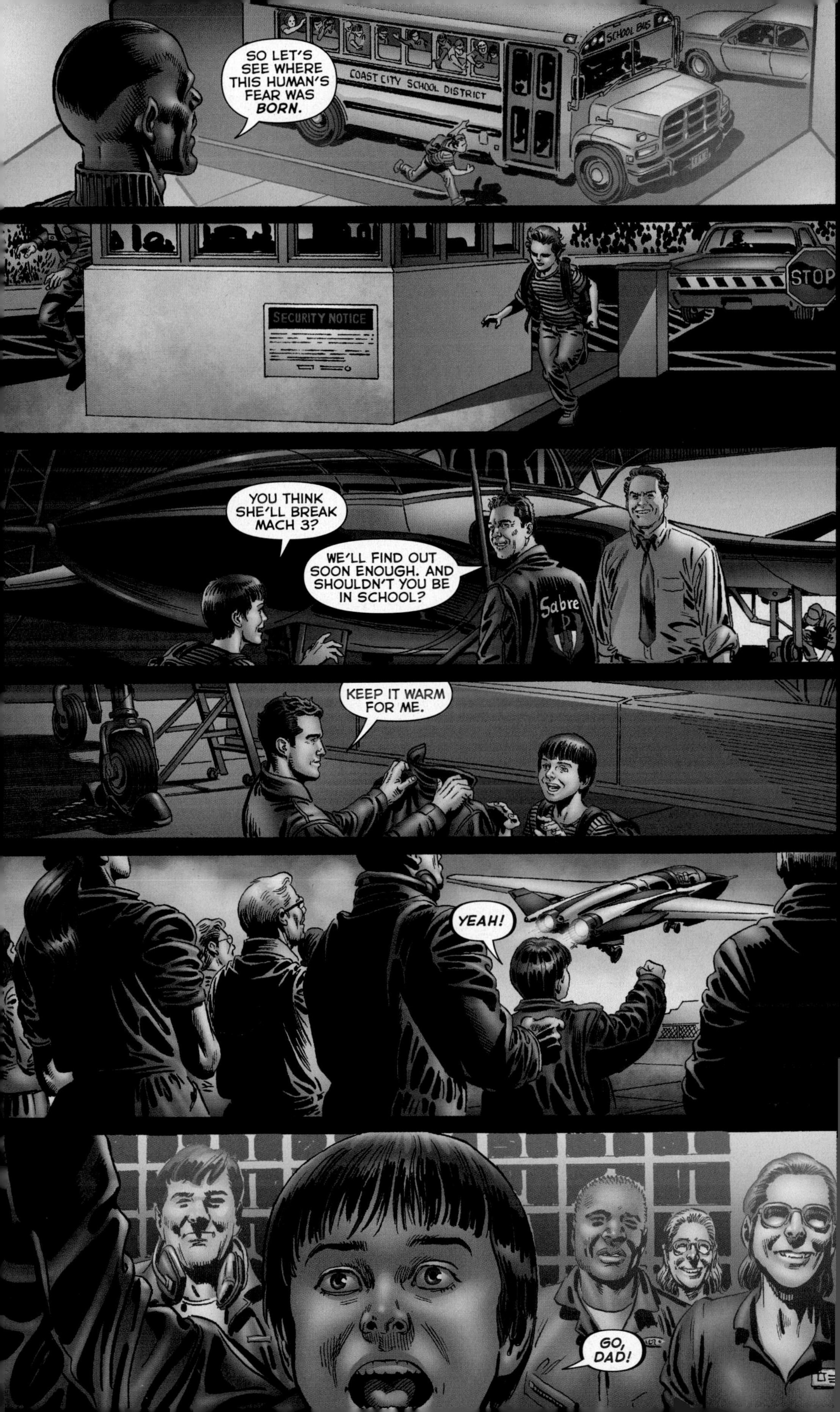
SO LET'S SEE WHERE THIS HUMAN'S FEAR WAS BORN.
SCHOOL BUS
COAST CITY SCHOOL DISTRICT
SECURITY NOTICE
STOP
YOU THINK SHE'LL BREAK MACH 3?
WE'LL FIND OUT SOON ENOUGH. AND SHOULDN'T YOU BE IN SCHOOL?
Sabre
KEEP IT WARM FOR ME.
YEAH!
GO, DAD!

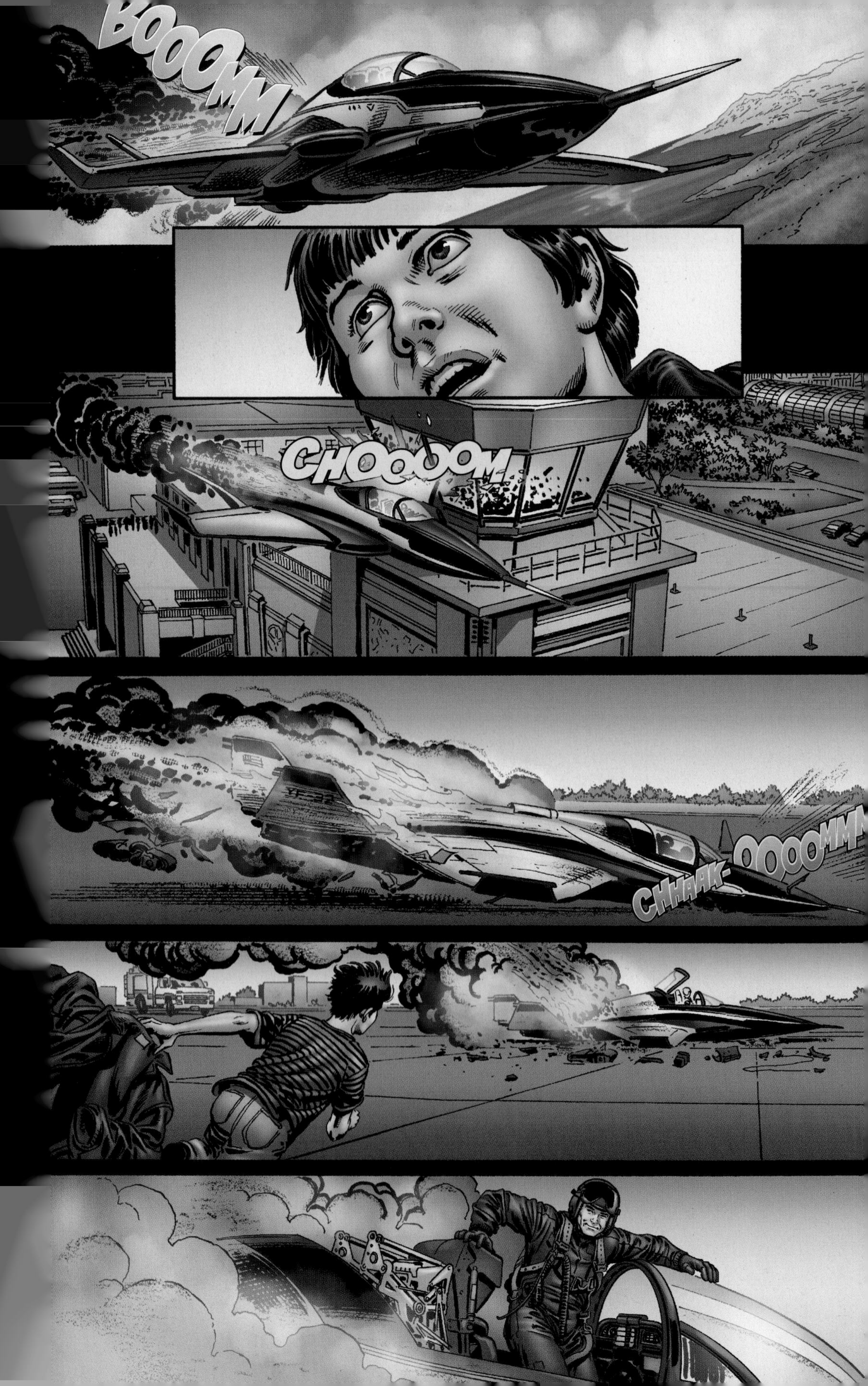
BOOOMM
CHOOOOM
CHHAAK-OOOOMMM

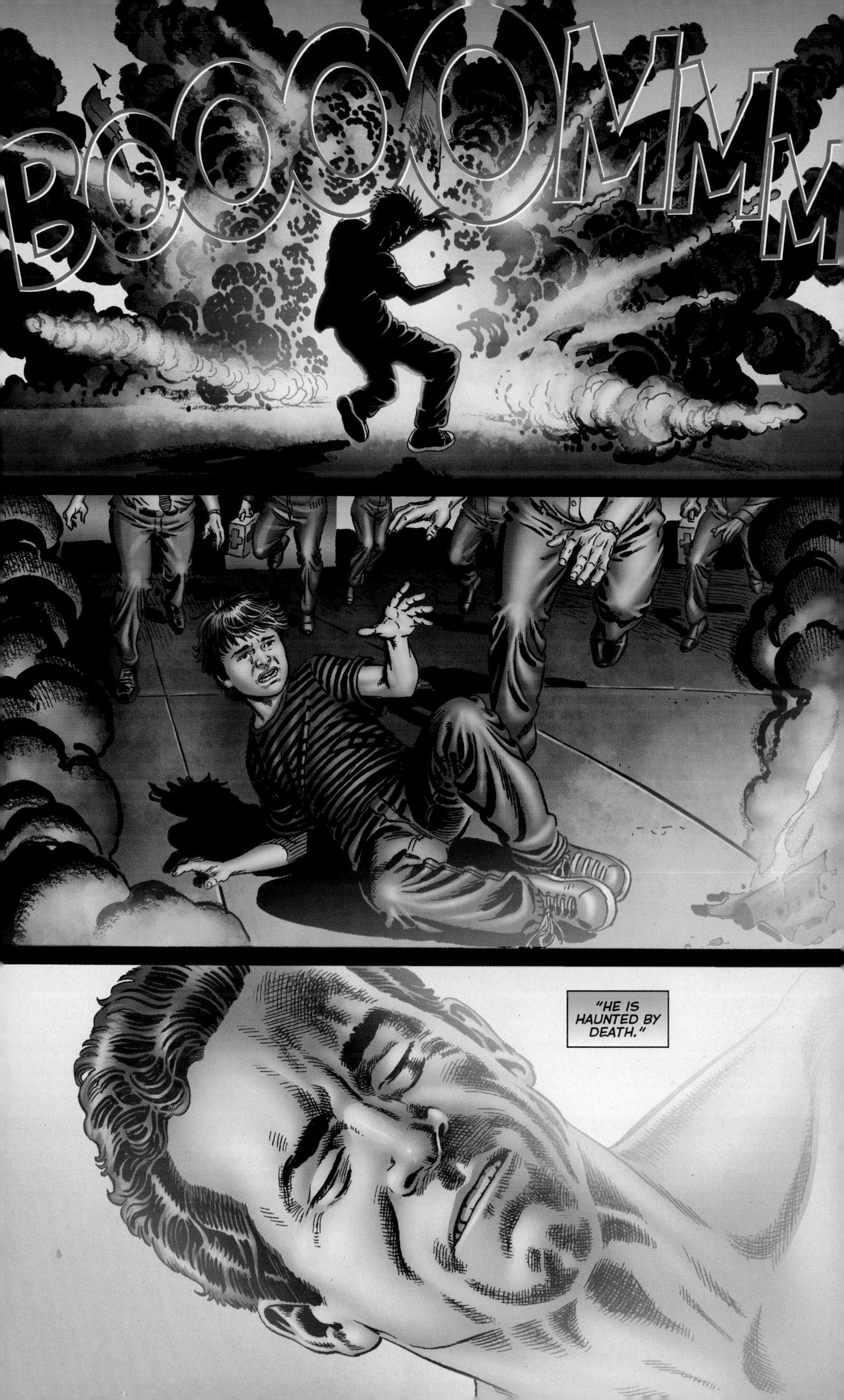
BOOOOMMMM
"HE IS HAUNTED BY DEATH."

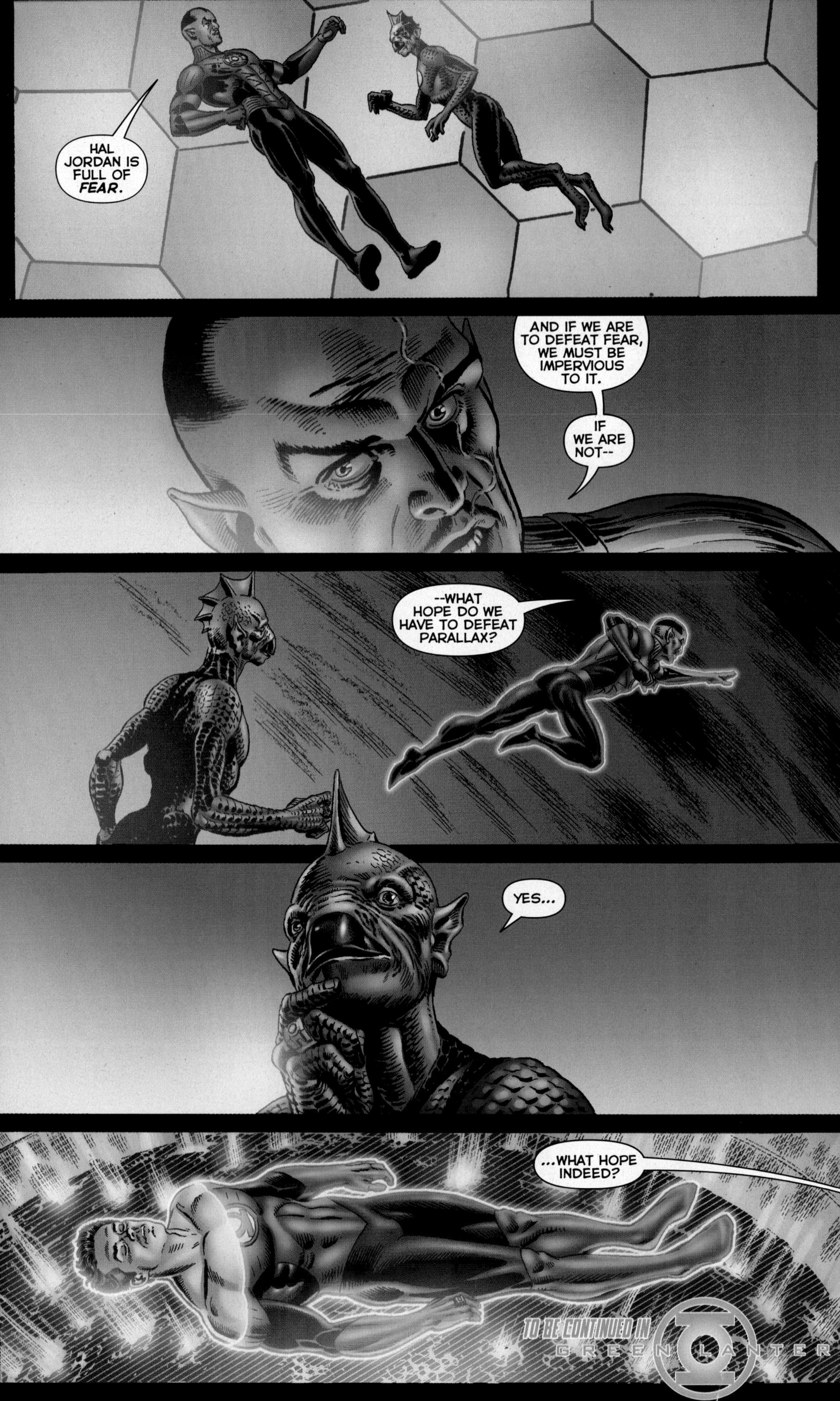
HAL JORDAN IS FULL OF *FEAR*.
AND IF WE ARE TO DEFEAT FEAR, WE MUST BE IMPERVIOUS TO IT.
IF WE ARE NOT--
--WHAT HOPE DO WE HAVE TO DEFEAT PARALLAX?
YES...
...WHAT HOPE INDEED?
TO BE CONTINUED IN
GREEN LANTERN

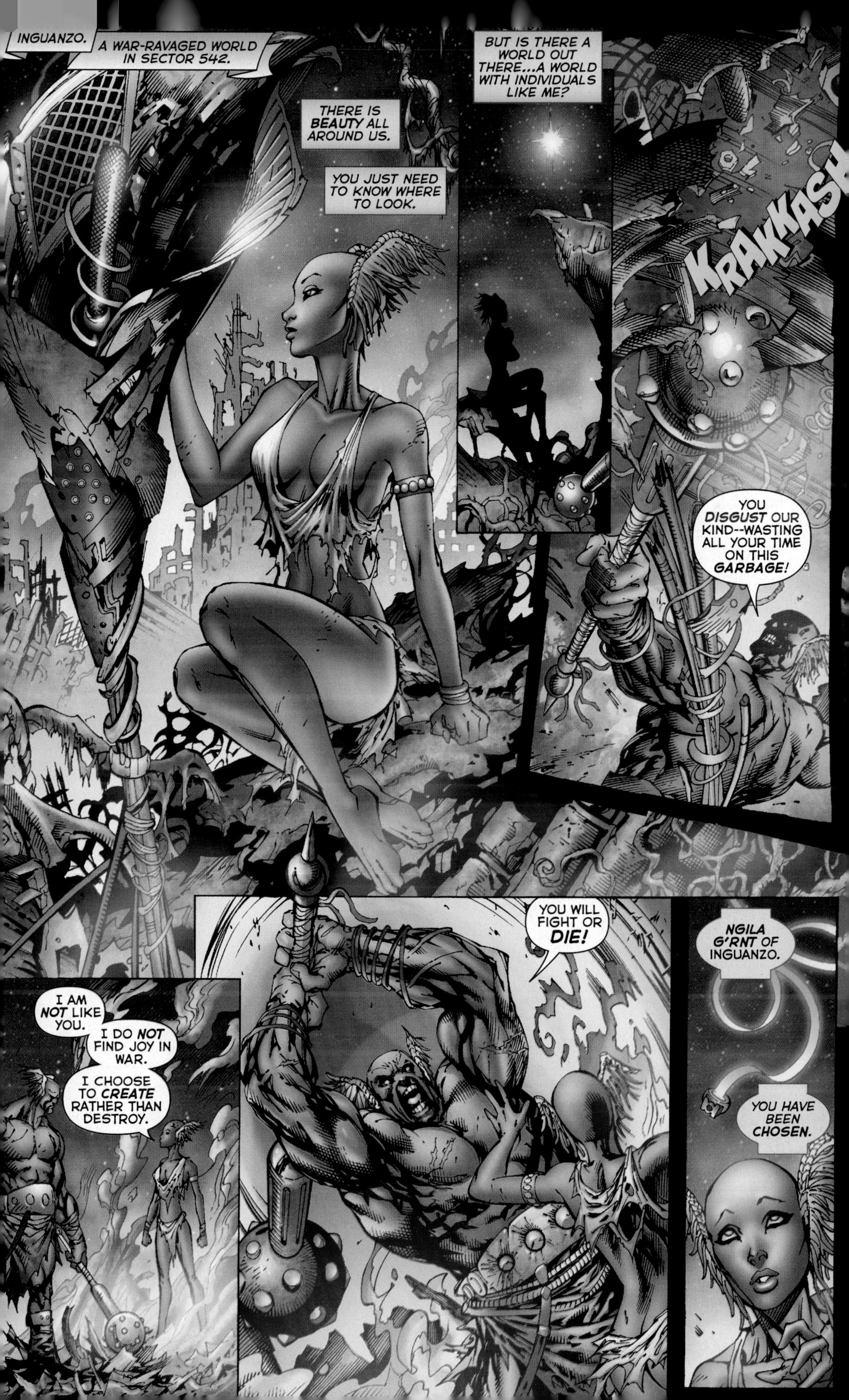
INGUANZO.
A WAR-RAVAGED WORLD IN SECTOR 542.
THERE IS BEAUTY ALL AROUND US.
YOU JUST NEED TO KNOW WHERE TO LOOK.
BUT IS THERE A WORLD OUT THERE...A WORLD WITH INDIVIDUALS LIKE ME?
KRAKKASH
YOU DISGUST OUR KIND--WASTING ALL YOUR TIME ON THIS GARBAGE!
I AM NOT LIKE YOU.
I DO NOT FIND JOY IN WAR.
I CHOOSE TO CREATE RATHER THAN DESTROY.
YOU WILL FIGHT OR DIE!
NGILA G'RNT OF INGUANZO.
YOU HAVE BEEN CHOSEN.

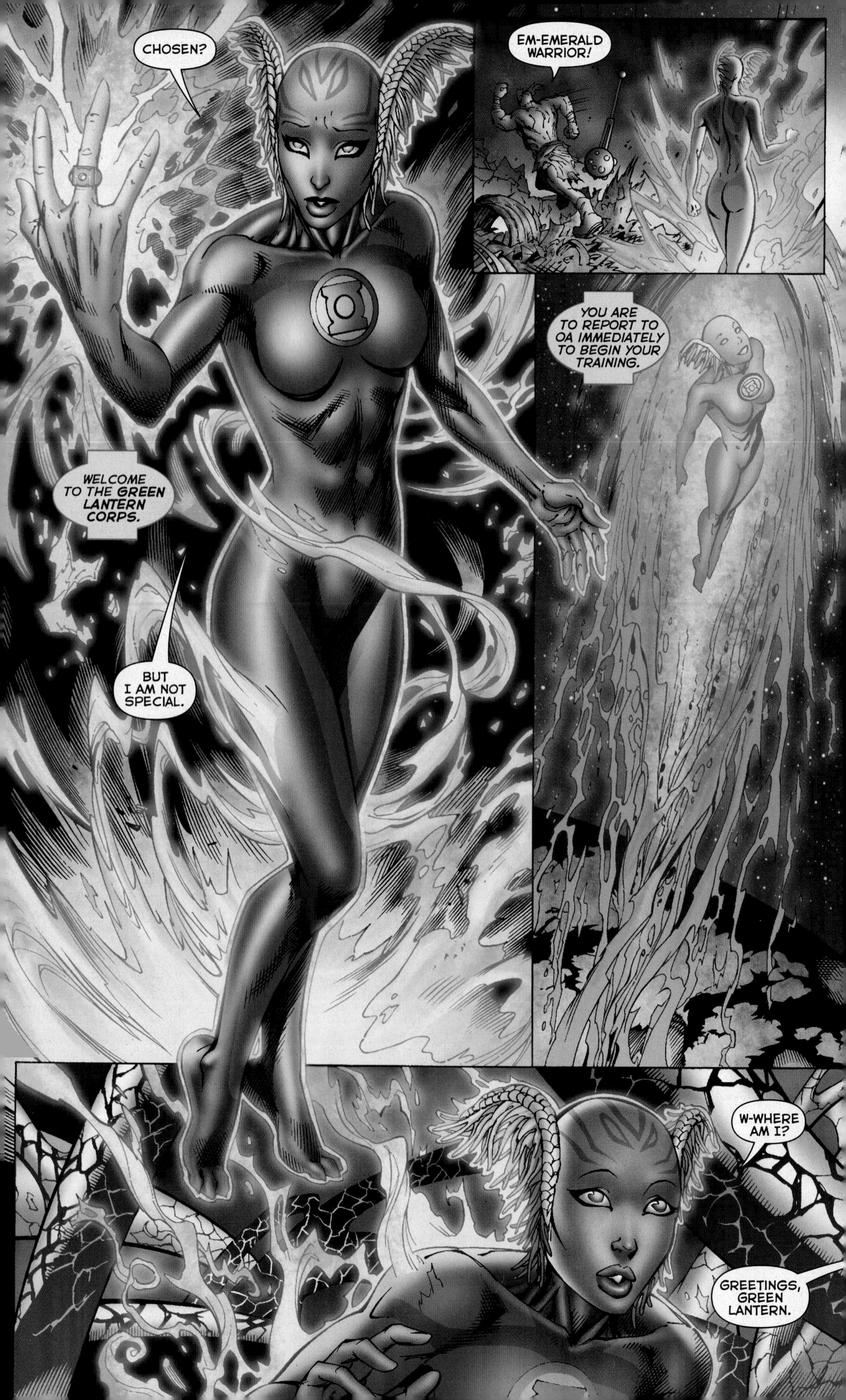
CHOSEN?
EM-EMERALD WARRIOR!
WELCOME TO THE GREEN LANTERN CORPS.
BUT I AM NOT SPECIAL.
YOU ARE TO REPORT TO OA IMMEDIATELY TO BEGIN YOUR TRAINING.
W-WHERE AM I?
GREETINGS, GREEN LANTERN.

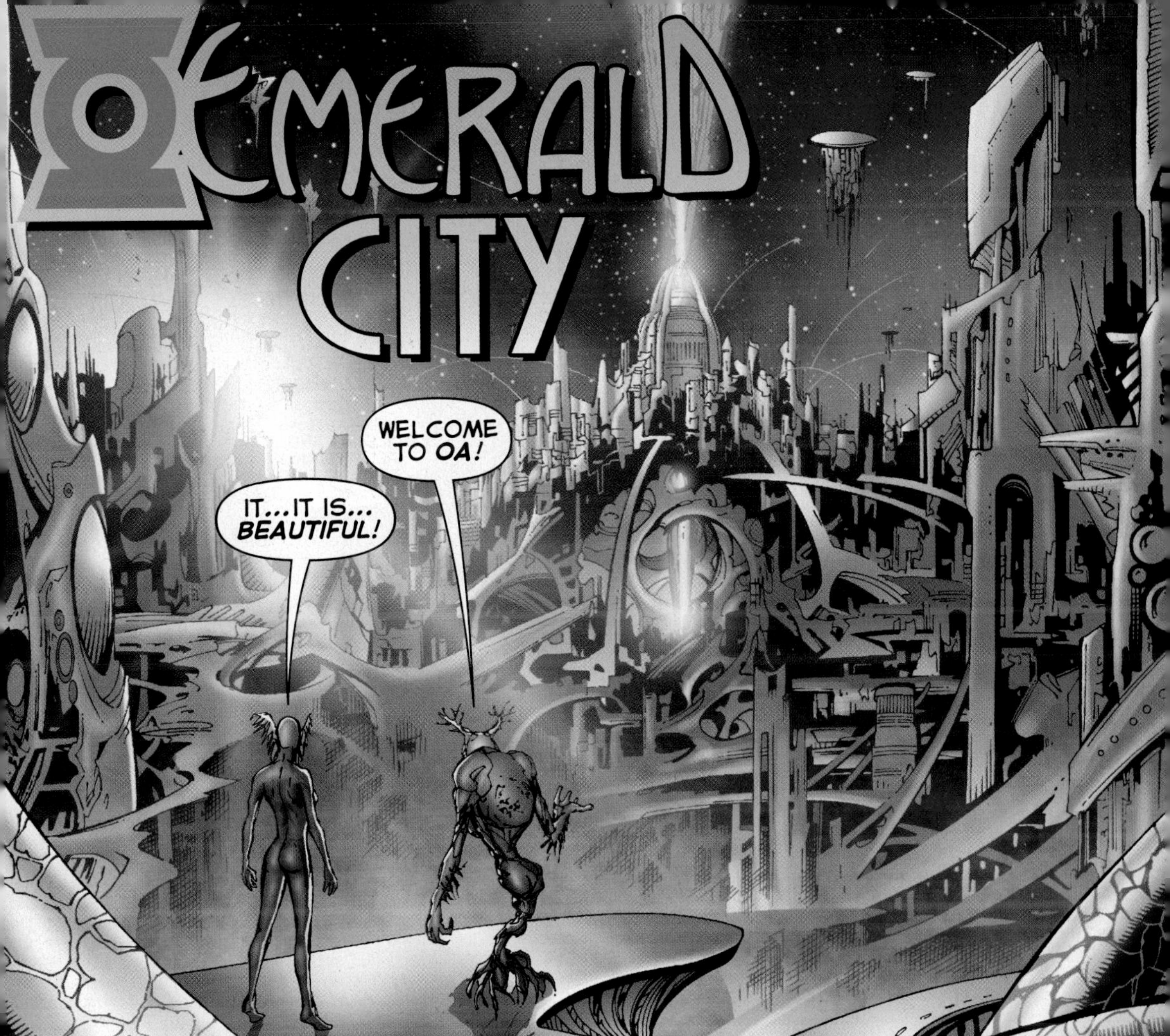
EMERALD CITY
WELCOME TO OA!
IT...IT IS... BEAUTIFUL!

WRITERS: DONALD De LINE AND ADAM SCHLAGMAN • PENCILLER: TYLER KIRKHAM
INKER: BATT • COLORS: RANDY MAYOR
LETTERS: CARLOS M. MANGUAL
ASSISTANT EDITOR: SEAN MACKIEWICZ
EDITOR: EDDIE BERGANZA

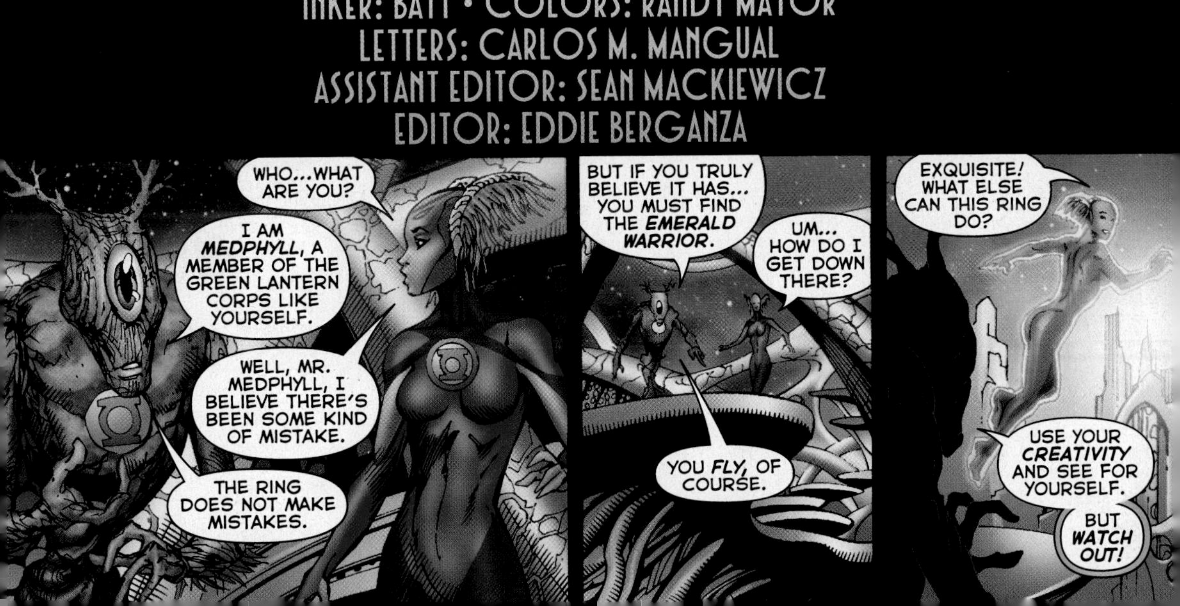
WHO...WHAT ARE YOU?
I AM MEDPHYLL, A MEMBER OF THE GREEN LANTERN CORPS LIKE YOURSELF.
WELL, MR. MEDPHYLL, I BELIEVE THERE'S BEEN SOME KIND OF MISTAKE.
THE RING DOES NOT MAKE MISTAKES.
BUT IF YOU TRULY BELIEVE IT HAS... YOU MUST FIND THE EMERALD WARRIOR.
UM... HOW DO I GET DOWN THERE?
YOU FLY, OF COURSE.
EXQUISITE! WHAT ELSE CAN THIS RING DO?
USE YOUR CREATIVITY AND SEE FOR YOURSELF.
BUT WATCH OUT!

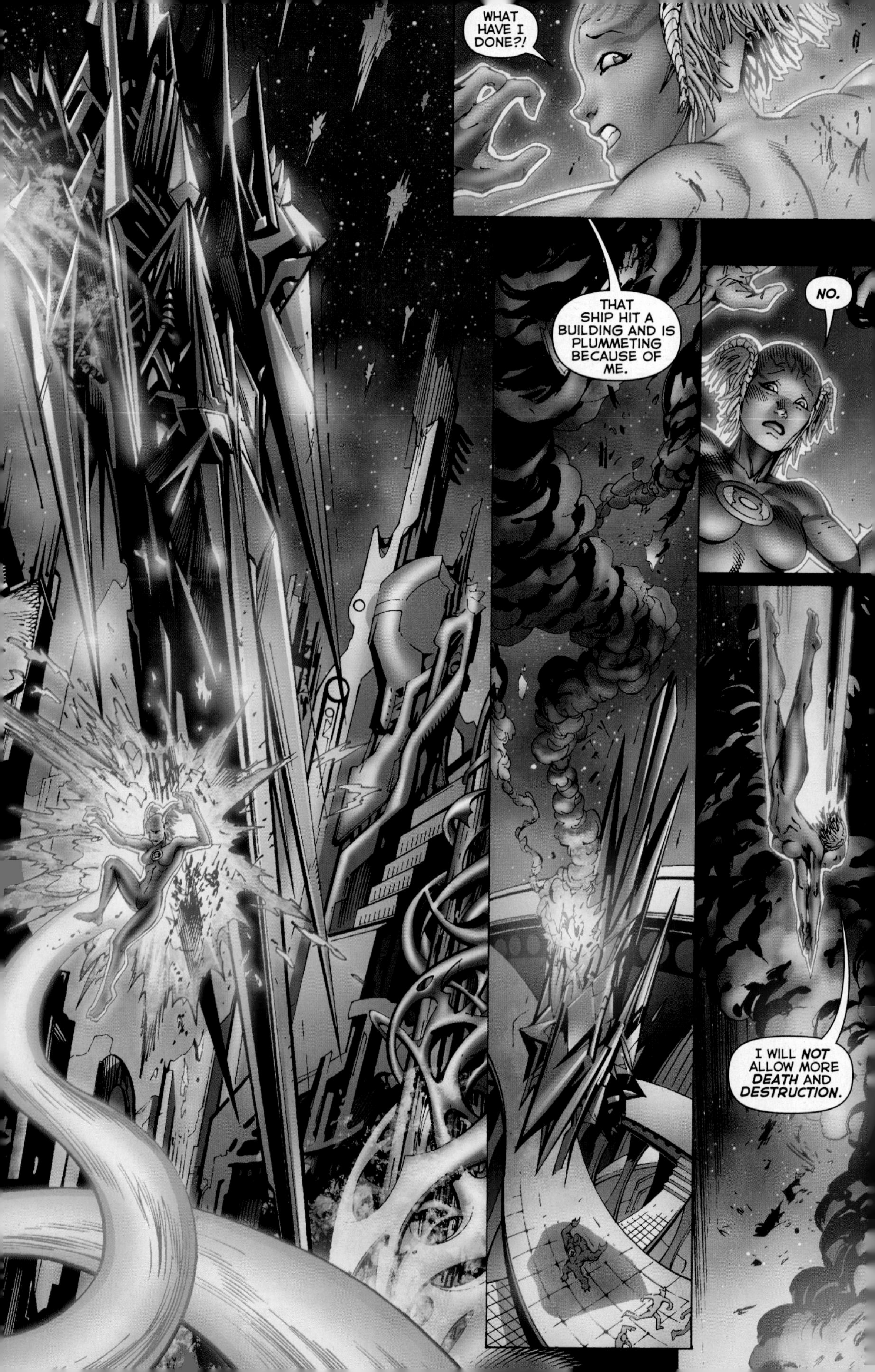
WHAT HAVE I DONE?!
THAT SHIP HIT A BUILDING AND IS PLUMMETING BECAUSE OF ME.
NO.
I WILL NOT ALLOW MORE DEATH AND DESTRUCTION.

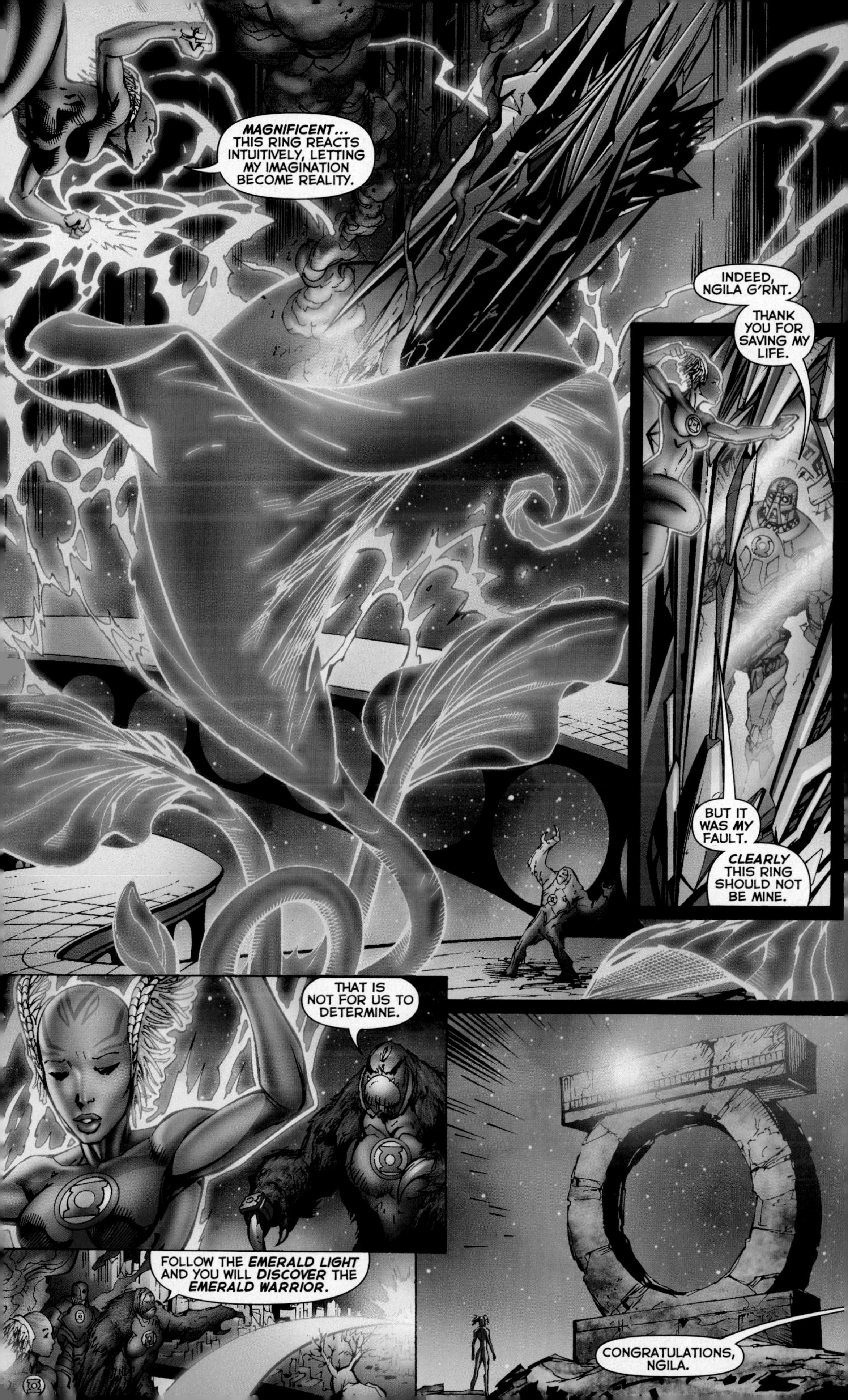
MAGNIFICENT... THIS RING REACTS INTUITIVELY, LETTING MY IMAGINATION BECOME REALITY.
INDEED, NGILA G'RNT.
THANK YOU FOR SAVING MY LIFE.
BUT IT WAS MY FAULT.
CLEARLY THIS RING SHOULD NOT BE MINE.
THAT IS NOT FOR US TO DETERMINE.
FOLLOW THE EMERALD LIGHT AND YOU WILL DISCOVER THE EMERALD WARRIOR.
CONGRATULATIONS, NGILA.

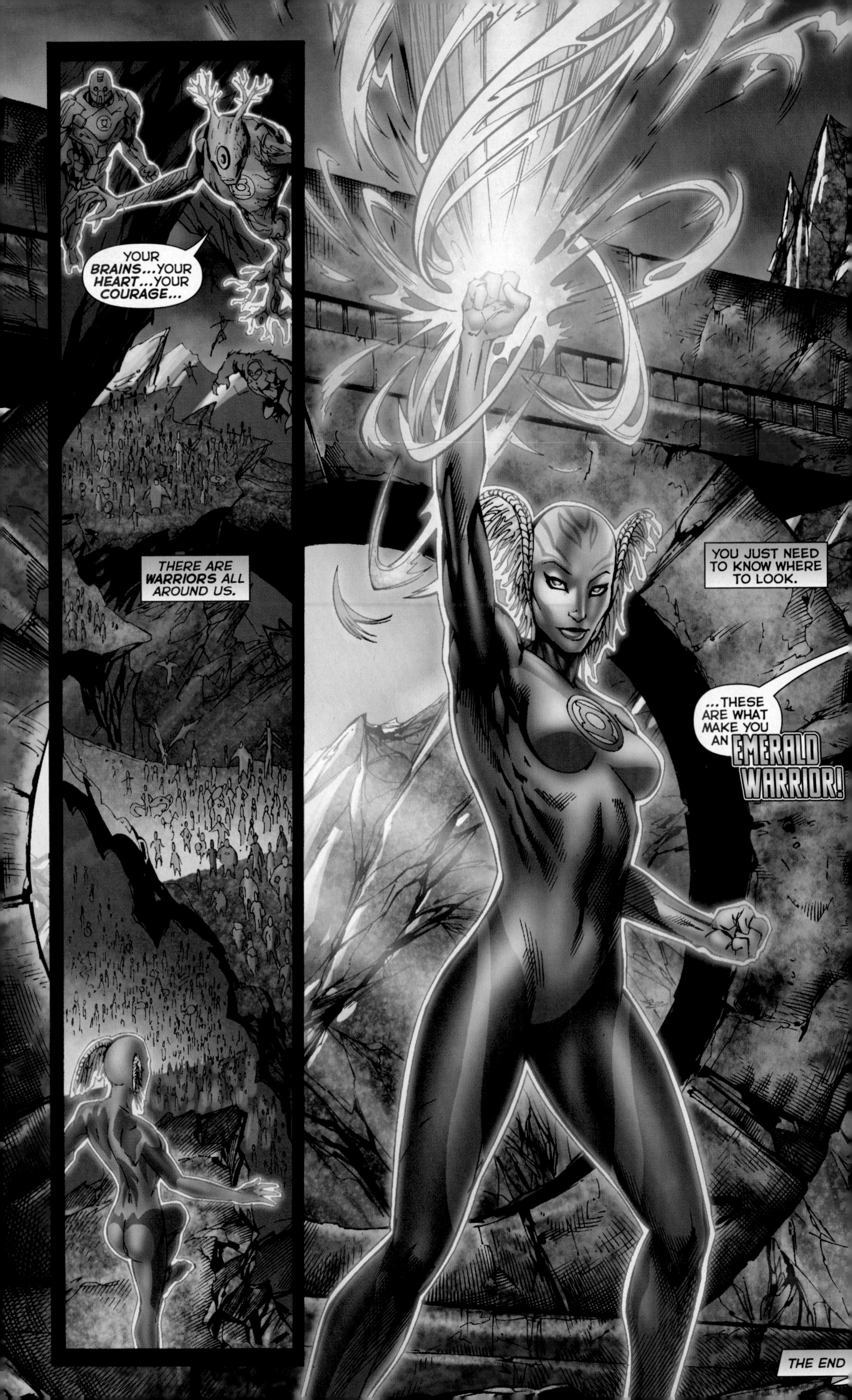
YOUR BRAINS...YOUR HEART...YOUR COURAGE...
THERE ARE WARRIORS ALL AROUND US.
YOU JUST NEED TO KNOW WHERE TO LOOK.
...THESE ARE WHAT MAKE YOU AN EMERALD WARRIOR!
THE END

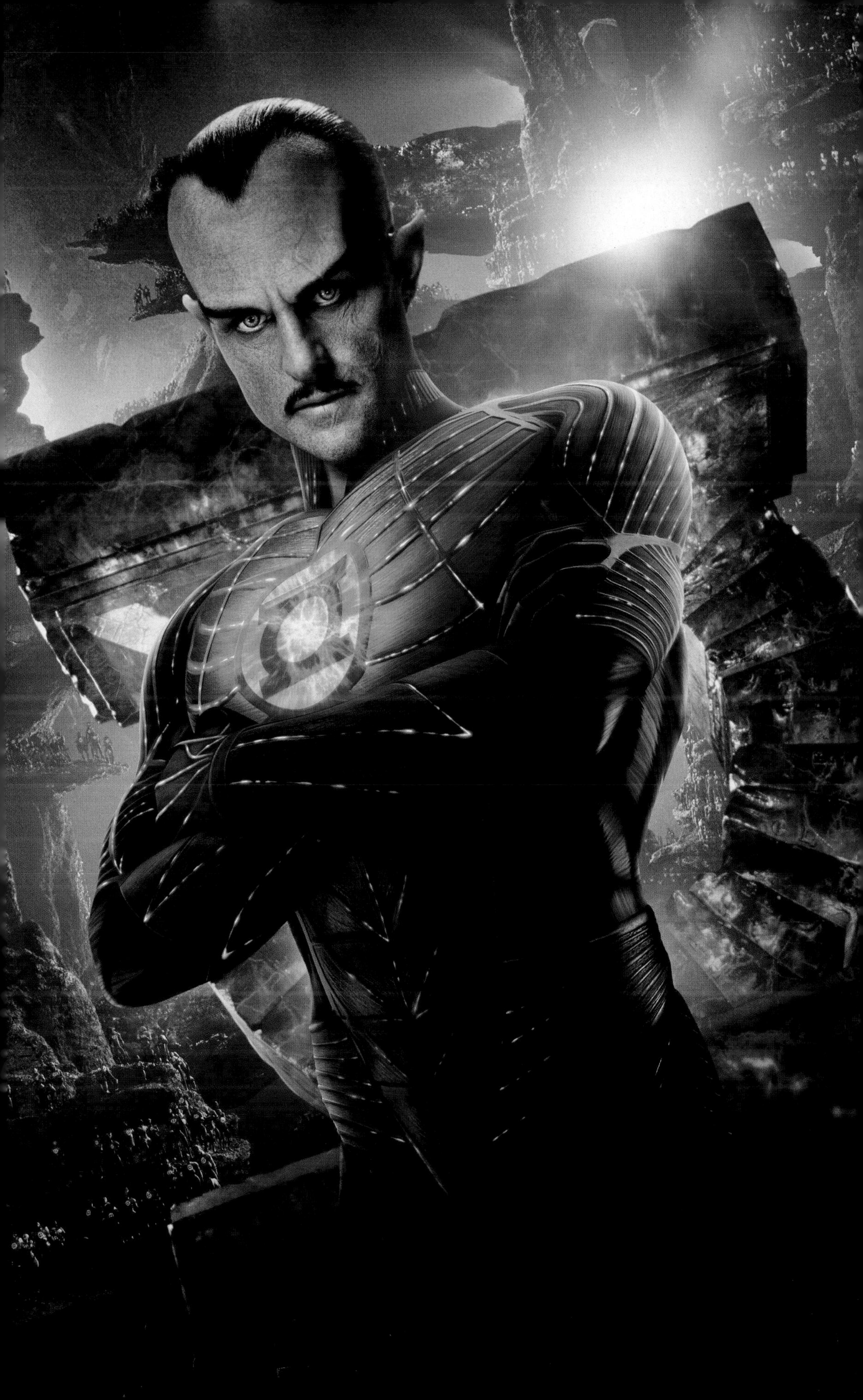

THE CHOSEN ONE

GEOFF **JOHNS** & MICHAEL **GOLDENBERG** writers

HARVEY **TOLIBAO**, CLIFF **RICHARDS** & JERRY **ORDWAY** artists

SECRET ORIGIN OF
THE GREEN LANTERN CORPS

GEOFF **JOHNS** & ADAM **SCHLAGMAN** writers

FERNANDO **DAGNINO** penciller

RAUL **FERNANDEZ** inker

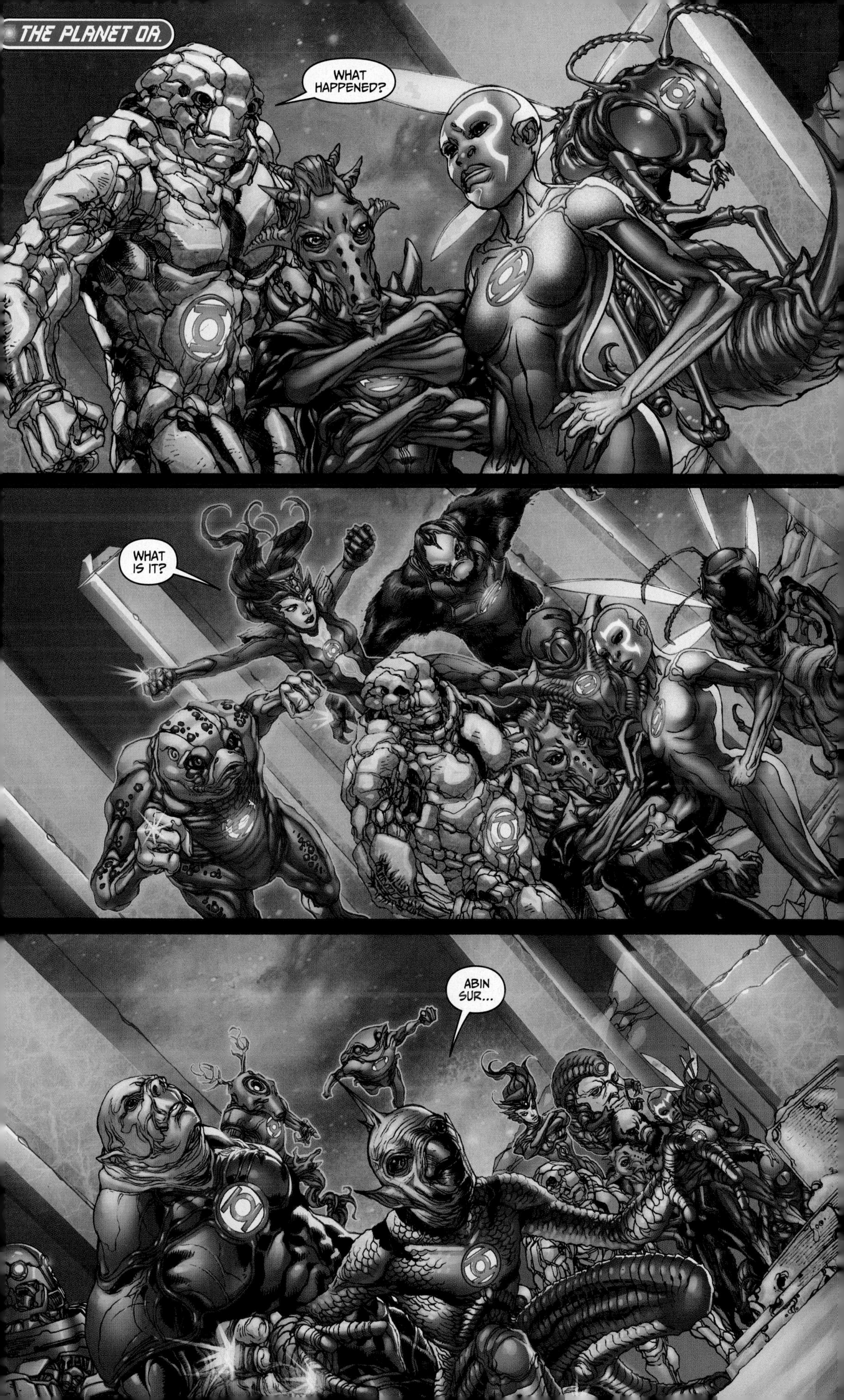
THE PLANET OA.
WHAT HAPPENED?
WHAT IS IT?
ABIN SUR...

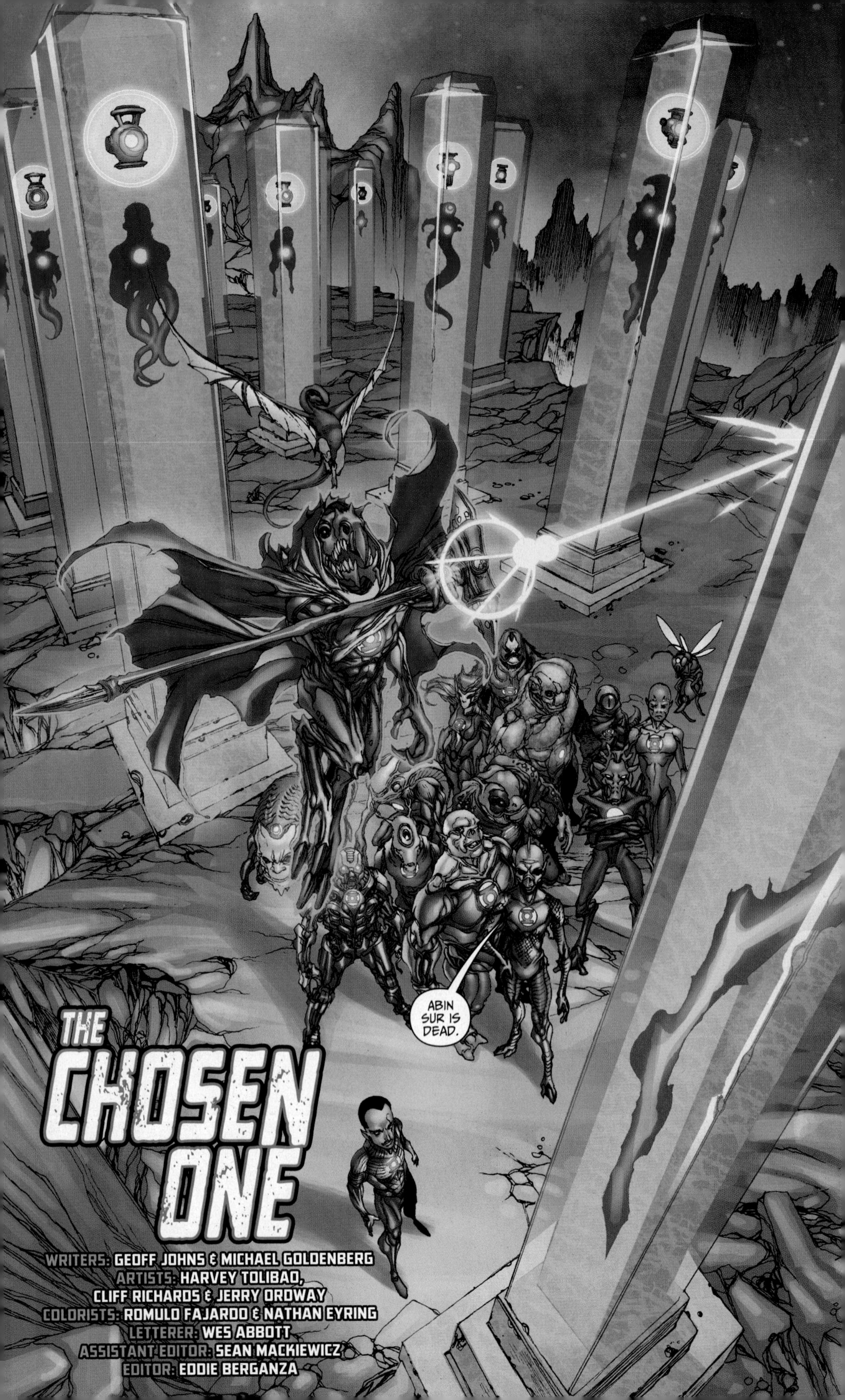
ABIN SUR IS DEAD.
THE CHOSEN ONE
WRITERS: GEOFF JOHNS & MICHAEL GOLDENBERG
ARTISTS: HARVEY TOLIBAO, CLIFF RICHARDS & JERRY ORDWAY
COLORISTS: ROMULO FAJARDO & NATHAN EYRING
LETTERER: WES ABBOTT
ASSISTANT EDITOR: SEAN MACKIEWICZ
EDITOR: EDDIE BERGANZA

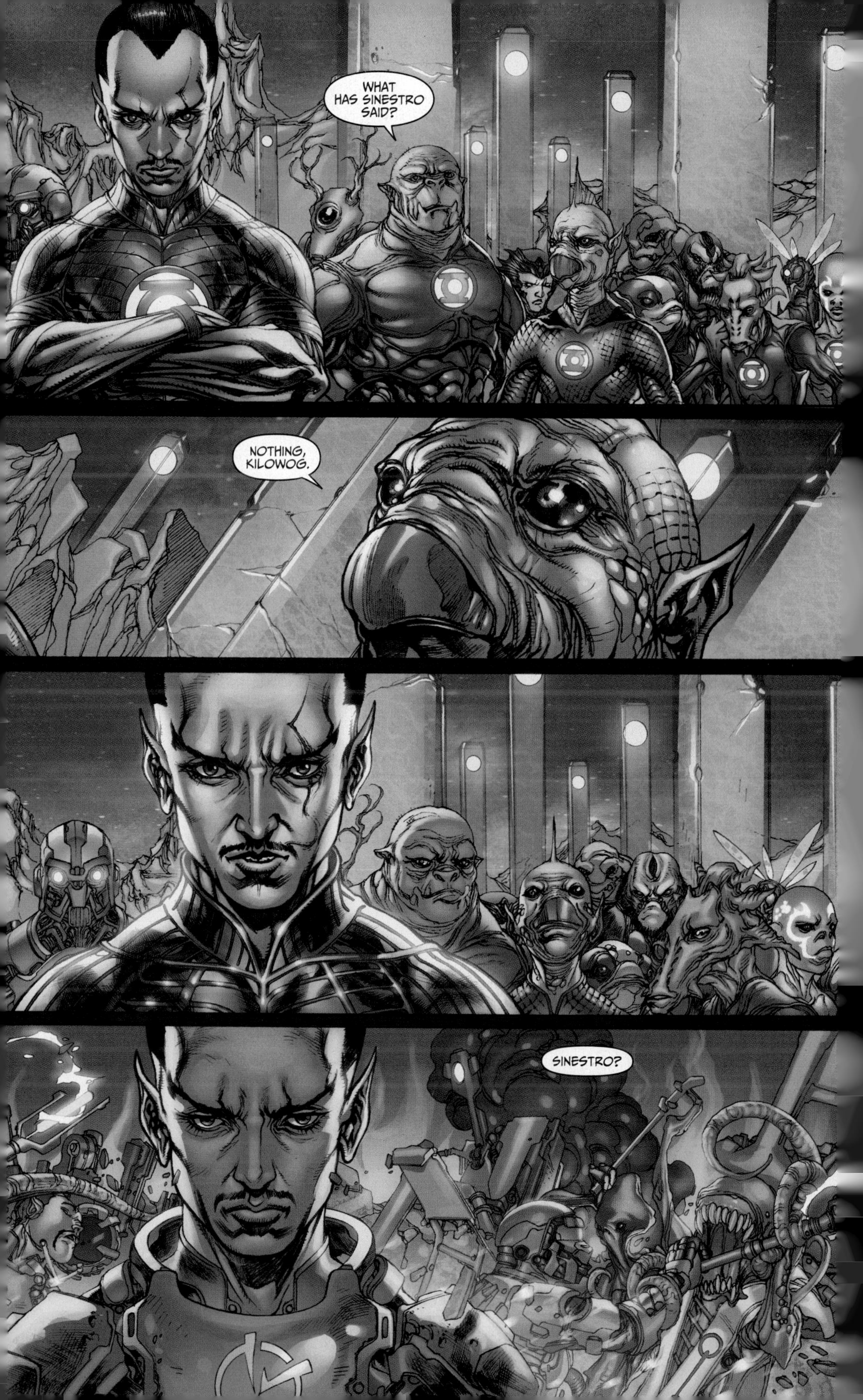
WHAT HAS SINESTRO SAID?
NOTHING, KILOWOG.
SINESTRO?

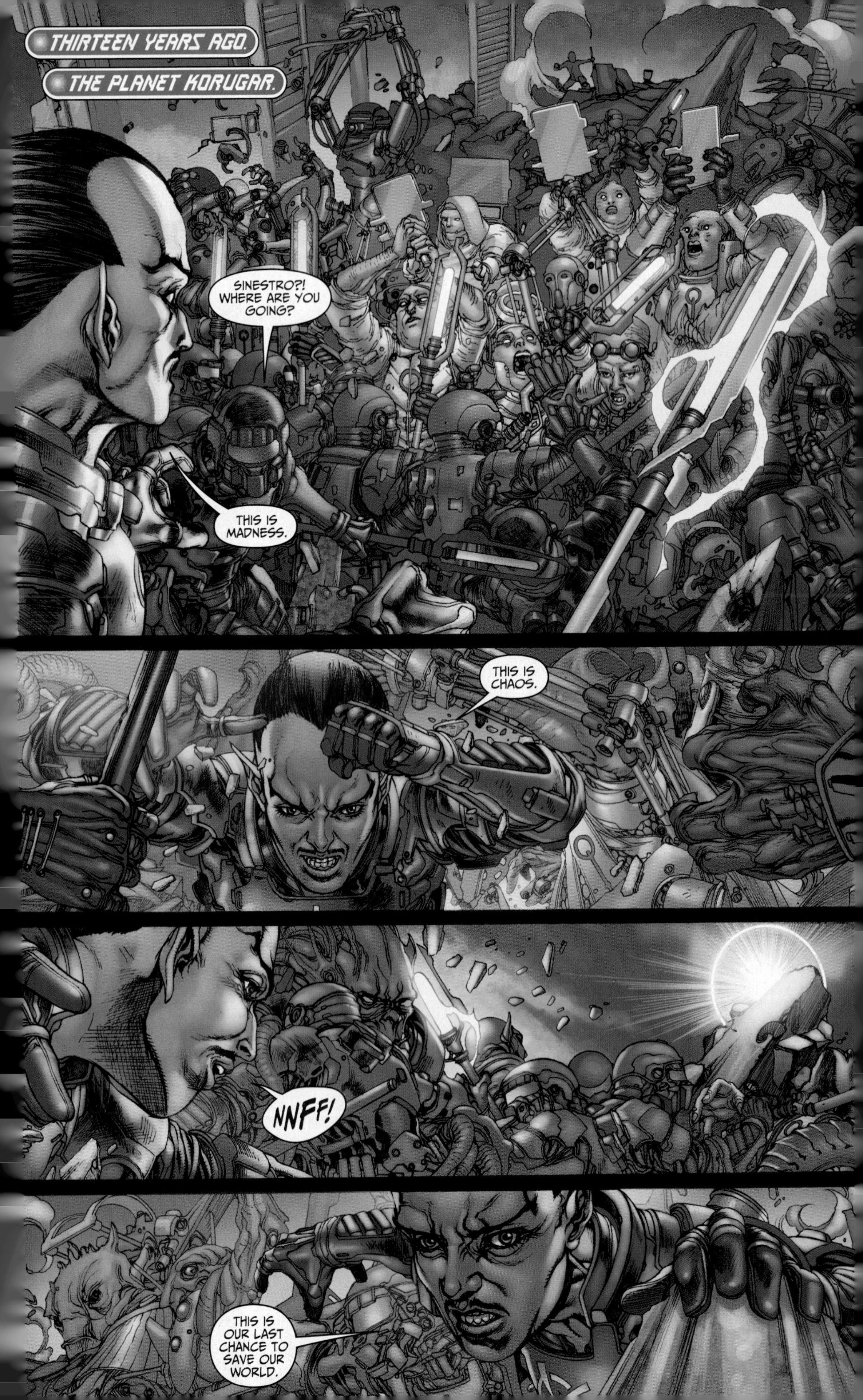
THIRTEEN YEARS AGO.
THE PLANET KORUGAR.
SINESTRO?! WHERE ARE YOU GOING?
THIS IS MADNESS.
THIS IS CHAOS.
NNFF!
THIS IS OUR LAST CHANCE TO SAVE OUR WORLD.

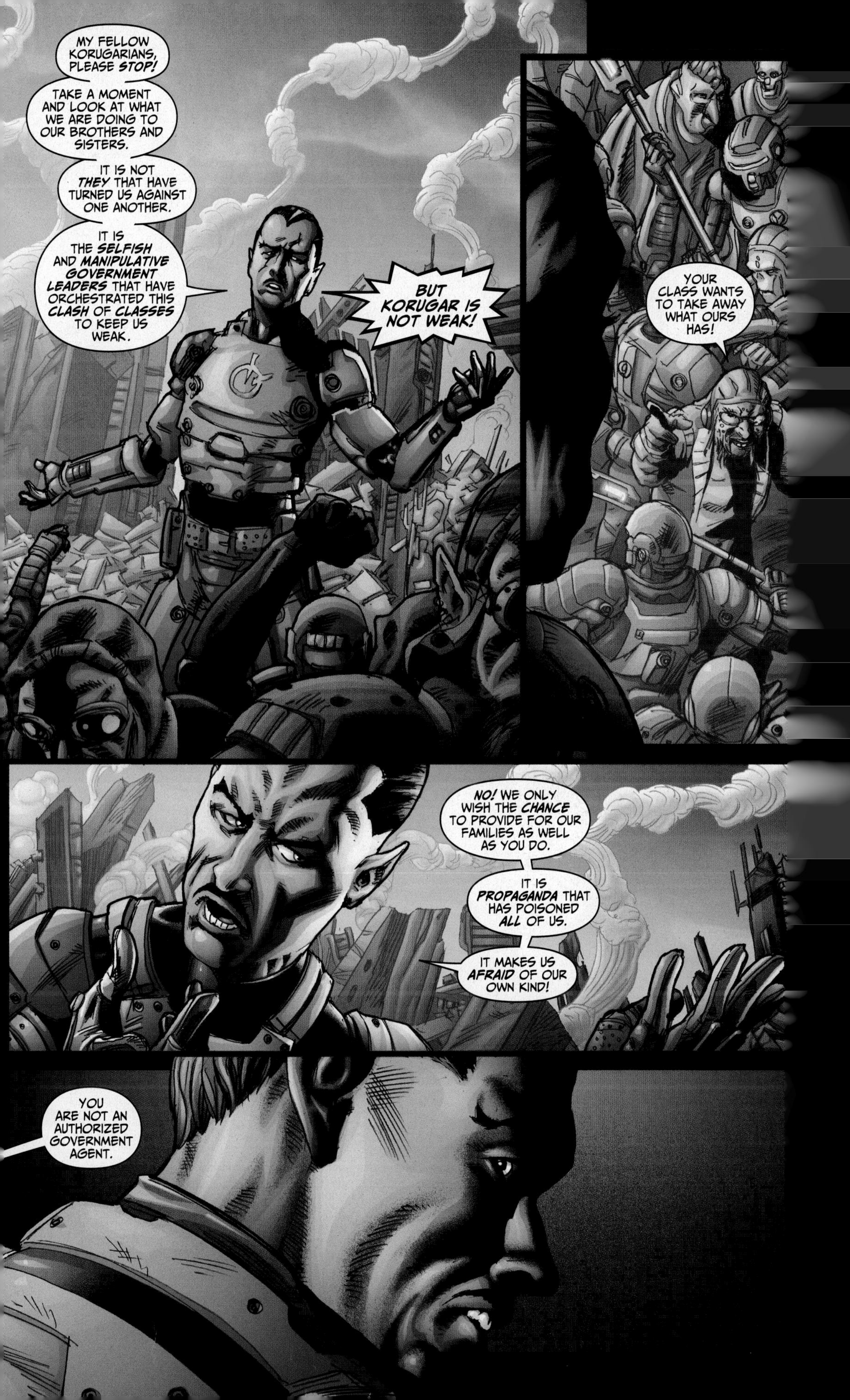

MY FELLOW KORUGARIANS, PLEASE STOP!
TAKE A MOMENT AND LOOK AT WHAT WE ARE DOING TO OUR BROTHERS AND SISTERS.
IT IS NOT THEY THAT HAVE TURNED US AGAINST ONE ANOTHER.
IT IS THE SELFISH AND MANIPULATIVE GOVERNMENT LEADERS THAT HAVE ORCHESTRATED THIS CLASH OF CLASSES TO KEEP US WEAK.
BUT KORUGAR IS NOT WEAK!
YOUR CLASS WANTS TO TAKE AWAY WHAT OURS HAS!
NO! WE ONLY WISH THE CHANCE TO PROVIDE FOR OUR FAMILIES AS WELL AS YOU DO.
IT IS PROPAGANDA THAT HAS POISONED ALL OF US.
IT MAKES US AFRAID OF OUR OWN KIND!
YOU ARE NOT AN AUTHORIZED GOVERNMENT AGENT.

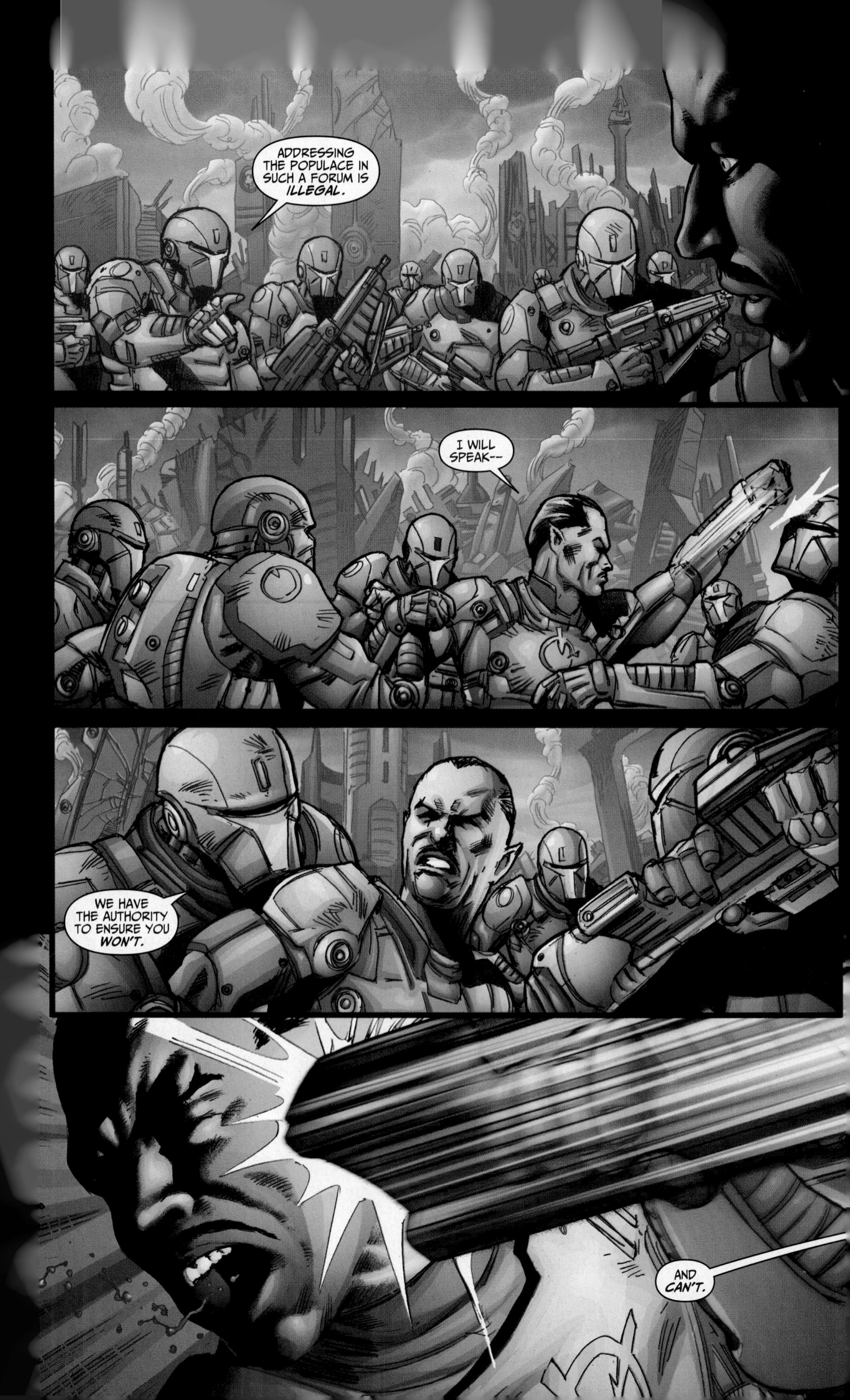
ADDRESSING THE POPULACE IN SUCH A FORUM IS *ILLEGAL*.
I WILL SPEAK--
WE HAVE THE AUTHORITY TO ENSURE YOU *WON'T*.
AND *CAN'T*.

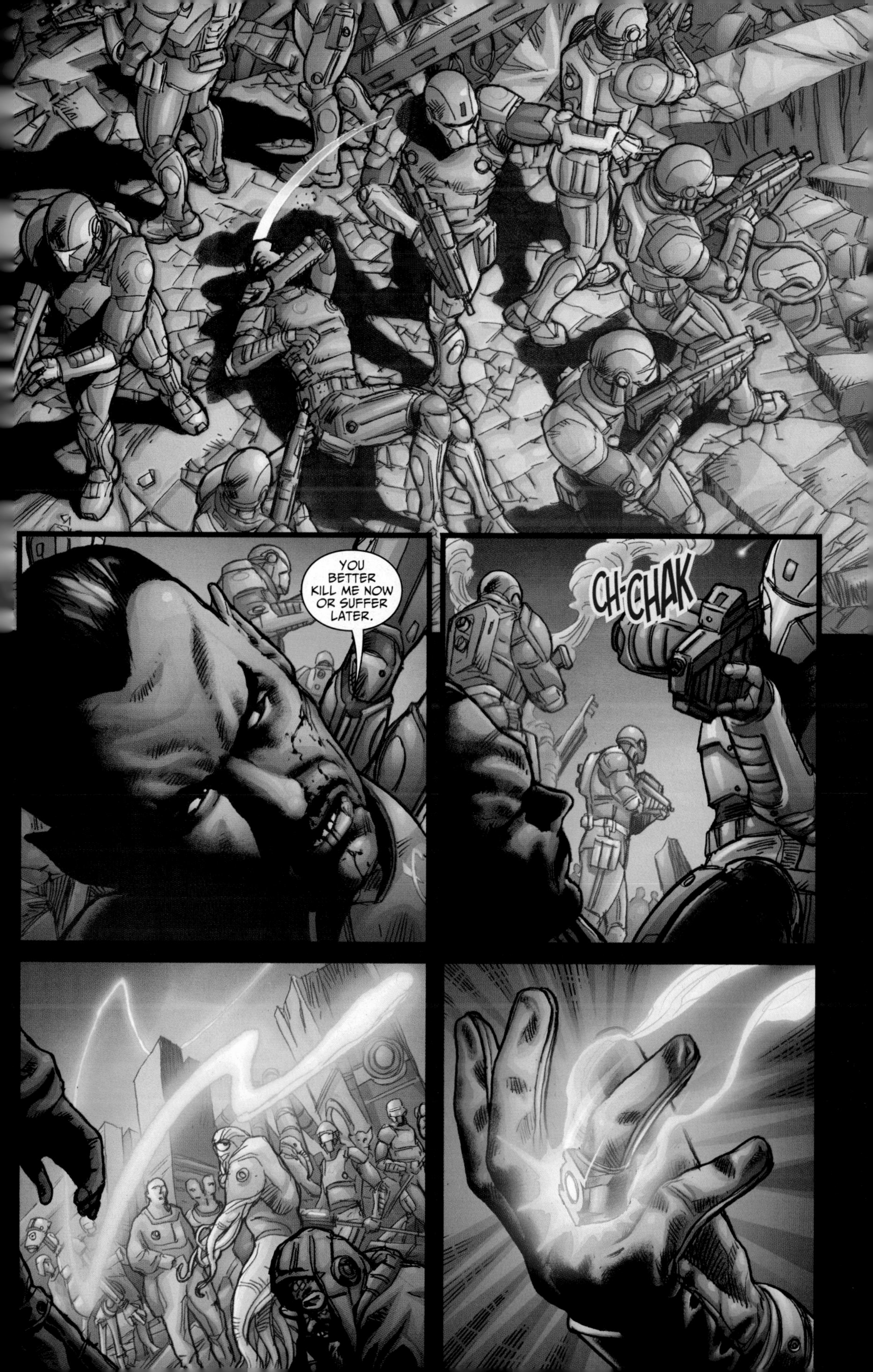
YOU BETTER KILL ME NOW OR SUFFER LATER.
CH-CHAK

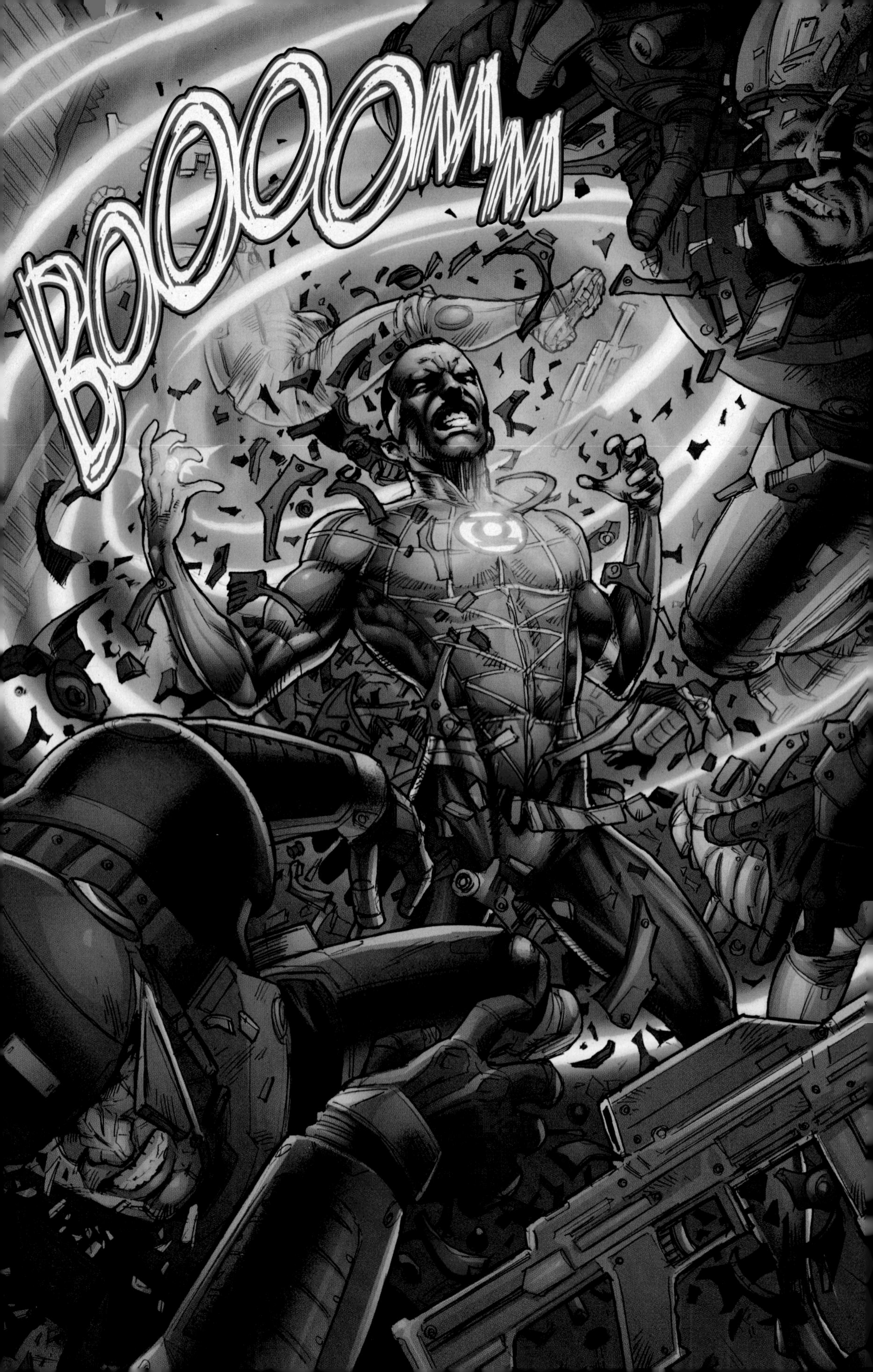
BOOOOOMMM

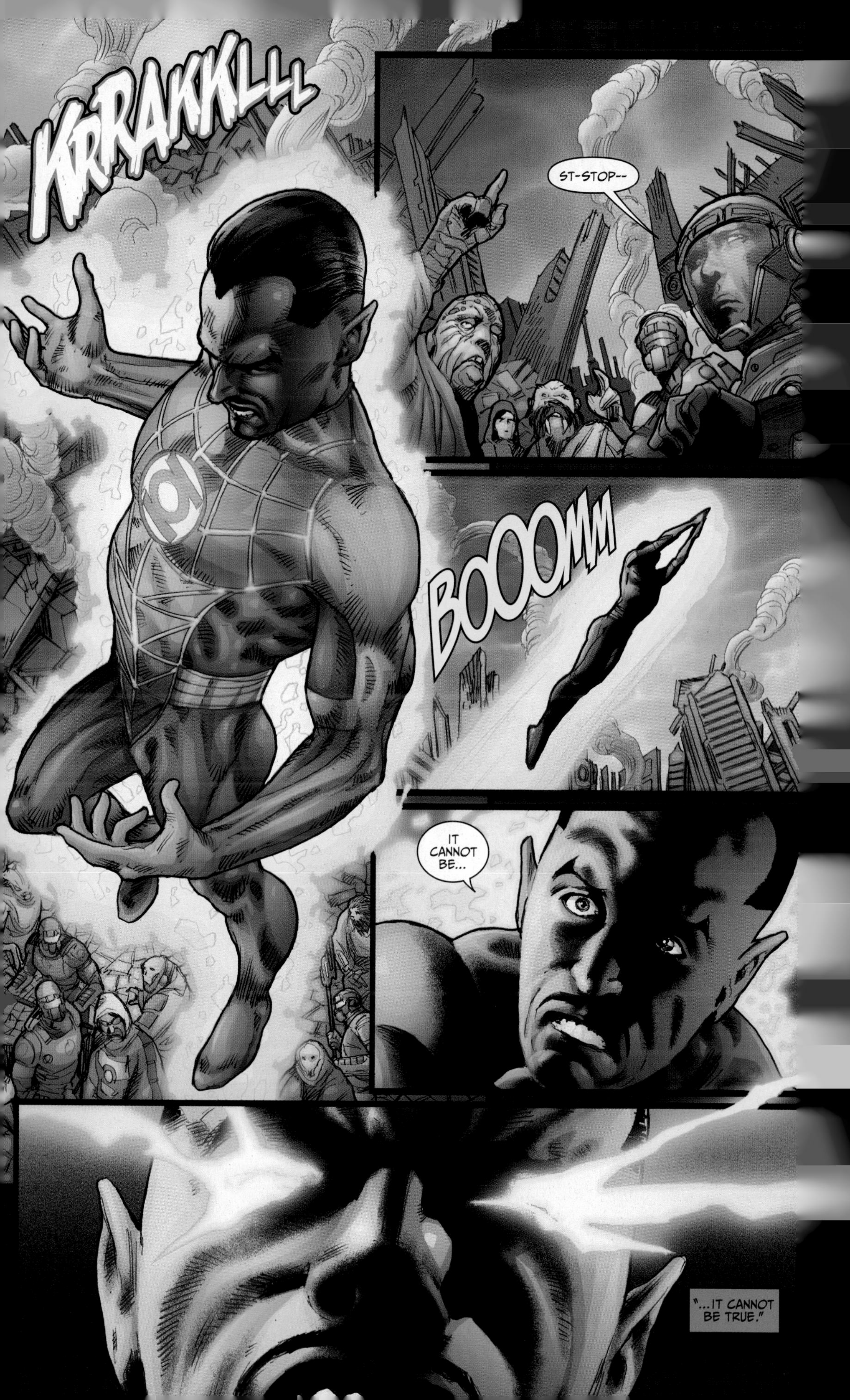
KRRAKKLLL
ST-STOP--
BOOOMM
IT CANNOT BE...
"...IT CANNOT BE TRUE."

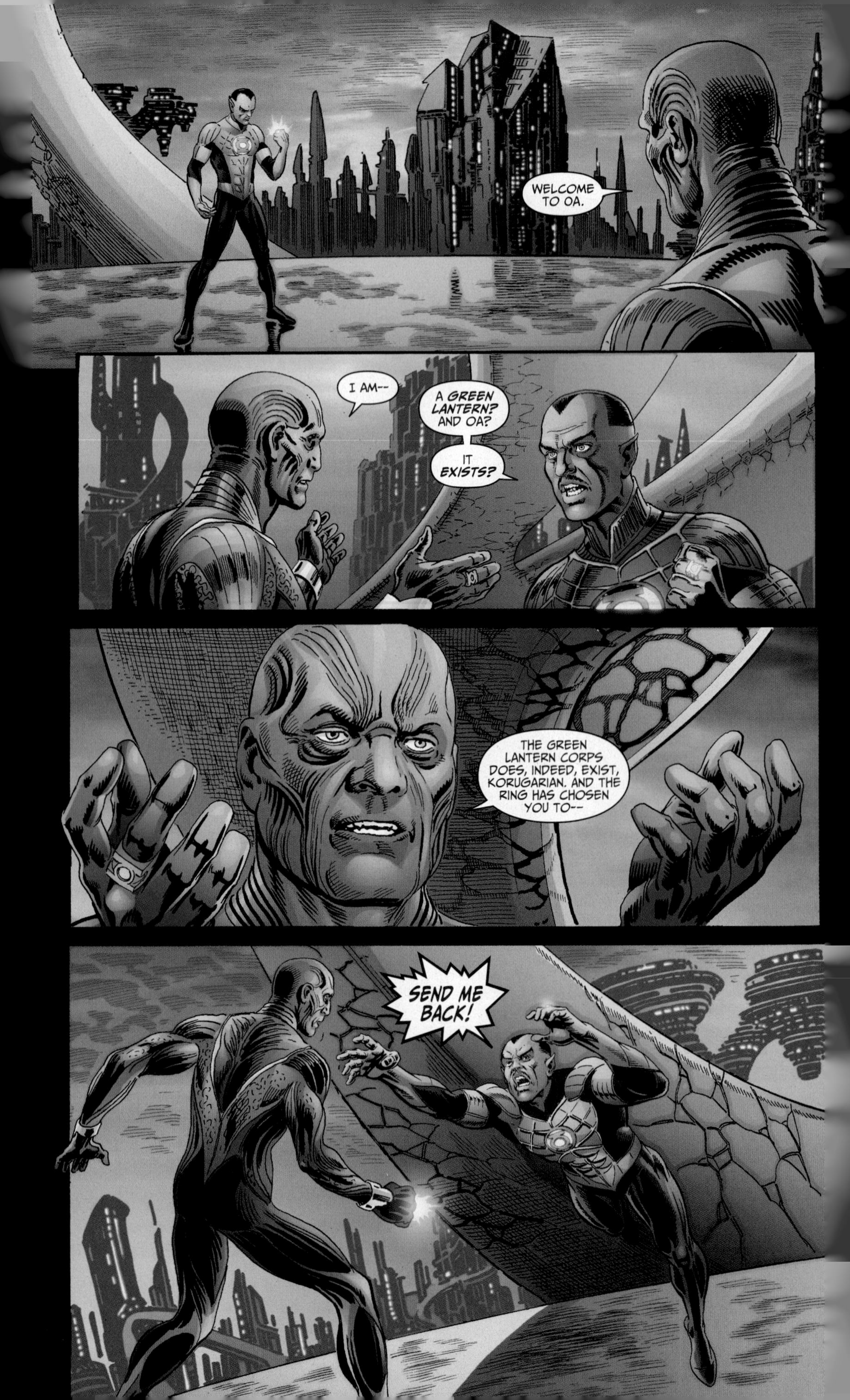
WELCOME TO OA.
I AM--
A GREEN LANTERN? AND OA?
IT EXISTS?
THE GREEN LANTERN CORPS DOES, INDEED, EXIST, KORUGARIAN. AND THE RING HAS CHOSEN YOU TO--
SEND ME BACK!

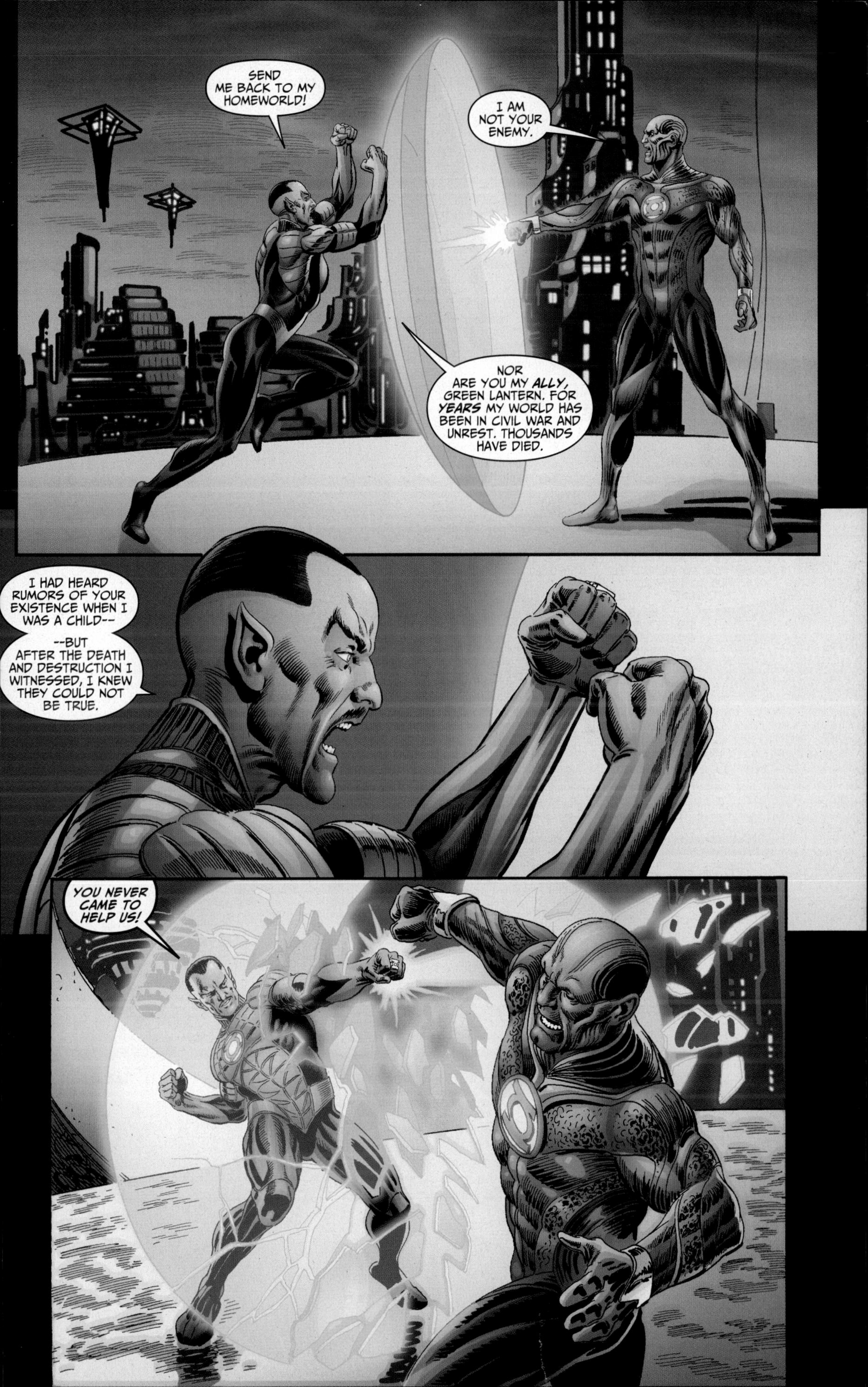
SEND ME BACK TO MY HOMEWORLD!
I AM NOT YOUR ENEMY.
NOR ARE YOU MY *ALLY*, GREEN LANTERN. FOR *YEARS* MY WORLD HAS BEEN IN CIVIL WAR AND UNREST. THOUSANDS HAVE DIED.
I HAD HEARD RUMORS OF YOUR EXISTENCE WHEN I WAS A CHILD--
--BUT AFTER THE DEATH AND DESTRUCTION I WITNESSED, I KNEW THEY COULD NOT BE TRUE.
YOU NEVER CAME TO HELP US!

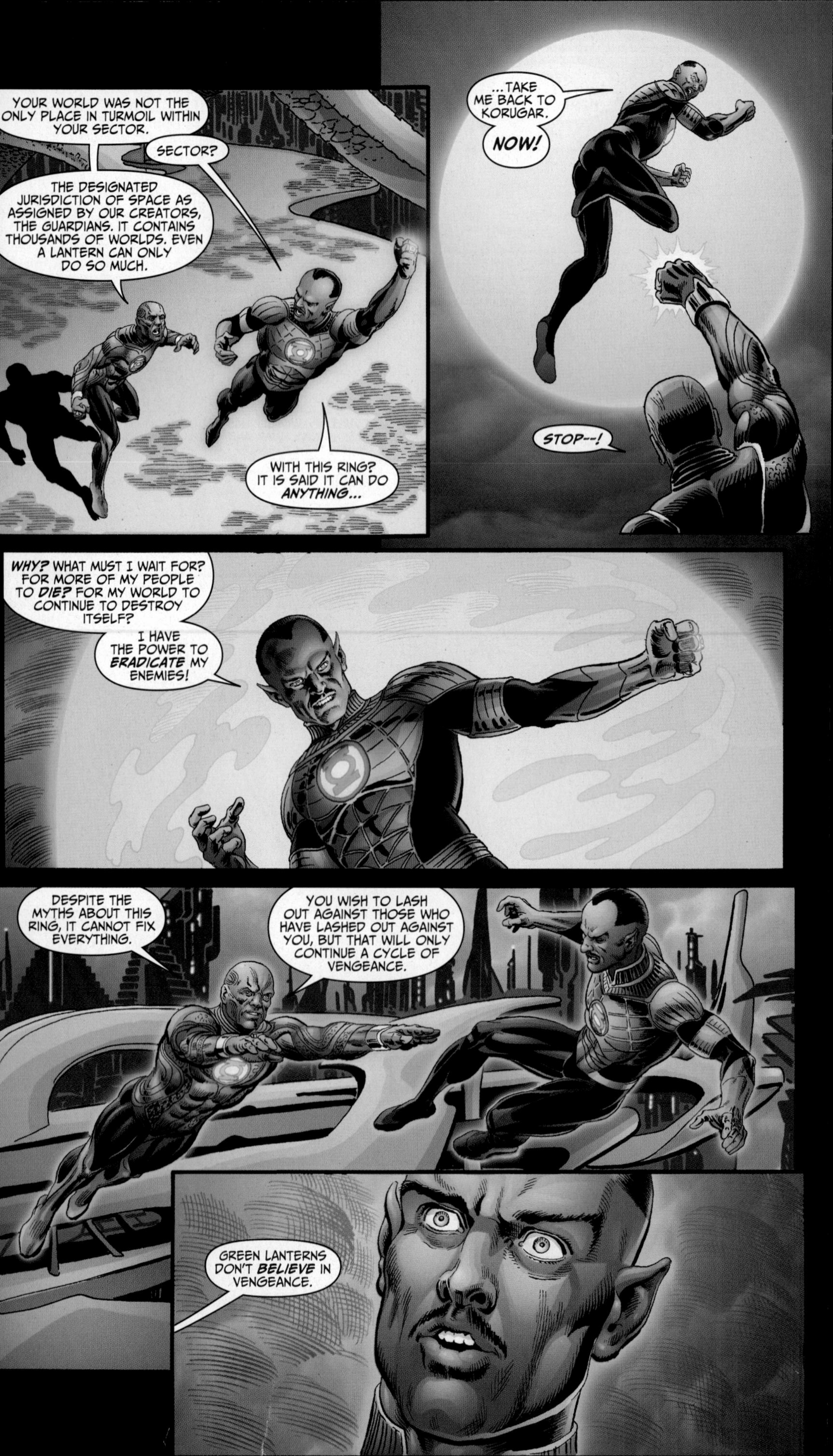
YOUR WORLD WAS NOT THE ONLY PLACE IN TURMOIL WITHIN YOUR SECTOR.
SECTOR?
THE DESIGNATED JURISDICTION OF SPACE AS ASSIGNED BY OUR CREATORS, THE GUARDIANS. IT CONTAINS THOUSANDS OF WORLDS. EVEN A LANTERN CAN ONLY DO SO MUCH.
WITH THIS RING? IT IS SAID IT CAN DO ANYTHING...
...TAKE ME BACK TO KORUGAR.
NOW!
STOP--!
WHY? WHAT MUST I WAIT FOR? FOR MORE OF MY PEOPLE TO DIE? FOR MY WORLD TO CONTINUE TO DESTROY ITSELF?
I HAVE THE POWER TO ERADICATE MY ENEMIES!
DESPITE THE MYTHS ABOUT THIS RING, IT CANNOT FIX EVERYTHING.
YOU WISH TO LASH OUT AGAINST THOSE WHO HAVE LASHED OUT AGAINST YOU, BUT THAT WILL ONLY CONTINUE A CYCLE OF VENGEANCE.
GREEN LANTERNS DON'T BELIEVE IN VENGEANCE.

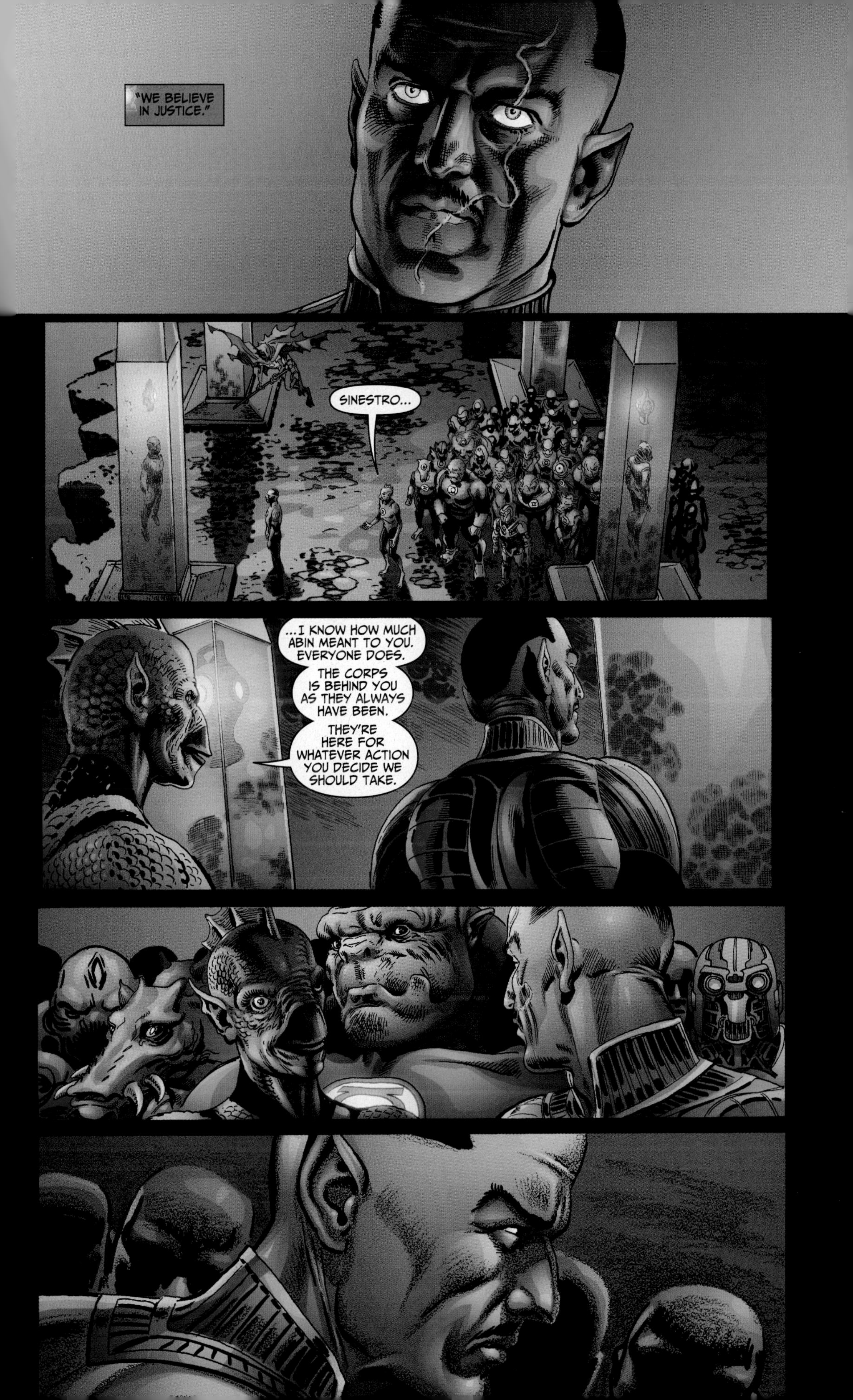
"WE BELIEVE IN JUSTICE."
SINESTRO...
...I KNOW HOW MUCH ABIN MEANT TO YOU. EVERYONE DOES.
THE CORPS IS BEHIND YOU AS THEY ALWAYS HAVE BEEN.
THEY'RE HERE FOR WHATEVER ACTION YOU DECIDE WE SHOULD TAKE.

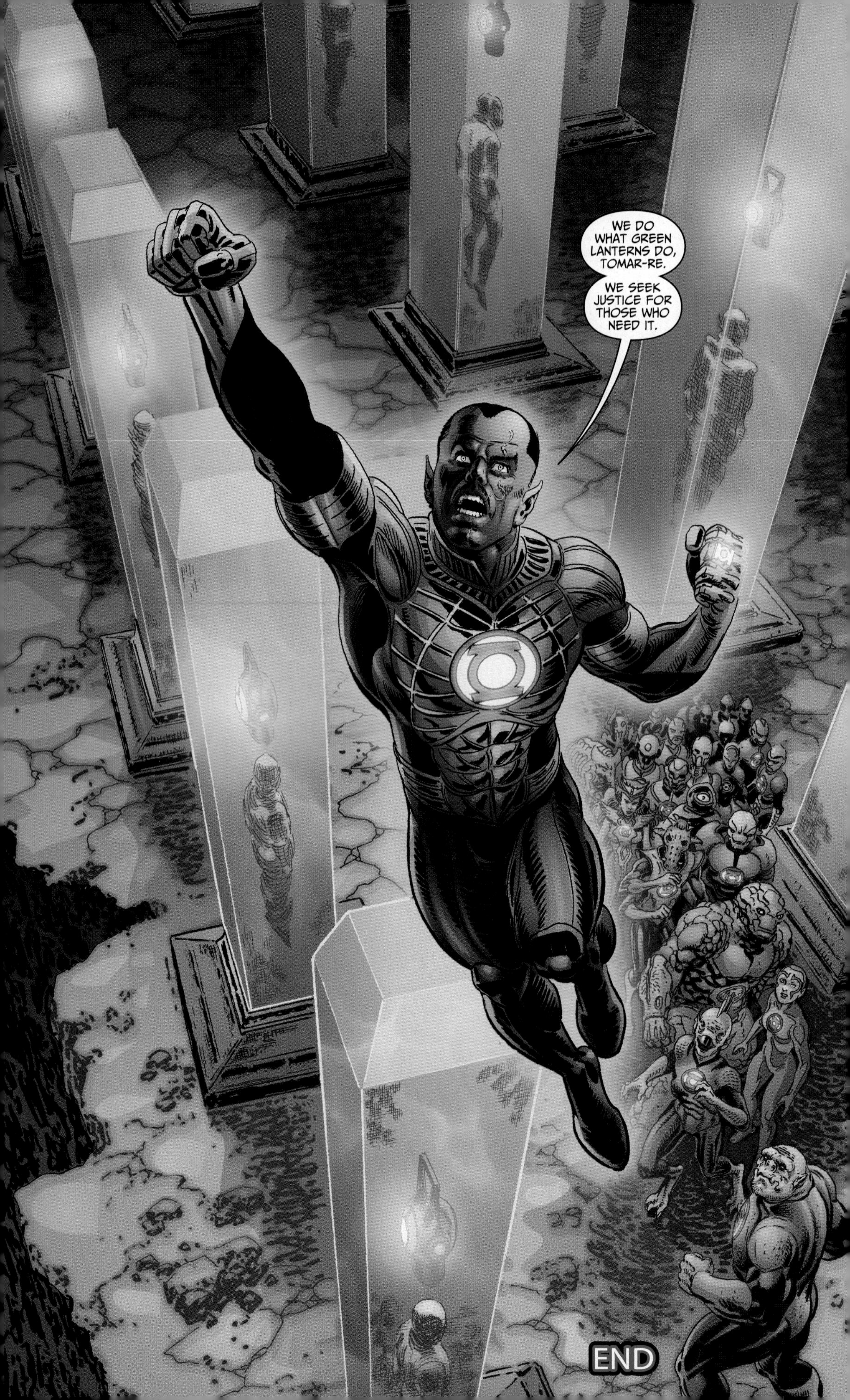
WE DO WHAT GREEN LANTERNS DO, TOMAR-RE.
WE SEEK JUSTICE FOR THOSE WHO NEED IT.
END

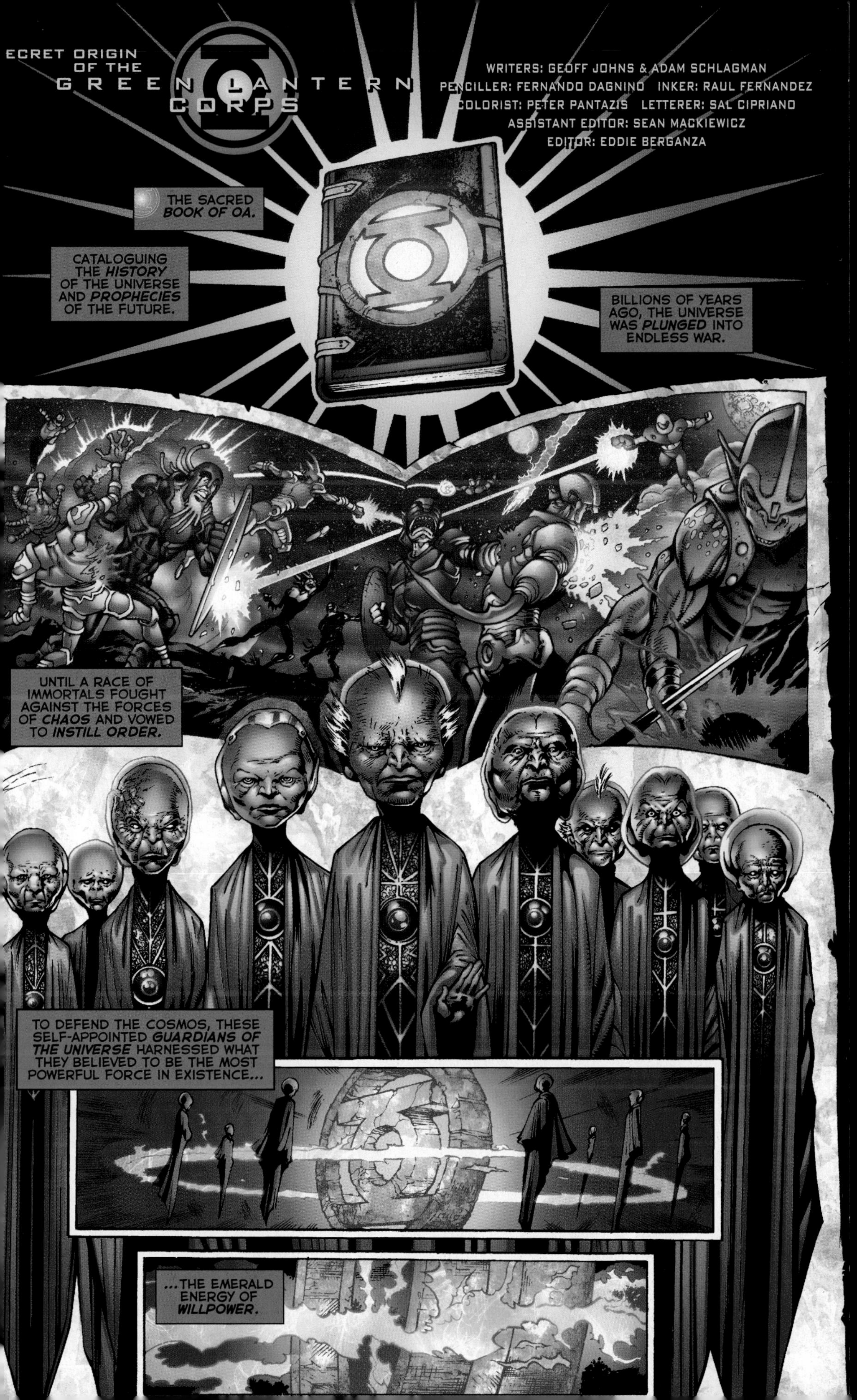

ECRET ORIGIN OF THE GREEN LANTERN CORPS
WRITERS: GEOFF JOHNS & ADAM SCHLAGMAN
PENCILLER: FERNANDO DAGNINO INKER: RAUL FERNANDEZ
COLORIST: PETER PANTAZIS LETTERER: SAL CIPRIANO
ASSISTANT EDITOR: SEAN MACKIEWICZ
EDITOR: EDDIE BERGANZA
THE SACRED BOOK OF OA.
CATALOGUING THE HISTORY OF THE UNIVERSE AND PROPHECIES OF THE FUTURE.
BILLIONS OF YEARS AGO, THE UNIVERSE WAS PLUNGED INTO ENDLESS WAR.
UNTIL A RACE OF IMMORTALS FOUGHT AGAINST THE FORCES OF CHAOS AND VOWED TO INSTILL ORDER.
TO DEFEND THE COSMOS, THESE SELF-APPOINTED GUARDIANS OF THE UNIVERSE HARNESSED WHAT THEY BELIEVED TO BE THE MOST POWERFUL FORCE IN EXISTENCE...
...THE EMERALD ENERGY OF WILLPOWER.

WITH THIS NEW POWER, THE GUARDIANS BUILT A WORLD FROM WHERE THEY COULD WATCH OVER THE UNIVERSE-- *THE PLANET OA.*

STORING THE ENERGY IN A *CENTRAL POWER BATTERY,* THE GUARDIANS *FORGED RINGS* CAPABLE OF CHANNELING IT.

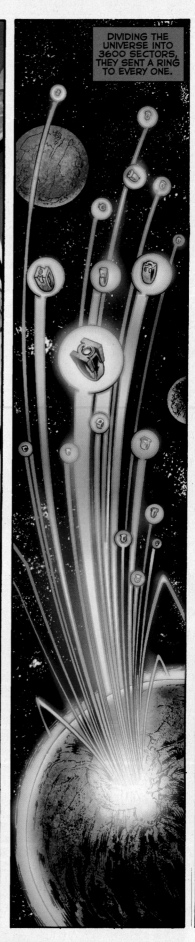

DIVIDING THE UNIVERSE INTO 3600 SECTORS, THEY SENT A RING TO EVERY ONE.

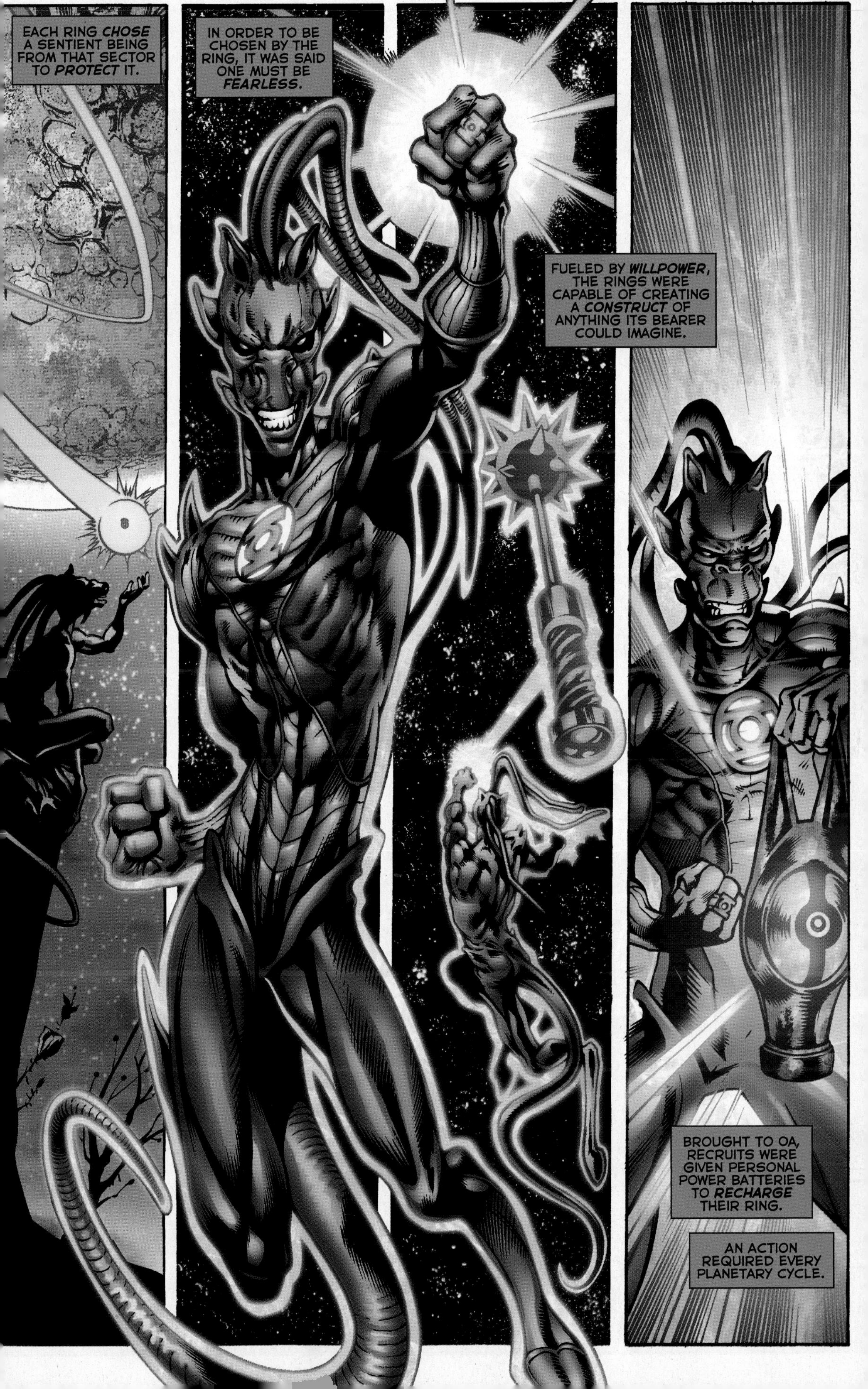
EACH RING CHOSE A SENTIENT BEING FROM THAT SECTOR TO PROTECT IT.
IN ORDER TO BE CHOSEN BY THE RING, IT WAS SAID ONE MUST BE FEARLESS.
FUELED BY WILLPOWER, THE RINGS WERE CAPABLE OF CREATING A CONSTRUCT OF ANYTHING ITS BEARER COULD IMAGINE.
BROUGHT TO OA, RECRUITS WERE GIVEN PERSONAL POWER BATTERIES TO RECHARGE THEIR RING.
AN ACTION REQUIRED EVERY PLANETARY CYCLE.

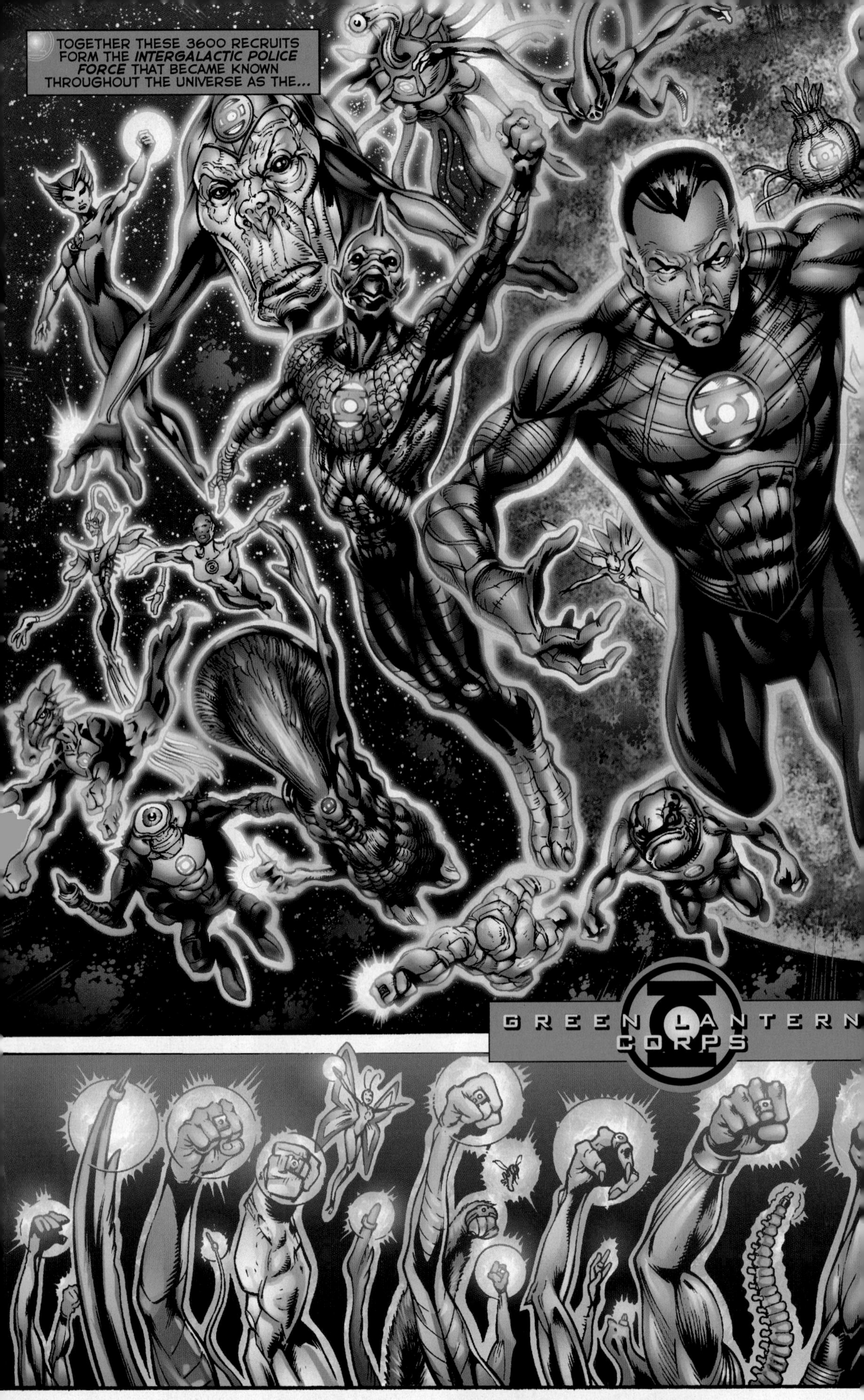
TOGETHER THESE 3600 RECRUITS FORM THE *INTERGALACTIC POLICE FORCE* THAT BECAME KNOWN THROUGHOUT THE UNIVERSE AS THE...
GREEN LANTERN CORPS

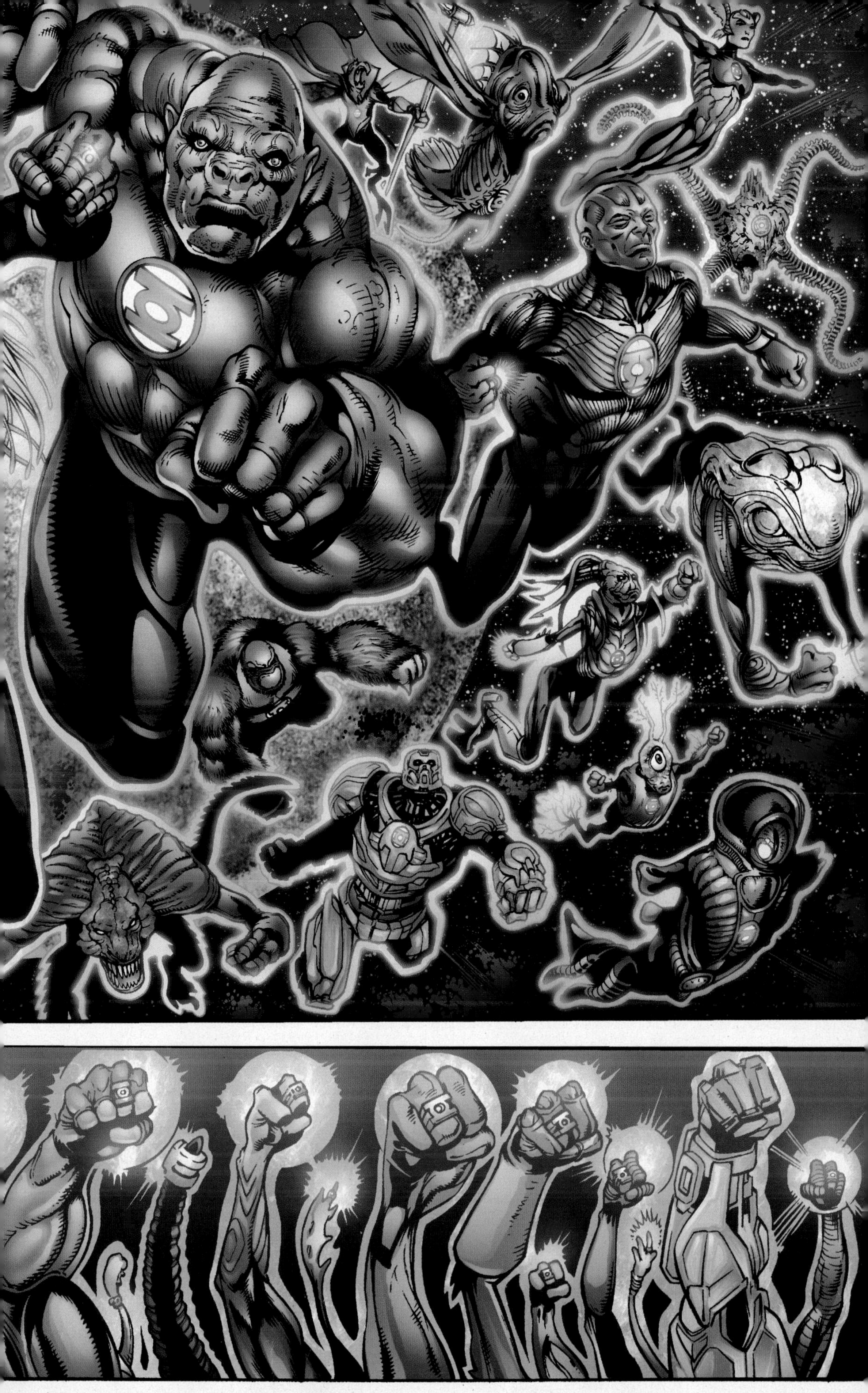

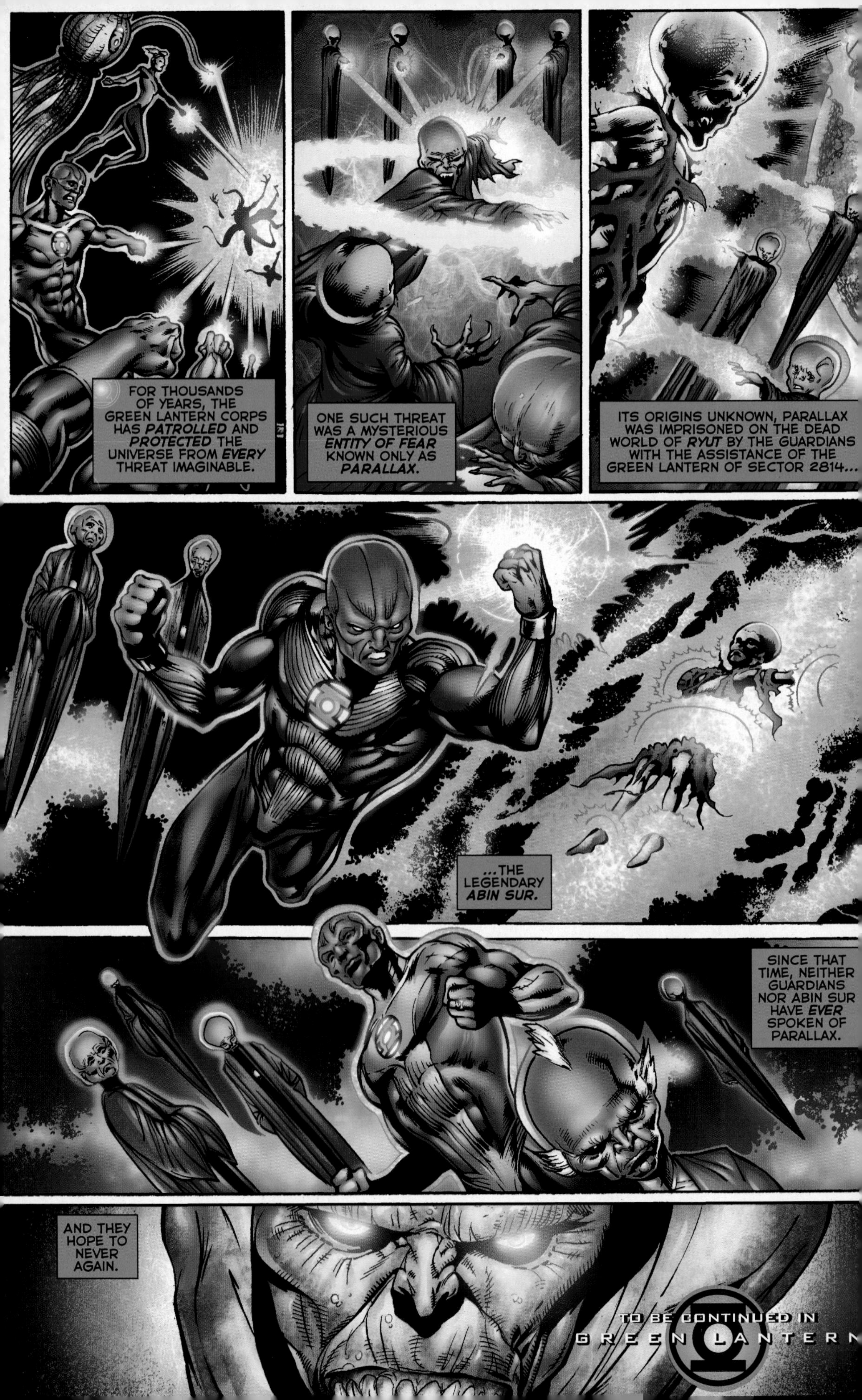
FOR THOUSANDS OF YEARS, THE GREEN LANTERN CORPS HAS PATROLLED AND PROTECTED THE UNIVERSE FROM EVERY THREAT IMAGINABLE.
ONE SUCH THREAT WAS A MYSTERIOUS ENTITY OF FEAR KNOWN ONLY AS PARALLAX.
ITS ORIGINS UNKNOWN, PARALLAX WAS IMPRISONED ON THE DEAD WORLD OF RYUT BY THE GUARDIANS WITH THE ASSISTANCE OF THE GREEN LANTERN OF SECTOR 2814...
...THE LEGENDARY ABIN SUR.
SINCE THAT TIME, NEITHER GUARDIANS NOR ABIN SUR HAVE EVER SPOKEN OF PARALLAX.
AND THEY HOPE TO NEVER AGAIN.
TO BE CONTINUED IN
GREEN LANTERN

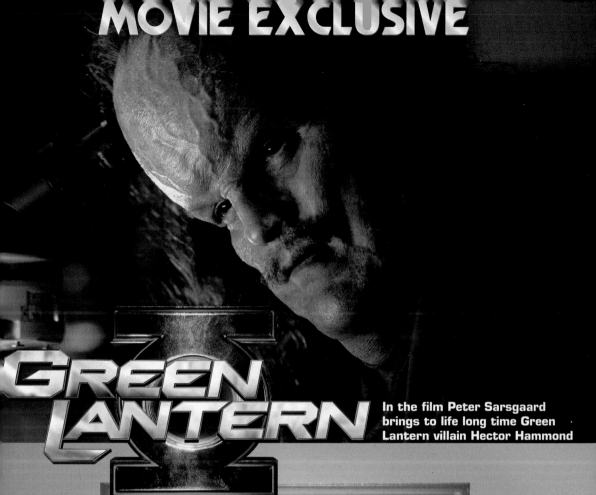

GREEN LANTERN

In the film Peter Sarsgaard brings to life long time Green Lantern villain Hector Hammond

Never let fear overcome you.

Since we reintroduced Hal Jordan and the Green Lantern Corps in 2004's GREEN LANTERN: REBIRTH, fear has been at the center of our stories. In our world, fear is a force in our lives that we can't touch or quantify, but it is very real. It's something that can keep us from following our dreams, it can create hate and it can paralyze us from living our lives with the freedom we all deserve. I wanted to make fear very real in the world of GREEN LANTERN, and I think that's part of the success of the characters. It's not that Green Lanterns are chosen because they have no fear, it's because they have the ability to overcome fear.

But not everyone does.

Some people give in to fear and live a life surrounded by it. This is exactly what happens to Doctor Hector Hammond in the GREEN LANTERN film. But before I briefly talk about Hector Hammond, let me back up and acknowledge that bizarrely cool still up there.

If you're reading this, chances are you already know of the release of the first-ever live-action GREEN LANTERN movie starring Ryan Reynolds as the quintessential Hal Jordan, the wonderful Blake Lively as Carol Ferris, Mark Strong as the perfect Sinestro and the unbelievable Peter Sarsgaard as Hector Hammond. If you didn't know we're that close to see-

ing Kilowog, Oa, Ferris Air and the Guardians of the Universe up on the big screen, now you do.

Last summer, I was on set down in smoldering New Orleans with producer Donald De Line during one of the scenes with Hal and Hector. (And to give you an idea of how into it Donald is, he was wearing his Green Lantern ring.) When Peter Sarsgaard walked on stage in full makeup it was scary. Hector Hammond has been a longtime character in the comics, someone I've enjoyed writing myself, but this scientist turned highly evolved telepath was never portrayed as frightening or as human as this. I was captivated watching director Martin Campbell (Casino Royale, The Mask of Zorro) work with Peter on getting a performance that, for me, elevated Hector Hammond to an entirely new level. Peter took the air out of the room. We were all speechless, mesmerized not only by the makeup that turned this grotesque longtime enemy of Green Lantern into a reality, but more important, by each and every word coming out of Peter's mouth. Hector Hammond has become a formidable and very real force for fear.

Coming up in the following pages you'll get looks at Hal's power battery and ring, the aliens of the Green Lantern Corps, Oa, the Guardians of the Universe and even the greatest Green Lantern that's ever lived…Sinestro!

All will be well,

Geoff Johns

Mark Strong IS Sinestro!

THE GREATEST GREEN LANTERN!

Before Sinestro fell from grace, becoming the ultimate Green Lantern villain and one of the greatest foes in history… he was the finest Green Lantern ever.

Respected by his Corpsmen and trusted by the immortal Guardians of the Universe, Sinestro is considered the greatest Green Lantern, having preserved definitive order in his sector. This regal Korugarian commands attention and needed an actor that could portray the same. Could anyone live up to the perfection of Sinestro?

Have No Fear, for Mark Strong IS Sinestro!

When Mark Strong (*Sherlock Holmes, Robin Hood, Kick Ass*) arrived on the set decked out in make-up and prosthetics, I thought Sinestro had walked right off the comics page. Take a look at that still… just incredible!

Back in August, I visited the Green Lantern movie set with Blackest Night and Sinestro Corps masterminds Geoff Johns and Ivan Reis — and what a trip it was. My mind is still blown from the experience. I was given the opportunity to hold the actual Power Battery and was able to wear the

Green Lantern ring… *In Brightest Day, In Blackest* — sorry, got carried away. I could go on for pages about the amazing production designs, how surreal Ryan Reynolds looked in Hal Jordan's flight suit, or how awestruck I was by early CG tests of Oa and the different alien Green Lanterns, but instead let me focus on the supreme highlight.

Sinestro.

I witnessed scenes of Sinestro in action, addressing the entire Corps, and speaking with the Guardians. The entire time I was glued to my seat, unable to turn away. Mark nailed it all. The voice — the demeanor — everything! Mark, like much of the film, has taken his inspiration from Geoff Johns's extraordinary run on GREEN LANTERN.

The same care and enthusiasm is being brought to the Green Lantern movie by visionary director Martin Campbell (*Casino Royale*), producer Donald De Line and the rest of the cast and crew. I am beyond excited!

Long Live the Corps!!!!

Adam Schlagman

Tomar-Re brought to life by Sony Imageworks.

IT'S ALL IN THE DETAILS...

...is a mantra Tomar-Re lives by which has aided him in becoming an honored and highly respected Green Lantern. It's also a mantra that the filmmakers, like production designer Grant Major, costume designer Ngila Dickson and visual effects supervisor Jim Berny have taken as their own. Producer Donald De Line and director Martin Campbell have assembled an amazing corps.

Growing up on the planet Xudar, Tomar-Re comes from a peaceful avian race that focuses their efforts on the arts and sciences instead of war. His nature to examine everything has led the Guardians of the Universe to appoint him the archivist and protector of the sacred Book of Oa. When not studying the nature of the Corps, Tomar-Re patrols sector 2813 where he developed a close friendship with neighboring sector 2814's Green Lantern, Abin Sur. Tomar has taken an interest in Abin's replacement Hal Jordan. Though Hal is *not* one for details, Tomar hopes to teach Hal what it means to be a Green Lantern.

Now the same thoughtfulness that Tomar-Re believes in is being utilized to bring him and the rest of the Green Lantern Corps to life on the big screen.

We've watched test after test supervised by digital effects master Jim Berney based on the amazing design work by Grant and Ngila. Their passion for detail is much like Tomar-Re's. Something I found extremely interesting was the mix of motion capture and straight-up animation they used in creating the Green Lantern Corps. Some of the more humanoid Corps members like Tomar-Re and Kilowog started with motion capture, but most of their flying and movement beyond simple interaction was animated, some based on the movement of insects or animals and others created completely from scratch – giving them all a unique, and alien, feel. It's this attention to detail – from the scales on Tomar-Re's skin to the way he turns when he flies into the air – that will give the Green Lantern Corps more life than it's ever seen.

With talented people like Grant, Ngila and Jim and his team pouring their heart and soul into this, it makes you realize even more than you might already how truly amazing the Green Lantern universe is.

Let's follow the advice that Tomar-Re would give to Hal: Follow your heart, believe in your will and never, ever disrespect Sinestro!

Geoff Johns

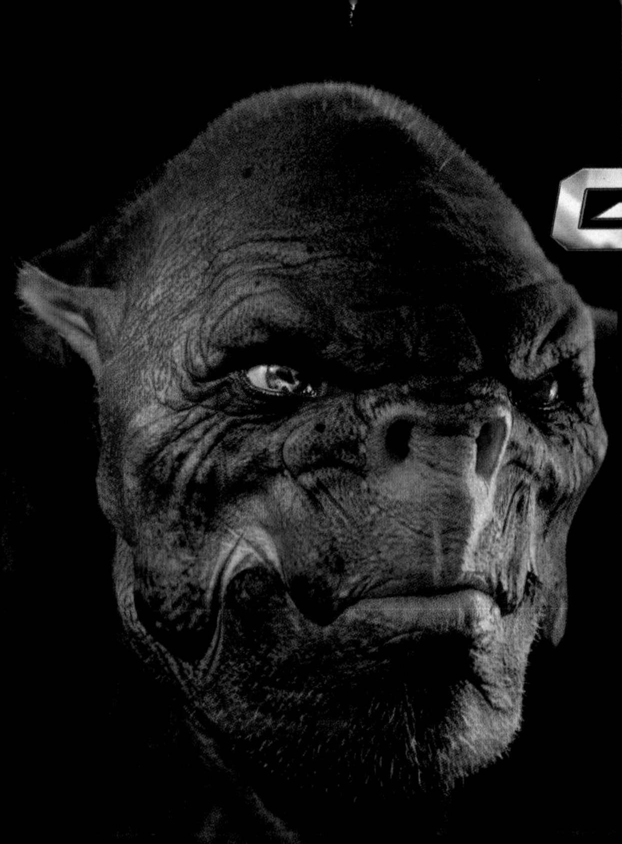

KILOWOG - as brought to life by Sony Imageworks

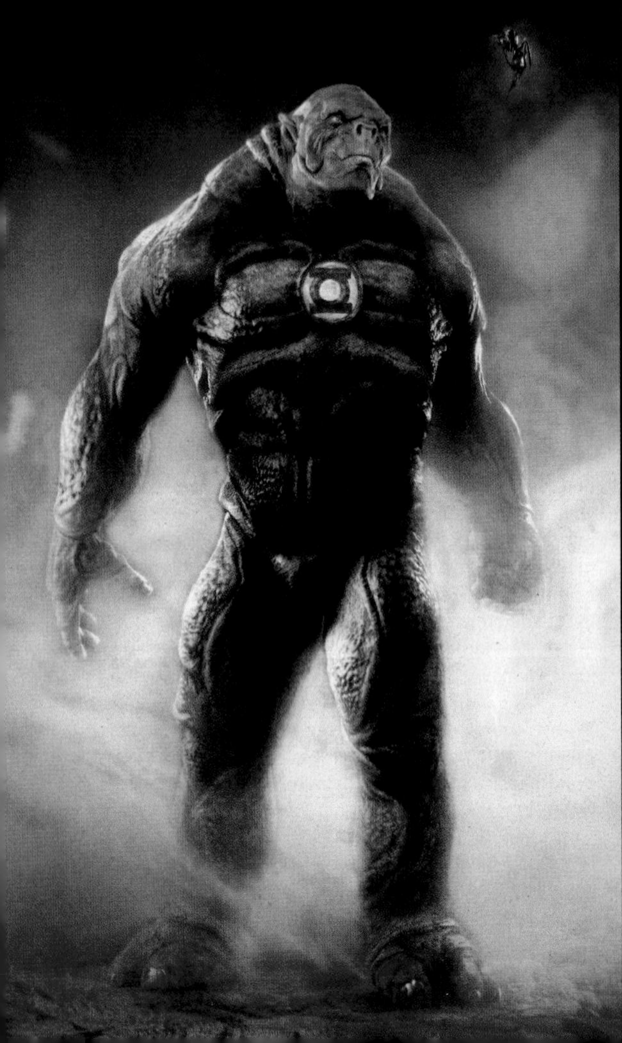

Green Lantern

One of the greatest challenges for the Green Lantern film is bringing the Green Lantern Corps to life. It falls to the work of dozens of people overseen by director Martin Campbell and led by production designer Grant Major and costume designer Ngila Dickson.

We've taken a look at the spiritual trainer of the Corps in previous issues with Tomar-Re, but this time the big guy takes the stage. Perhaps the most popular alien Green Lantern – next to Sinestro, of course – is the one member of the Green Lantern Corps that can whip any rookie Lantern into shape. Even an Earthman named Hal Jordan.

If the saying "Beware my power" were true for any other Corps member, it'd be the Green Lantern known as KILOWOG.

Along with every other GL fan, my introduction to this brute of a GL was in 1986's *Green Lantern Corps* #201. Kilowog looked among the most alien of the existing GLs of the day. The lone survivor of his home world Bolovax Vik, he came from a society of decidedly Socialist views—ideal for a police force where there is no rank. Now, of course, he spends most of his time on the Corps' headquartered world of Oa.

And yet, his tough exterior and demeanor belies a thoughtful soul, and one couldn't ask for a better ally in letting no evil escape your sight. Kilowog might be tough as a rhino on his trainees, doing anything he can to motivate and educate them. Without a family to call his own, he embraces his rookies as if they were, with a tough love designed to keep them alive and do right by the ideals of the Corps.

The filmmakers have captured the essence of Kilowog perfectly in the film. And with film, there's an entirely new dimension to Kilowog and the rest of the Corps members. You'll see them brought to life with detail and power you could never imagine.

Beware his power!

Brian Cunningham
Green Lantern Editor

, DC Nation,

is year, Green Lantern is primed to take the world by orm with WAR OF THE GREEN LANTERNS in the comics, e GREEN LANTERN: ANIMATED SERIES this fall, GREEN ANTERN: RISE OF THE MANHUNTERS videogame, an nazing line of consumer products and of course the GREEN ANTERN film. Everyone will understand the mantra NO FEAR nd will be reciting the sacred oath.

got my first look at the beginning of August 2010 when I visited e Green Lantern Movie Set with team GREEN LANTERN/ .ACKEST NIGHT, Geoff Johns and Ivan Reis. And what a trip was. My mind is still blown from the experience, but read on r some of the highlights I'm allowed to spill.

'hen we arrived on set, producer Donald De Line greeted us. onald is working closely with Chief Creative Officer Geoff hns, to ensure that the Green Lantern Feature Film stays true the characters. Donald excitedly brought us to view some nimatronics; we were awestruck to see a flythrough of Oa d CG tests of the different alien Green Lanterns. Production esigner Grant Major and costume designer Ngila Dickson oth Academy Award winners!) have been working tirelessly bring the world of Green Lantern to life.

nd some items had already been created... the props. I was ole to clutch the Power Battery in my hand and wear the reen Lantern ring. Check out these photos of Ivan and me arging up.

nd there's Geoff near Hal Jordan's cockpit.

e man steering the film is visionary director Martin Campbell *'asino Royale*). He has embraced the intricacies of the ythology and is bringing the world of Green Lantern to the g screen in an immense way. After a nice conversation about mic book flicks, it was time for filming.

oon entering the stage, we found ourselves completely rrounded by blue screens. You may ask why blue and not een screens? Well, that's because the green, in the Green ntern costumes and their constructs, would be difficult to stinguish from a green background.

ere's Ryan Reynolds, and he's wearing Hal Jordan's flight it. So cool! Ryan even swung by to say hello. Geoff John's REEN LANTERN: SECRET ORIGIN is Ryan's bible and spiration.

ddenly Mark Strong, who plays Sinestro, arrived. Just jaw opping. It's like Sinestro literally walked right off the comic ge. We were able to witness scenes of Sinestro in action, ldressing the entire Corps and speaking with the Guardians. ark nailed 'em all!

m so pleased and grateful to the cast, crew and staff for such incredible time and for their amazing vision, dedication d determination in making this movie as great as it can be. e Green Lantern Corps couldn't be in better hands.

ng Live the Corps!!!

Adam Schlagman

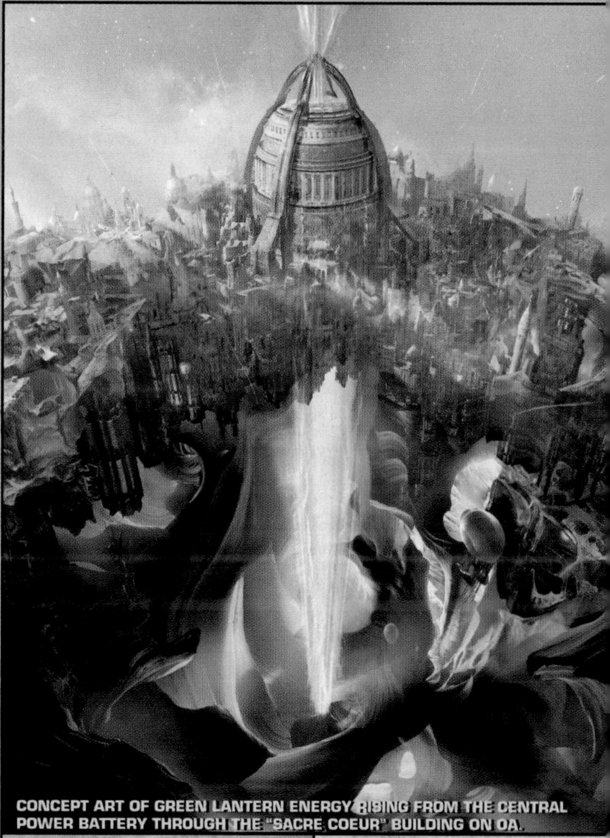

CONCEPT ART OF GREEN LANTERN ENERGY RISING FROM THE CENTRAL POWER BATTERY THROUGH THE "SACRE COEUR" BUILDING ON OA.

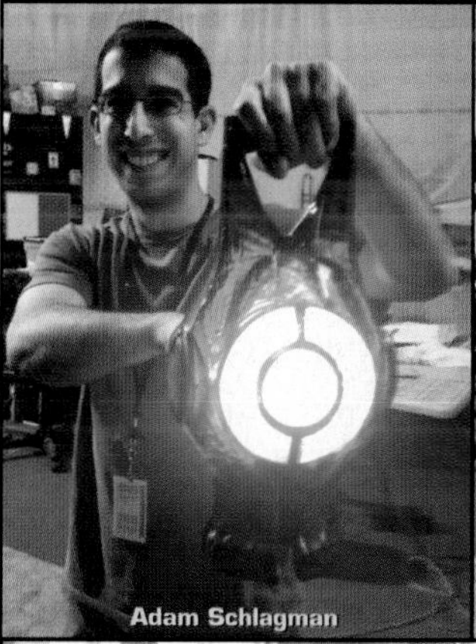

Adam Schlagman

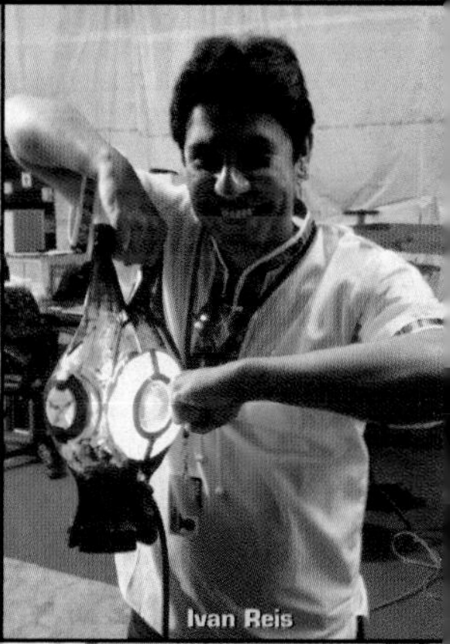

Ivan Reis

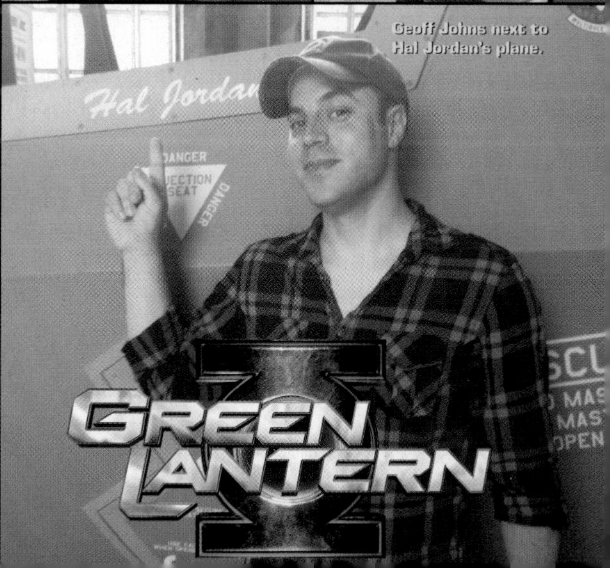
DANGER
GREEN LANTERN

Geoff Johns next to Hal Jordan's plane.

GREEN LANTERN

Actor Temuera Morrison brings the doomed
Green Lantern officer to life on screen.

Every story has a beginning.

So it's only fitting that in the ordered world the Guardians of the Universe seek that their most legendary Green Lantern starts with an "A."

Abin Sur, portrayed in the GREEN LANTERN film with pitch-perfect nuance by Temuera Morrison (best known for his role as Jango Fett in *Star Wars: Episode II—Attack of the Clones*").

A courageous alien from the planet Ungara, this Green Lantern was charged with protecting sector 2814. His deeds were grand, but he gained true immortality with his actions in the moment of his death. Having crashed to Earth in his vessel, he sent his power ring to seek out a successor – someone worthy to carry on the mantle. It selected a man capable of overcoming great fear – test pilot Hal Jordan.

The rest is cosmic history told in the Book of Oa.

We saw the first glimpse of Abin at Comic Con as his dead body was placed on display. But here we get to see how Abin is brought to life on screen – and how amazingly and vibrantly the emerald light flows off him.

It's clear that the movie team has taken great care to translate to the silver screen the amazing artwork and designs of former GREEN LANTERN artist Ivan Reis concocted in the "Secret Origin" arc that inspired the film.

Abin Sur, and the GREEN LANTERN feature film, has summoned movie audiences to witness Abin's final instrumental act as Hal Jordan is chosen as the new Green Lantern of Sector 2814!

Eddie Berganza
DC Comics Executive Editor

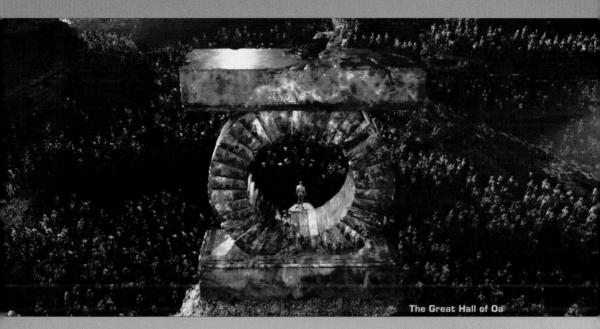

The Great Hall of Oa

GREEN LANTERN is an epic sci-fi adventure!

The feature film transports us on a journey through the stars to the alien planet Oa — the central precinct of the Green Lantern Corps.

With an abundance of futuristic spacecraft and ancient alien architecture and unique Green Lanterns, Oa is a world like no other. Production Designer Grant Major and Sony Imageworks have put great effort into the creation of the planet, its detailed features and the Corps members that inhabit it. On this very page you can catch a glimpse of the Great Hall featuring the Green Lantern Corps gathered together.

The Green Lantern Corps is composed of thousands of unique alien creatures spanning the universe from diverse worlds, extraterrestrial cultures and strange societies. Many of these Lanterns are featured in the film. Playing key roles are the legendary Abin Sur, drill-sergeant extraordinaire Kilowog, the detail-oriented Tomar-Re and of course the greatest of them all, Sinestro.

But there are many other fan-favorite alien corpsmen sprinkled throughout. See if you can spot some of these fearless Lanterns in the film:

- Boodikka, one of the fiercest warriors
- Bzzd, the smallest and boldest
- Hannu, the Lantern who would prefer to use his fists before his ring
- Larvox, the friendly insectoid
- Green Man, the most dedicated and loyal
- Medphyll, the experienced veteran plant life-form
- Morro, the caretaker of the Crypts
- R'amey Holl, the recent majestic recruit
- Rot Lop Fan, an enigma
- Salaak, the ultimate multitasker
- Stel, the battle-driven sentient robot
- Voz, the no-nonsense Warden of the Sciencells

In Green Lantern, they are joined by the very first Earthman: Hal Jordan!

-Adam Schlagman
Creative Executive

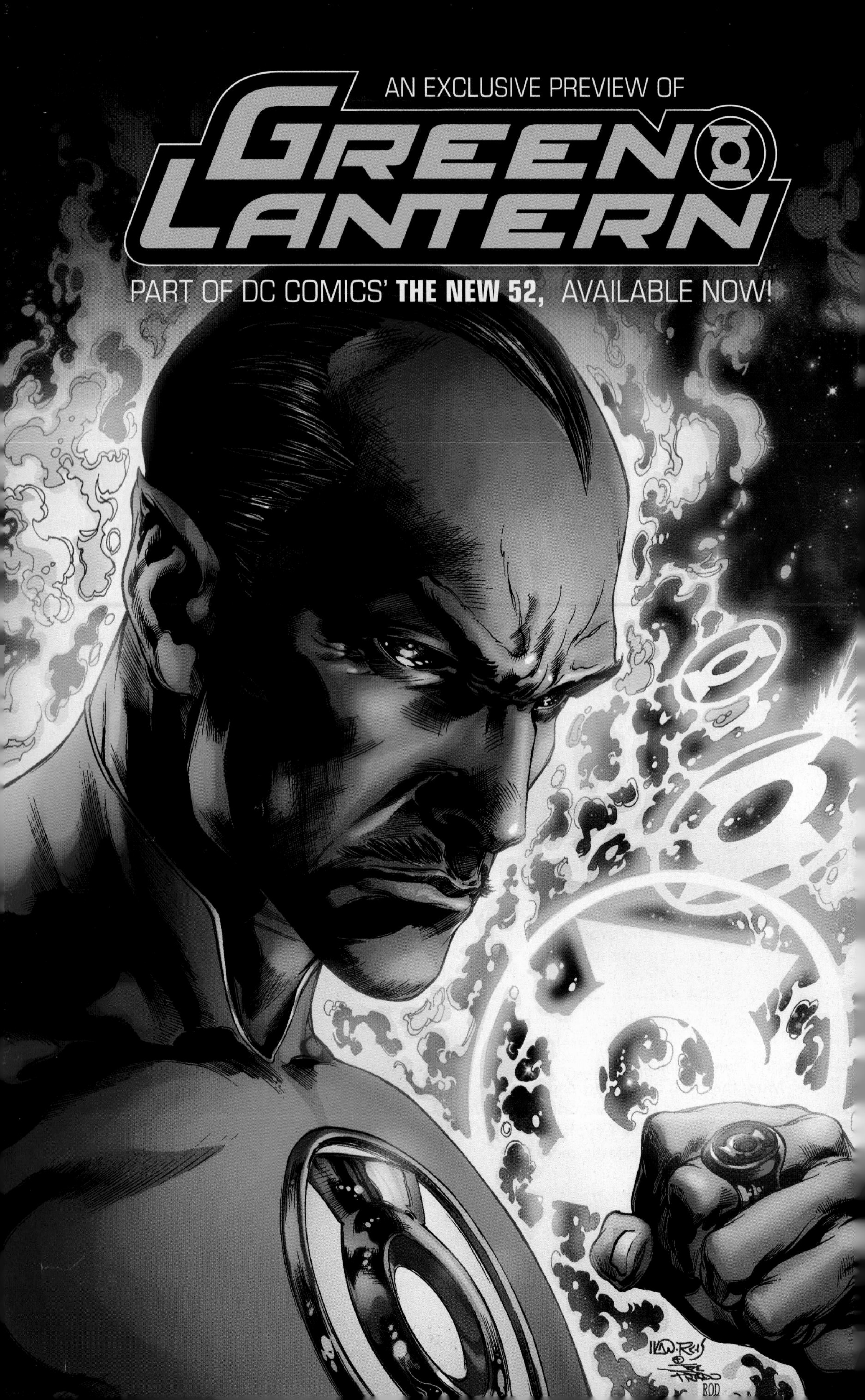
AN EXCLUSIVE PREVIEW OF
GREEN LANTERN
PART OF DC COMICS' THE NEW 52, AVAILABLE NOW!

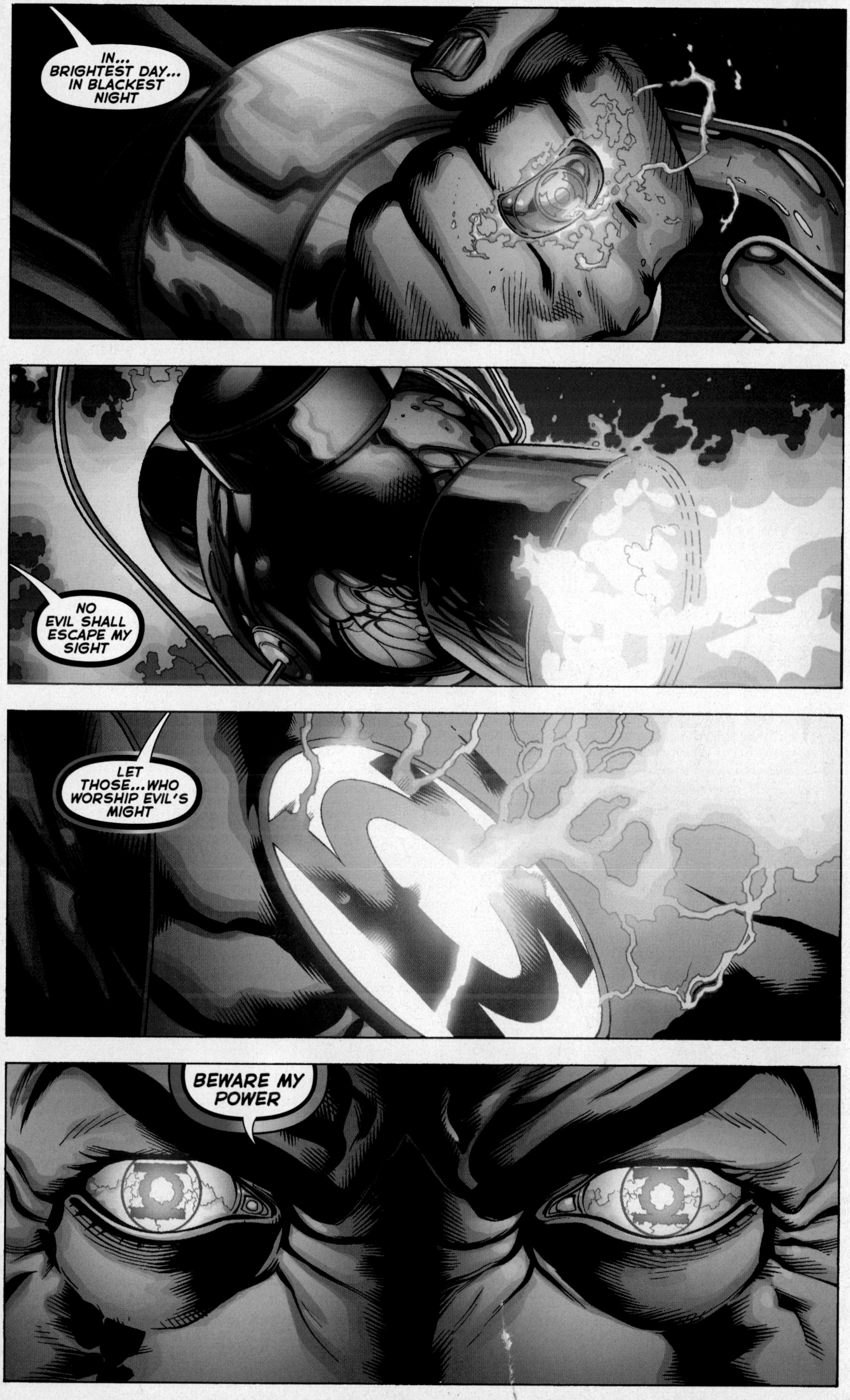
IN... BRIGHTEST DAY... IN BLACKEST NIGHT
NO EVIL SHALL ESCAPE MY SIGHT
LET THOSE...WHO WORSHIP EVIL'S MIGHT
BEWARE MY POWER

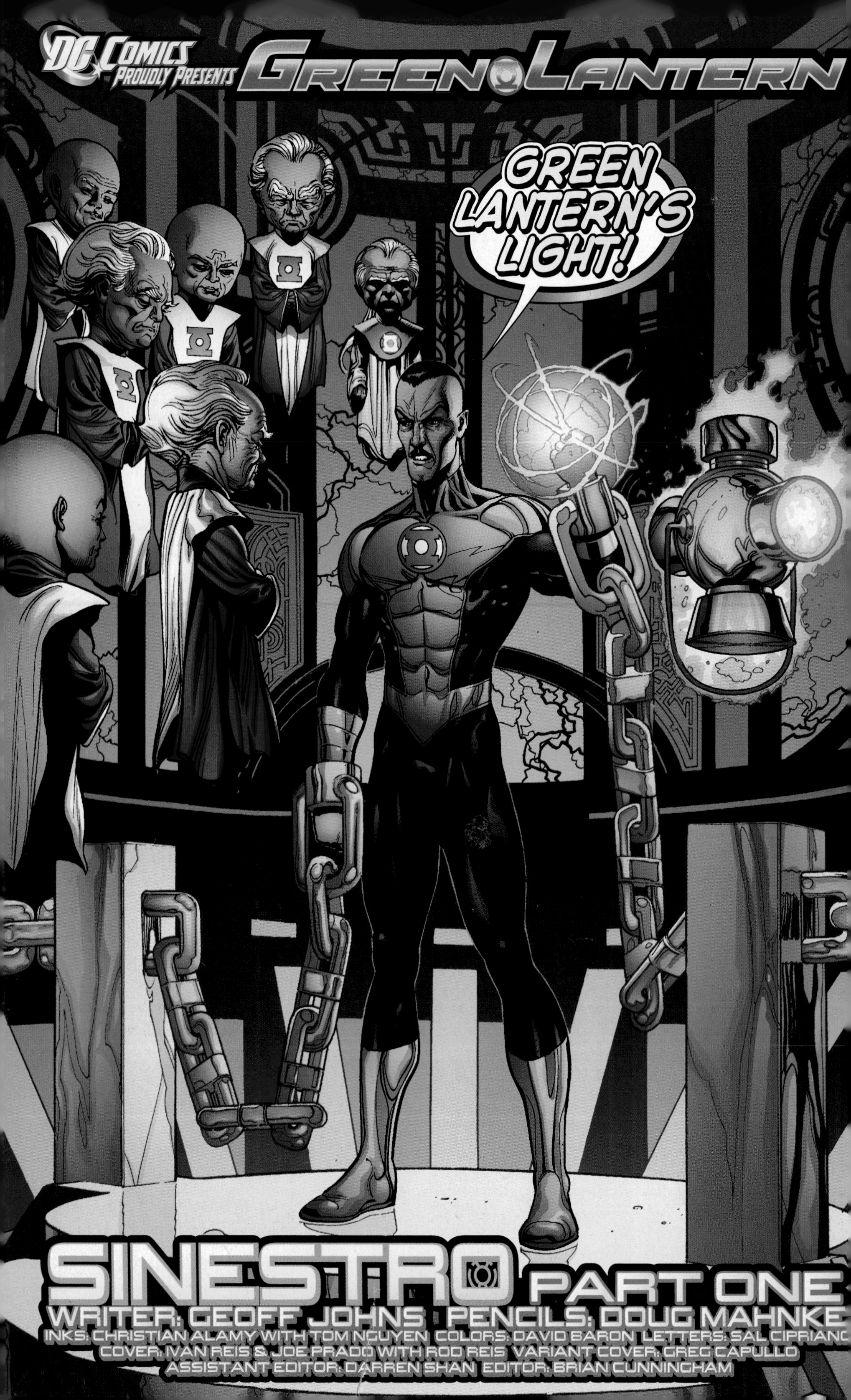
DC COMICS PROUDLY PRESENTS
GREEN LANTERN
GREEN LANTERN'S LIGHT!
SINESTRO PART ONE
WRITER: GEOFF JOHNS PENCILS: DOUG MAHNKE
INKS: CHRISTIAN ALAMY WITH TOM NGUYEN COLORS: DAVID BARON LETTERS: SAL CIPRIANO
COVER: IVAN REIS & JOE PRADO WITH ROD REIS VARIANT COVER: GREG CAPULLO
ASSISTANT EDITOR: DARREN SHAN EDITOR: BRIAN CUNNINGHAM

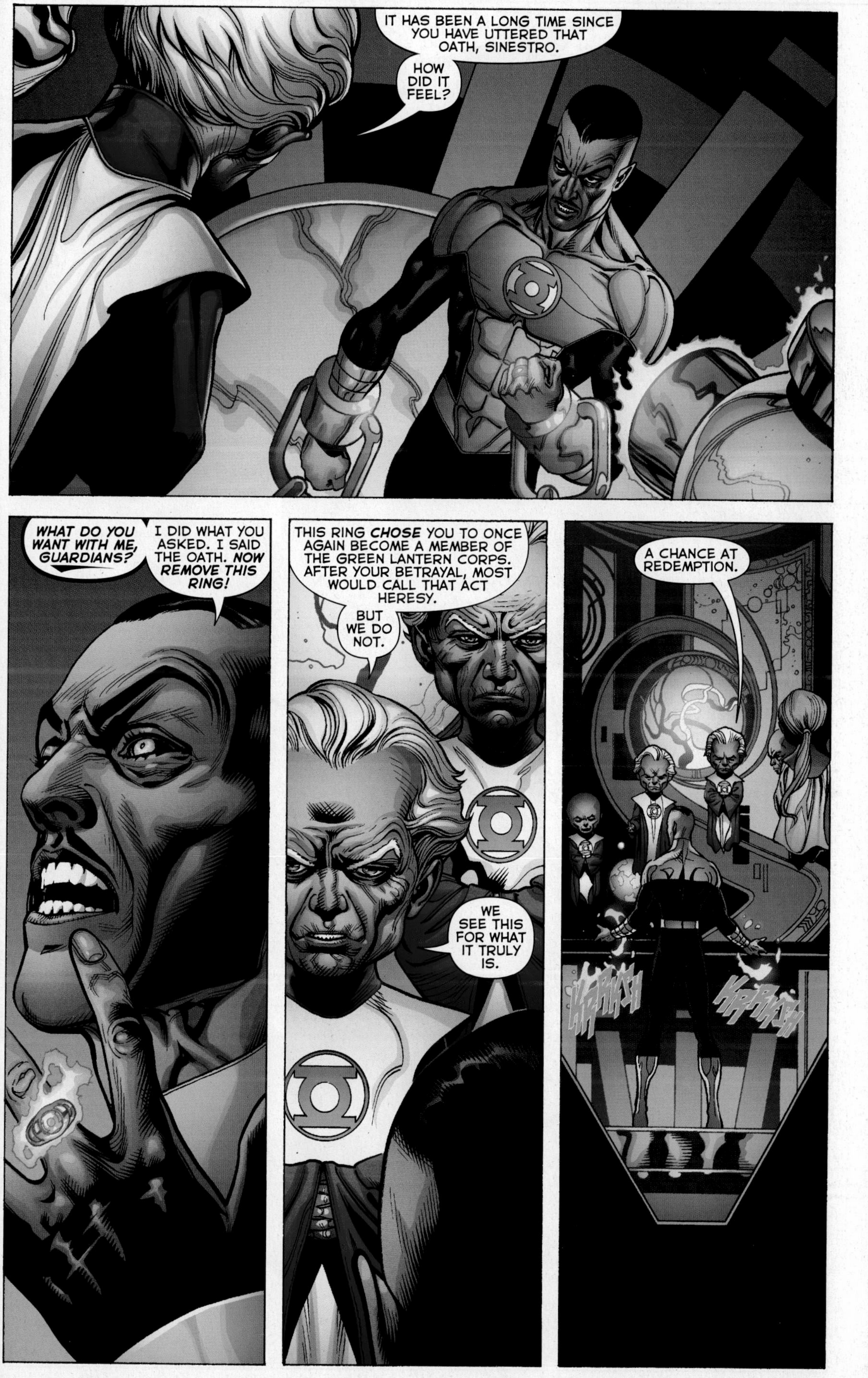
IT HAS BEEN A LONG TIME SINCE YOU HAVE UTTERED THAT OATH, SINESTRO.
HOW DID IT FEEL?
WHAT DO YOU WANT WITH ME, GUARDIANS?
I DID WHAT YOU ASKED. I SAID THE OATH. NOW REMOVE THIS RING!
THIS RING CHOSE YOU TO ONCE AGAIN BECOME A MEMBER OF THE GREEN LANTERN CORPS. AFTER YOUR BETRAYAL, MOST WOULD CALL THAT ACT HERESY.
BUT WE DO NOT.
WE SEE THIS FOR WHAT IT TRULY IS.
A CHANCE AT REDEMPTION.
KRRKSH
KRRKSH

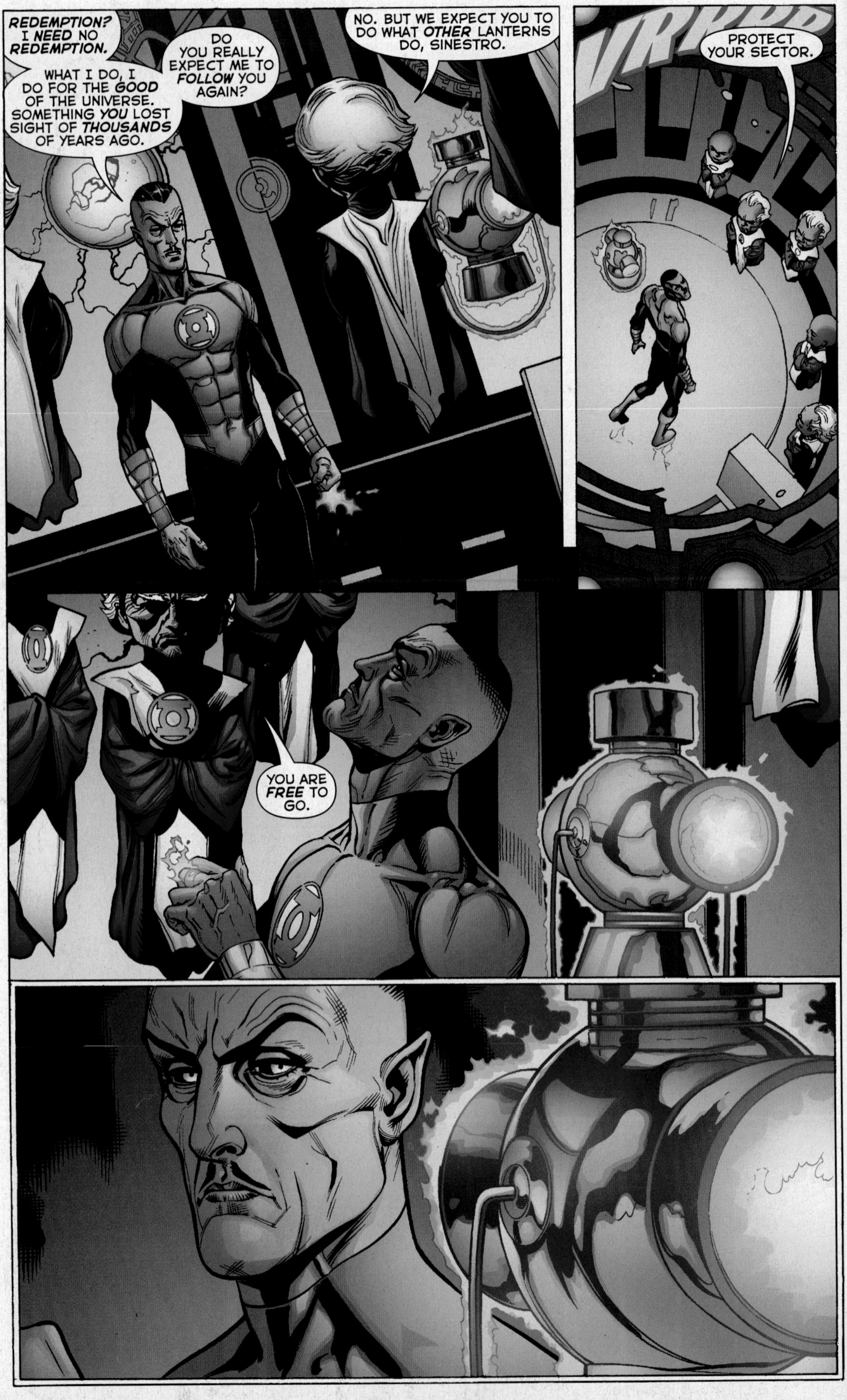
REDEMPTION? I NEED NO REDEMPTION.
WHAT I DO, I DO FOR THE GOOD OF THE UNIVERSE. SOMETHING YOU LOST SIGHT OF THOUSANDS OF YEARS AGO.
DO YOU REALLY EXPECT ME TO FOLLOW YOU AGAIN?
NO. BUT WE EXPECT YOU TO DO WHAT OTHER LANTERNS DO, SINESTRO.
PROTECT YOUR SECTOR.
YOU ARE FREE TO GO.

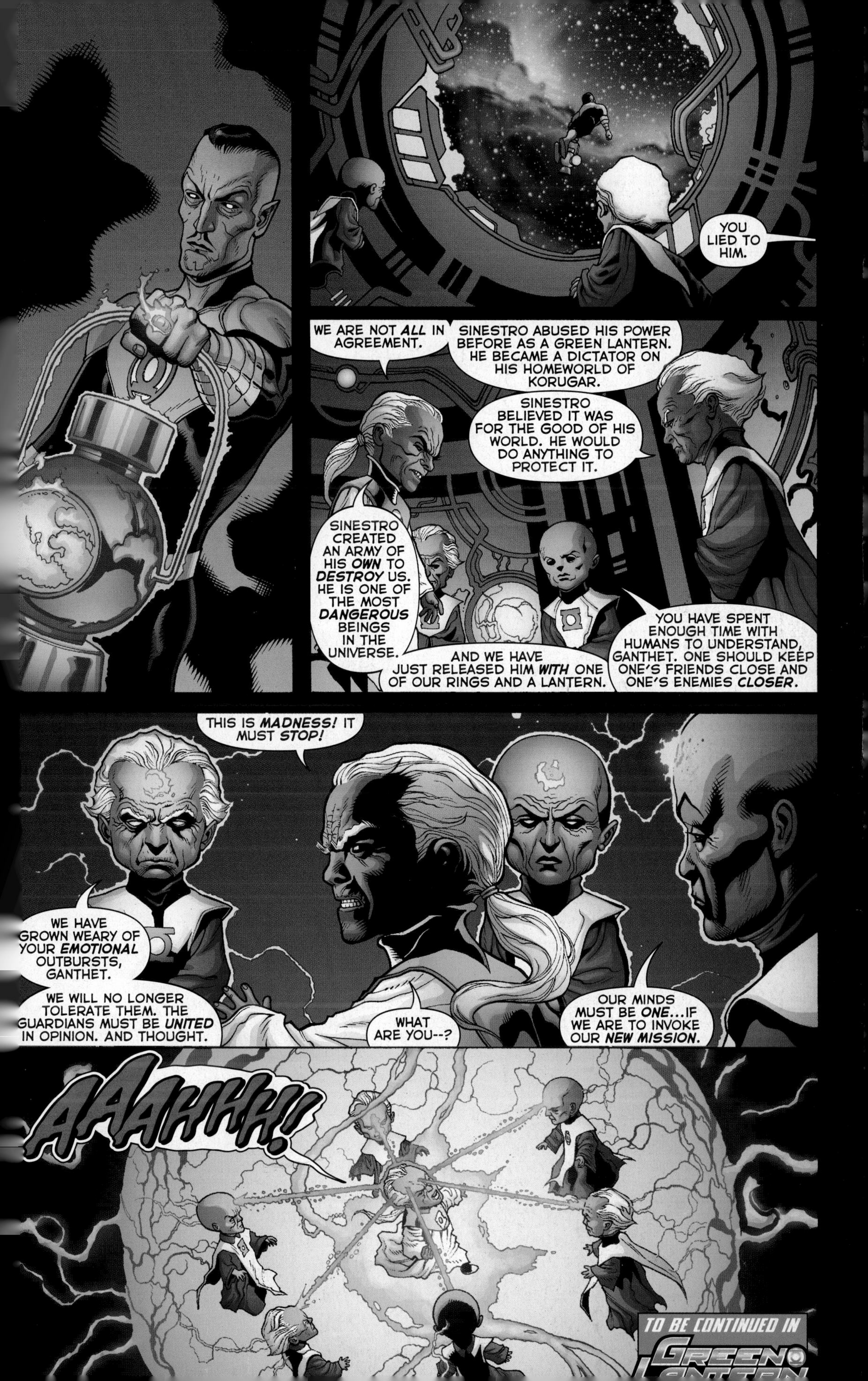
YOU LIED TO HIM.
WE ARE NOT ALL IN AGREEMENT.
SINESTRO ABUSED HIS POWER BEFORE AS A GREEN LANTERN. HE BECAME A DICTATOR ON HIS HOMEWORLD OF KORUGAR.
SINESTRO BELIEVED IT WAS FOR THE GOOD OF HIS WORLD. HE WOULD DO ANYTHING TO PROTECT IT.
SINESTRO CREATED AN ARMY OF HIS OWN TO DESTROY US. HE IS ONE OF THE MOST DANGEROUS BEINGS IN THE UNIVERSE.
AND WE HAVE JUST RELEASED HIM WITH ONE OF OUR RINGS AND A LANTERN.
YOU HAVE SPENT ENOUGH TIME WITH HUMANS TO UNDERSTAND, GANTHET. ONE SHOULD KEEP ONE'S FRIENDS CLOSE AND ONE'S ENEMIES CLOSER.
THIS IS MADNESS! IT MUST STOP!
WE HAVE GROWN WEARY OF YOUR EMOTIONAL OUTBURSTS, GANTHET.
WE WILL NO LONGER TOLERATE THEM. THE GUARDIANS MUST BE UNITED IN OPINION. AND THOUGHT.
WHAT ARE YOU--?
OUR MINDS MUST BE ONE...IF WE ARE TO INVOKE OUR NEW MISSION.
AAAHHH!
TO BE CONTINUED IN